Molo
Hope you enjoy doing it
much as I enjoyed doing it
Barry Howard
4/5/2013

WOW,
AND THEY EVEN PAID ME!

By Col. Lucky

AKA COL. BARRY J. HOWARD, USAF, RET.

This book is dedicated to my Granddaughters
Evan and Bryn Howard

This book is dedicated to my wonderful Texas granddaughters Evan and Bryn who have made this old fighter pilot very proud. With the help of their parents, my son Mike and his beautiful wife, Marla, they have achieved every goal they established and they continue to climb their mountains with success and class. Along their way, their Aunt Barrie Lynn has contributed to their achievements in many ways.

Evan recently graduated from Oklahoma University, I frequently scratch my head trying to figure out why a pretty and smart Texas gal would go to OU, but she did and did very well at OU!

Evan was employed in association with the Summer Olympics, in England. I am told that she truly proved herself with her work performance. While in England she was fortunate enough to see the future King "William" which thrilled her. Her experience and an already strong resume recently provided her the opportunity to obtain a new job in Dallas, TX in her career field. She also maintains a small secondary job. Additionally, she recently worked the Super Bowl XVLII in New Orleans for the same company she worked for during the summer Olympics in England.

Her sister, Bryn, and one who has truly understudied her older sister, recently started at the University of Texas, Austin, in engineering, and she is already attacking the program and frankly watering some eyes with her early achievements! She is a bit concerned about some of her liberal professors talking politics rather than concentrating on the subject! She is blessed with her cousin, Larry Brogdon, a Texas leader in fracking, who will mentor her.

Bryn had to test to establish herself in the engineering school in Austin, and I am told that she beat most male applicants and was one of the very few who passed the test on the first try. In fact so many failed the test that they all retook the test and she finished second of the whole class! These Howard gals are special and they both know how to work and make money!

I am extremely proud of them and their parents who had so much to do with their upbringing and establishing the right set of morals and character in them. Hopefully, Evan and Bryn won't be shocked about some of the tales in the book, but I had to tell the truth and spell it all out.

TABLE OF CONTENTS

ACKNOWLEDGEMENTS

This book has had the support of many people either directly or indirectly. However, one person provided her computer skills, design capability, and just plain support, Sandra Schakel, my beautiful Lady. Additionally, Dr. David Albright and Dr. Bob "Hawkeye" Turner contributed so much in various ways to this challenge!

The following provided the inspiration for portions of this book by providing me leadership, mentoring, encouragement, and friendship. Unfortunately, most have passed away:

Congressman, Ralph Harvey, formerly of the Fifth District Indiana

Maj. Gen. George Patton Jr., my TAC Officer as a Major, mentor, friend, hero

Gen. Charles Gabriel, former Chief of Staff, USAF

Gen. "Chuck" Donnelly, former 5th AF and Commander USAFE, boss, friend

Gen. Andrew "Andy" Isoue, former Commander ATC, longtime friend

Lt. Gen. Howard Leaf, Longtime Test and Evaluation expert, friend

Maj. Gen. Hoyt "Sandy" Vandenberg, USAF Operations, mentor, boss

Maj. Gen. "Willie P" McBride, TAC Director of Operations, hero, boss, friend

Maj. Gen. "Fat" Fred Haeffner, PACAF Vice-Commander, boss, friend

Maj. Gen. Neil Eddins, boss twice and Thunderbird Leader, friend

Maj. Gen. Billie Joe Ellis, USAF Operation, longtime friend, boss

Maj. Gen. Ed McNeff, short-time boss and mentor

Brig. Gen. Wendel Bevan, combat boss and mentor

Brig. Gen. CA Martin, Commander, Williams AFB, boss, friend

Col. Donald "Gridley" Riley, friend, supporter and true Air Force leader

Dipak Parekh, formerly of Flatiron CO., boss, friend, and mentor

PREFACE

This book is about *courage*. But the word *courage* appears only in this preface. I had the privilege of observing courage in my parents and others throughout my life. As a fighter pilot, I flew 229 combat missions in Vietnam, primarily in the F-4. I am not sure how many times my aircraft was hit by enemy fire, because, after the fifth time, I decided I didn't want to know anymore and stopped counting. I think it was about twelve times. I flew a few combat missions in other airplanes and I fought other types of near-combat battles, with both feet on the ground!

The persons who taught me and those who fought along with me understand that *courage* is something you do, not something you talk about!

In and out of combat, I, and those I respected, have been willing to continue to fight on principle. To fight well, I worked hard and pursued every opportunity to improve my skills. I also had more than a lot of fun along the way.

During my adult life, I have probably said hundreds of time, "Wow, and they even paid me!" This is my story of a happy and exciting life and the story of those who challenged and inspired me, and that is why this book is titled:

Wow, and They Even Paid Me, by Col. Lucky!

INTRODUCTION

A recent horoscope I read might give the reader some insight about me, an Aries (March 25)!

Aries: The Daredevil (Mar 21–Apr 19) Energetic. Adventurous and spontaneous. Confident and enthusiastic. Fun. Loves a challenge. EXTREMELY impatient. Sometimes selfish. Short fuse. (Easily angered.) Lively, passionate, and sharp wit. Outgoing. Lose interest quickly—easily bored. Egotistical. Courageous and assertive. Tends to be physical and athletic

Sounds pretty good to me, and I guess it does point out that I might have had an exciting life, and I have! This is why I decided to write this for my grandchildren and actually my children because, like my father, I seldom talked much about my young or adult life. Around Barrie and Mike, our children, I was the tall noisy Daddy but seldom talked about my life; but we did try to teach them not to make the mistakes Dorlyne and I made during our lives.

I have lead a blessed life, being the first child on both sides of the family. Of course, I was spoiled rotten with truly very loving parents who were strong but really caring!

A couple of examples follows that clearly demonstrate my tall Father's silence which probably contributed to him being known as "Handsome Harry." When I was in junior high school, I started playing a lot of tennis for a period, and I thought that I was getting pretty good, as I beat most others I played. Consequently, I challenged Dad to some tennis, thinking that I could finally beat him in something! We weren't on the tennis court five minutes when I realized that once again, I was learning something about my Dad that had never been mentioned before. This occurred after never being able to return *one* of his serves. I asked him about his playing tennis before. He said, "That he had been the national high school doubles champion many years ago."

My next realization was when we moved to 607 Neely Avenue in Muncie, Indiana, in the winter, and the house had a pool table in the basement. Naturally, since Indiana winters are so miserable, I really spent lots of time at the pool table. Again, thinking that maybe I had a chance to beat Dad, I challenged him to a game of pool. Being foolishly confident, I offered him to do the break. What a break, where not one but two balls went in a pocket! After the break, he quickly cleaned the table without missing a shot. I was standing there with my mouth wide open, and he said, "Son, when I grew up in Pratt, Kansas, I hung out at the Catholic church, since they had such great youth programs and we shot a lot of pool." One more lesson for Barry!

MY INTERESTING YOUNG LIFE, 1936-1954

I have never forgotten the time I was sitting playing cards with the madam of the world-famous Dolly's whorehouse on south Mulberry Street in Muncie, Indiana. I was a thirteen-year-old batboy for the Cincinnati class D baseball team and the game had been rained out. The team members, including me, all went to Dolly's. I was playing gin rummy with the madam, and in walked the local FBI agent, making his required regular visit. The tall, handsome FBI agent in his fedora walked in, nodded to the madam, and simply looked at me and said, "Hi, son," and then walked into the madam's office to privately talk with her, as he was required to do regularly. This was shortly after World War II, and he did tell me sometime later that those establishments were very patriotic, which is why he was required to regularly visit Dolly's for possible information.

A few days later at a Sunday baseball game (Dolly's was closed on Sundays), my Mom and Dad had box seats right behind where I, as the batboy, sat when the other team was at bat. One of those never forgotten incidents occurred. All of the Ladies from Dolly's were attending the game and had seats close behind my parents. For some reason, they all recognized me at the same time, stood up, and shouted in unison, "Hi, Barry, honey!"

Needless to say, Martha Howard, lovingly known as "Little Napoleon" almost burned my eyes out with her flaming and devastating stare. I noted my dad lean over and whisper something to her, which seemed to quiet her a bit! Hopefully, he told her that I was simply playing gin with the madam on a rain-canceled game day, which was true!

Along the way, I have been very lucky because I had many folks who helped me achieve my goals. I have found that the harder I worked, the *luckier* I became. My *"luck,"* coupled with the example set by my parents, who were wonderful role models for me, gave me a road map on how to achieve my goals. Martha Francis Howard (or "Little Napoleon" as Dad lovingly called Mom, all five feet of her) and Harry Francis Howard, (a big six-foot-one and known as "Handsome Harry" to those he worked with in law enforcement) constantly demonstrated to me how to face my challenges.

I need to digress a bit at this point and begin introducing in detail the wonderful ladies or girls who all had a great impact on my life! Few real men fail to admit that the women in their life have been extremely important and have been crucial to their successes or failures. If they do not admit it, they are fools, or they are fooling themselves!

I am and always have been a very *lucky* guy; in general, my female associates or friends were and still are not only pretty but extremely sharp and *with it*! I guess I loved them all in a special way, which in most cases was not in a sexual manner. *Prude* is a word that described the younger Barry Howard. For a long time in my life, "going all the way" was reserved for marriage. Those wonderful ladies will be listed around the time

2

they entered my life and possibly some of the effects and/or control they had on my life. As you will see, my ladies had a tremendous impact on my life, and God love 'em, they made life exciting!

MY MOM, MARTHA FRANCIS HOWARD, 12/5/1910-3/17/1987

My mother was the most influential woman in my life, not by her overt acts but just by my watching and learning from her. Her personal strength, determination, and ability to control her family and our life were unique. Actually, her mother, Hattie McIntyre, was probably her role model. We referred to her as "Hop-Along Hattie" because when she would get bored with Wichita, Kansas, where she lived with my grandfather, Frank "Mac" McIntyre. She would take a taxi to the bus station and get on a cross-country bus to visit my mom, wherever we lived.

At some stop along the way, she would call and say that she was coming, and usually she would knit a sweater en route! Grandma's independence and strength demonstrated to Mom how she should live. Grandma Mac was really a modern, independent woman who women's libbers should have modeled themselves after. That is why Mom was unique! Mom stood at least six feet tall in strength at actually was only five feet tall, but everyone knew not to mess with her, because she could swing

4

a broom fiercely! I am convinced that Little Napoleon was the backbone of the Harry Howard family. I remember seeing pictures of her when she was a lifeguard; no wonder Handsome Harry chased and caught her—she was absolutely beautiful, and what a body!

Mom and Dad never said we boys (Barry, Kent, and Alan) had to go to college; it was just a given in all conversations that after high school, we went to college. It was up to us to decide where we wanted to go and what we wanted to take. This atmosphere prevailed even though Dad attended only two years of college; and Mom, none.

Along the way I had heroes or mentors such as Ralph Harvey, gentleman farmer, from the Fifth Congressional District of Indiana, who allowed me to take the tests for the military academies during my senior year of high school. At this time I began to realize that I had been a very *lucky* individual, and, if I worked hard to address any roadblocks I encountered, I could usually overcome them.

Early in my life as I mentioned, I was a batboy for a Class D Cincinnati farm club baseball team in Muncie, Indiana, and that was a real exposure to life and the challenges of young men. Thanks to the team coach, Mike Blazo, I grew under his guidance.

The next summer, I traveled alone to Wichita, Kansas, to be a mascot for a baseball team, the Fort Wayne Pistons, from Fort Wayne, Indiana, in the National Semi-pro Championship play-offs. I had written a letter to the team saying I would be in Wichita and would like to be their batboy and I was previously the batboy with the Muncie Class D team. My mentor with the Pistons was "Stumpy" Coleman, home-run hitter and the catcher! Our team won the championship and to my grandfather McIntyre's (Mom's dad) delight, I was in a picture on the front page of the *Sporting News*, then the baseball Holy Bible!

Next this city boy traveled for two summers to Colorado to work on a wheat ranch. While there, I learned to drive vehicles including a jury rig of twin John Deere model D tractors pulling a thirty-two-foot sweep plow with which I would plow from before sun up to dark 5 1/2 days a week. Additionally, I learned to drive, load, and off-load a large truck of wheat. I even learned to milk cows (I hated it).

Again, my cousins Richard and Wirt Goodloe mentored me by teaching me to be a competent young wheat farmer and minor mechanic and just plain how to think and solve problems. I also learned how to take live chickens, depart their heads, and prepare them for the dinner table.

Following my two summers farming in Colorado, I worked as a *gandy dancer* on a railroad crew and I could drive spikes with the best of them. The permanent *gandy dancers,* Old Mike and Tony mentored me on the railroad work crew. Old Tony arrived in the US from Italy as a young boy speaking no English, and did he have exciting tales to tell! Mike and Tony later suggested that I become acting foreman, which I did for part of the summer. It seems I had the natural ability to detect defective ties or problems with the track.

The last two jobs were primarily in hopes that I could gain some weight to play high school football. Playing HS football at very skinny 135 pounds and six foot tall was hazardous to my health. I was so skinny that I did have to eat seven pounds of bananas to make the minimum weight for the Naval Academy but that is another story!

As you will see on the following pages, there were many other challenging jobs and mentors. In most cases my hard work located and won the jobs, but some jobs, others, primarily my father, had suggested I try for them. However, I did earn the job, do the work, and was pretty successful. Certainly from my many jobs, I learned a lot that prepared and gave me a firm foundation for my future with many military and later civilian challenges.

Congressman Ralph Harvey, of Indiana's Fifth District, the gentleman farmer from nearby New Castle, Indiana, gave me the chance to attend the US Naval Academy. Even my initial decision to want to attend West Point opened new and exciting challenges for me. While I wanted to go to West Point, I tested for Congressman Harvey, along with twenty-one others; a fellow named Wayne Day, who was attending Ball State University (then it was Ball State Teachers College), Muncie, Indiana, for two years, beat me. I then was offered the Naval or the Coast Guard Academy, talk about *lucky*! I selected the Naval Academy– *yes*! That decision occurred in 1954, around March. I then had to report in June to Annapolis. Probably going to the Naval Academy was the best thing that happened to me! I had already won a Naval ROTC scholarship to either Notre Dame or Purdue, but the Academy was my ultimate goal. However, my high school girlfriend, Sandy Maldaner, was probably a bit disappointed at the time since we planned to go to Purdue together.

Two events follow that demonstrate how *lucky* I was! While at the Naval Academy, an upperclassman named, Len Benzi, rescued me from one of his fellow classmates who was physically and emotionally seriously harassing me not because anything I did, but because of what my assigned "Firstie" (academy senior classman who was selected as my Firstie, to guide me through plebe year) had done to Roger Lyle, my nemesis. My Firstie had cited him for being drunk and almost had Lyle kicked out of the Academy! This was a major event in my life as I was flirting with getting kicked out of Annapolis after I beat the hell out of this upperclassman (But more on this later.)

I wanted to fly when I graduated, but my eyes weren't quite up to the stringent requirements for flight school, as many others weren't, because of the four years of intensive studying at the Academy. First I talked the Navy, and I was told that I had to go to sea for three years and then I could go to fly. The Air Force

Representative said, "When you physically qualify, off to flying school you'll go." Unfortunately, he forgot to tell that to the Air Force personnel system! But again, hard work addressing the problem resolved that roadblock. One day I met Maj. Bill Frasca, an older US Naval Academy graduate and a general's aide at my first assignment out of Intelligence school at the Barksdale AFB Officer's Club Bar. After telling him my sad story, with a simple phone I was off to flying school three days later—*lucky* again!

I had many more mentors along the way, and they will be highlighted in the following pages. They were fellow officers, senior enlisted men, and many others from various walks of life. I know I had many challenges but I learned early on, that they will always be there, but they can be defeated with good work and a little *luck*!

MY BEGINNING and FAMILY, 3/25/1936-Present

I have been blessed with an exciting, sometimes demanding, and truly fun life ever since I can remember. Of course it didn't hurt that, as I said earlier, I was the oldest son of parents who dearly loved their children, and also that I was the oldest grandson of both families.

I think I was born a warrior, probably because my father, Harry F. Howard, was a warrior his whole life: Cop, FBI agent, and Sheriff. As a Cop, he was made Night Captain of the Wichita, Police Department at the tender age of 23. My mother, Martha F. Howard, in her own way was a warrior too; you didn't want to get on the wrong end of the kitchen broom when she was upset with you, because all five feet of her could make you suffer from her wicked right-handed strike! Mom and Dad met as lifeguards at a pool in Wichita, Kansas, and what a pair they have made: a little bitty beauty with big "Handsome Harry!"

I have been blessed with being part of some events that most would only fantasize about. When I was the thirteen years old bat-boy for the Cincinnati Reds Class "D" baseball team in Muncie, Indiana I had a chance to experience older life at a young age! It was a real experience-builder and certainly exposed me to the *older* young man's world! As I said earlier, they took me every-place they went, even to Dolly's Whorehouse.

We, many of the baseball team, normally went there on "rain days," when the ball game had been called for rain. While being the batboy, I even had the opportunity to escort the famed, Satchel Page, for a day and even batted against him. It was something that any baseball fan would be thrilled and honored to do. When he threw the ball at you, it was scary, and you had no idea where it was coming from. I suspect, at the time, he was at least fifty or older. Since I was able to hit his pitching, he told me that I had a future in baseball. Although Cincinnati indicated that they might want me, I decided that the baseball life wasn't for me.

My early life was in some ways normal for a boy in a small Indi-ana town: riding bikes, playing basketball, baseball, and fishing. Hell, even one summer in my life, I, along with Gerald McBride, we fished every day of the summer, even though I still worked a summer job. We fished the White River, a couple of gravel pits, and a few streams. Because Indiana grows lots of beautiful and delicious tomatoes, we frequently would help ourselves to some of them from the nearest field, cool them in the water, and always have a saltshaker with us for a snack.

About this time two young ladies came into my life. The first girl that I suppose I had affection for was Wanda Welch, because she was so *neat*. She enjoyed the same things that we guys did: tackle football, hanging out, and just talking and being one of the guys. Yet we all had a special regard for her; she was good-looking, exciting, fearless, and fun. She was really well built and very well endowed, something that we knew was good, but we had not yet developed that special attention that older guys give to good-looking girls who are well endowed.

I guess that she was our big sister. We spent lots of time at her house and just liked to be around her. The last time I saw her with her husband, a friend from long ago, Mike Concannon, she still stimulated me in a special but really a very nice way. I still liked her a lot in a way that I can't explain. I suspect there is a deep thought somewhere in my head that said, "You should have chased her as a sexy woman, not someone to tackle or to be treated as a sister." My friend Mike was a lucky man. Unfortunately, Mike passed away a few years ago, but he and Wanda had built a great life, family and business together.

A bit later in junior high I met Sally Bays, who was the first girl I kissed a lot, maybe because it was the thing to do. In fact, she scared the hell out of me one time when I walked her home. But had I met her later in life, I would have chased her with a fury. She had that slender and well-built figure that truly turned me on, especially as I got older—I guess because she was somewhat advanced of me in the field of boy-girl relations, and I was probably a bit afraid of her. Girls weren't really important to me at that time, as my home life and sports were really the center of my world.

At home our family did resemble a *Leave It to Beaver* family, in that nights at home after a family dinner might involve family bridge, canasta, or other card games. Frequently the family had deep discussions involving all members of the family on various subjects that were of interest at the time. We insisted that every member participate and everyone's opinion was to be listened to and discussed. This was good because Alan, the youngest, was surely the best-read and probably the smartest.

My brothers Alan Robert, eight years younger, and H. Kent, four years younger than me, were truly blessed, as I was, with caring and participating parents, Martha (Little Napoleon) and Harry (Handsome Harry). This is not to say that Mom and Dad were perfect, but from my eyes, they were! They encouraged, lightly directed, disciplined, and were extremely proud of their children. Then, without our knowledge or any fanfare, they established in our minds that college was part of normal growth and critical to success. It obvious worked better with my brothers, who each have more than one college degree compared to my one. But, there never was a minute that any of us did not plan to attend college. More importantly, our parents set examples that have lasted for our adult lives: the knowledge that hard work resulted in success, reading expanded the mind, and to be honest with integrity.

Some may say that there was a drinking and smoking problem in our family. I would say that drinking and smoking was simply part of our family, but it never was a problem. Alan has been off drinking and smoking for well over thirty five years; Kent drinks less than he used to and has stopped smoking cigarettes but usually will have a cigar. I usually have a couple of drinks a day (normally red wine). This is a result of my visit to the Air Force Hospital at Brooks AFB around the age of twenty-eight. Brooks is the major hospital for the Air Force and the cardiologist I saw said, "Two drinks a day, preferably red wine, are good for you, and someday everyone will know this."

I, of course, have followed or improved on his direction as best I could and I have an occasionally cigar and as a President has said, "I never inhaled!" But, I never smoked cigarettes.

To understand our family life, it is important to know my mother, Martha. Mom was tough as nails. She truly ran the family although to others it appeared that big Harry was in charge as she controlled him through the "Honey-do method." Dad affectionately called Mom "Little Napoleon", which was certainly apropos. I suspect all of the Howard boys have suffered Little Napoleon with a broom as a weapon of discipline. In high school, we frequently brought our friends home to eat, even though Mom wasn't a great cook but since we had lived in many other parts of the nation, our friends thought we had wonderful meals designed from her experiences in the south, east coast or the west that our friends may not have experienced before. They especially liked the Mexican food Mom prepared!

Dad was known as "Handsome Harry", and in his FBI attire—dark suit, dark tie, and fedora—he was Hollywood handsome. Before the FBI, Dad was a Cop, and I am told he was really a great and tough cop! He also was the Night Captain on the Wichita, Kansas, Police Force. Why? Because the previous Mayor had been impeached, and the new Mayor said, "Who is the toughest cop we have"? The answer was Harry Howard, because he had the black beat and had never been whipped, although he had a fine scar on his upper lip from a knife! "Make him night captain," said the reform mayor, "and don't worry about his age of twenty-three!"

When Dad retired from the FBI, he became a golf-course fashion plate and in my entire life, I can't ever remember him in casual clothes looking scrubby, without a shave, or wearing jeans or shorts. After a short retirement from the FBI, he was then elected Sheriff of Delaware County, Indiana, for the allowed two terms. Unfortunately, he then ran for mayor and suffered his only loss in his adult life. After that defeat, a local Muncie, Indiana, silent but concerned leader hired him as the head of plant security for a local meat-packing company.

Dad fiercely protected his family, especially his children. One time during high school, I was walking on the street returning from having lunch at the YMCA; I unconsciously or maybe intentionally flipped a parking meter, which caused a coin not fully in, to drop in, thus starting the clock. Apparently the coin had been inserted by an off-duty police officer who saw me do it and came roaring at me, pushing and putting me against the bank wall that we had been passing. This officer read me a riot act and frankly scared the hell out of my friends and me. Dad found out about it. Sometime later a police officer friend, who later became the Chief, told me that Dad had confronted the officer and he physically lifted him up and carried him to the nearest wall. He then said, holding him against the wall without his feet touching the ground, "If you ever touch one of my boys again, I will seriously kick your ass." It is even rumored that once Dad fired his pistol at a couple of guys who beat up one of my brothers in an alley.

Handsome Harry was a very tough guy and a real old-fashioned cop who loved to teach others. When he was elected Sheriff, it gave him the golden opportunity to take young men and mold them into exceptional law-enforcement officers or leading citizens. He had several deputies who have since retired from his beloved FBI, and one deputy, named Greg Williams, who went on to law school and eventually became a dean of a law school. Greg later became President of a College in New York City. What was especially unique was that Greg was black! That was significant because that was in the '50s, when he worked for Dad as the Sheriff, and those things just didn't happen very often in those days in Muncie, Indiana.

Dad had several other deputies who became FBI agents or community leaders. Handsome Harry made an impact and his many "sons" as he called them, made him, as he said, "Damned proud!"

Once, after his first election to Sheriff, I do remember him saying, "I can see why my opponents fought so hard to win this job! I could make a mint, if I wanted." Rather than line his pockets, which he did *not* do, he used what previous sheriffs' had pocketed from the snack machines and turned it around into a catering service for those in jail. The prisoners went from *day-old rolls and coffee* for breakfast, to catered meals. Dad used the jailed men and women to work on the roads and pick up litter, which they told me they loved to do, because instead of sitting around in the jail, they got out in the fresh air. Of course the ACLU challenged it. (I wonder if most readers are aware that the

ACLU, when first formed in 1920, initially, only represented early members of the Communist Party?)

As I mentioned earlier, our folks set limits for us boys but they never insisted or directed our lifestyles. As a result, each of us followed different paths and approaches to life. I, being the oldest, was the most outspoken and in charge or, as Mom used to say, "Big brassy and bossy Barry." While in school I was always a class officer. In most of the clubs that I was in, I was the president or was an athlete who tried hard, but I had very limited ability. My academic grades were pretty good, but I never made the Honor Society because I had a "D" in the ninth grade biology from a junior high school teacher named Miss Alldage, or "Miss All-Dog," as I had said, and she was one who really didn't like me. (My story!)

I am very proud of a few things that I contributed to while in high school. I did what I thought could to make our life in high school have a little less racial prejudice. One time, as a couple of us walked home from football practice, John Casterlow—our tall, black basketball center and football end—and I, stopped in the local very popular drive-in to get a hamburger. John was refused service and I blew my stack and promised them that we would close them down. After a few days of no high school visitors to their restaurant they assured us that John and others would be served in the future.

I was in charge of the Senior Ball dance; I selected Katy Crawford, a beautiful artistic tall black girl, to be Chairman of the Ball. Later in life, when we as a family were visiting my in-laws in Texas and my father-in-law constantly used the N word; actually, truly not negatively but just to refer to his friend, the black lady, who was at his morning coffee shop, the Whistle Stop. She stirred his coffee for him because of the mess he made because of his terrible palsied hands. I asked him to please stop using the N word in front of our children, which he just couldn't do. So we curtailed our visit by a week.

About this time, I picked up a young hitchhiker, black, who said he was looking for a job. I asked him if he had considered the Air Force. He said, and I will never forget it, "How much will it cost me?"

My middle brother, Kent, was quiet and studious and a little devious but normally accomplished his goals. One time when I was home from the Academy on leave, I found him standing in front of a mirror wearing my academy uniform. Naturally, he took the exams for the Academy and did very well, except on one exam on which he skipped a question, thus causing all the remaining answers to appear wrong. The academy administrators allowed me to see the test he had failed, and I was able to convince them of his error. He was allowed to retake the test the next year; he passed and was accepted. Unfortunately, while waiting to get into Academy, he attended DePaul College in DePaul, Indiana. Once he experienced the freedom of college, he realized that Academy life was not for him, and he lasted only a few weeks as a midshipman. He returned to Ball State, in Muncie, Indiana, and later he attended Harvard Law School. He attended Harvard as part of an experiment that Harvard Law School developed that brought in older, very accomplished, and experienced students.

He was at Harvard during the Vietnam War, and I had fun visiting him by flying in my F-4 fighter to the Boston area and wearing my flight suit at various bars in Harvard Square. I don't think it resulted in any major barroom fights, but there were a few very minor confrontations—but we also received many more free drinks, and we were treated wonderfully by the Harvard Square folks!

My youngest brother, Alan, was the brains of the family. As a small child, he actually read a full set of encyclopedias and was a reader extraordinaire. Alan also won a prized *Storer scholarship*, which he used at Yale, where he became the family communist. His college test scores were record-setting for Muncie. There was, however, a minor sibling rivalry about who scored the highest on the measured intelligence tests. My memory for numbers failed me, but I know I had a bit higher score than Brother Kent.

Mom and Dad encouraged all of us to earn money at an early age. My first real job was selling various concessions at the famous, now destroyed, Baltimore, Maryland, baseball stadium. My start came from a friendly policeman who suggested I get in the concession business and stop climbing the fence to get in free, as he had seen me do several times. I don't remember a lot about my ability to sell, but I know Mom and Dad were very proud of my successes.

After a short after-school job at the corner drugstore when we were living in Wichita, Kansas, my next venture was to be batboy, first for the Muncie, Indiana, Class D Cincinnati Reds baseball team. Following that, I did the same for the Fort Wayne Pistons, a National Semi-pro baseball team, at the National Semi-pro Championship tournament held in Wichita. I got the job as batboy by writing the Pistons saying I would be in Wichita for the tournament and I was from Muncie, Indiana. The Pistons won the Championship again that year, as they had before, and I believe it was by a bases-loaded home run by the catcher, my mentor, whose nickname was *Stumpy* (Colman) because of his short but husky stature. He gave me his bat that he hit the winning home run with it!

My grandfather McIntyre (Mom's dad) was absolutely thrilled when my picture with the team was on the front page of his beloved *Sporting News* (at that time, the premier baseball publication). He said, "It was a dream, come true!" What could be more exciting than being the batboy at a championship affair? And to make your living grandfather on cloud nine—can't beat that, and you get paid for it too! I was beginning to get a message: working can be fun, and you make good money! Most importantly, I learned that by taking the initiative and attacking if you see something that interests you, you probably can achieve your goals!

My other grandfather, Harry Burns Howard, died early in our life, but what a man he was when he was alive! He was an old-style cowboy, drank his share of whiskey, slept with a .44 pistol under his pillow, and ate tons of Fig Newton (which I still love). I loved to spend the night at his apartment, because I got to sleep with him! Grandpa Howard did love to gamble on Saturday night, and, of course, he would drink his share! Occasionally, a beat cop would escort him home in his patrol car; *they did that in the old days*! Grandpa would always use a fictitious name, because he was the father of my Dad, the Night Captain. (Dad used to say, "He damned well better!") But Grandpa would always send the officer who took him home a box of cigars. Grandpa was a hell of an athlete, and I remember his walking around the block he lived on, *on his hands* for me one time, and it was a big block!

Dad, as a Wichita, Kansas, Police Officer, had been recruited by J. Edgar Hoover for the FBI around 1938 or 1939. He had already accepted a position as a Texas Ranger, as he thought his father or grandfather had been one, but I have never really been able to confirm that! As an FBI agent, he was one of the first of a bunch of agents who Hoover personally recruited for his newly restructured FBI, and was one of the few without a college degree. Dad had risen to Night Captain in Wichita at age twenty-three, because he was the "toughest cop on the force." Dad, like any Howard, worked very hard at being the Night Captain, riding a motorcycle around at night, going to where the action was! I still remember a picture of Dad in the *Wichita Star*. He was in his motorcycle uniform—high, polished boots and all—with his right hand on the throat of a *Peeping Tom* on the garage floor, as he was about to hit him with a left. (The good old days!)

Dad was a tough guy but a "softie" for his family and their well-being. Dad had been a significant athlete (unlike me) during his high school years in football and was even in the National Tennis Championship Tournament by winning the doubles championship. Being the son of an FBI agent during WW II meant that you would be moving frequently. Starting in Wichita, Kansas, we then moved to Baltimore, Maryland; followed by Boston, Massachusetts; Duluth, Minnesota; Houston, Texas; Wichita, Kansas; and finally, Muncie, Indiana.

I need to tell my story of Duluth, as it was a short but exciting experience for me. First, the neighborhood boys my age used to hitchhike almost every day to a dammed-up stream that was our swimming hole. I will never forget the day several water moccasins decided that we boys were in their territory and swam toward us as we made a mad exit from the old swimming hole. It snowed on the Fourth of July, and it was great fun making snowballs with firecrackers in them. The most exciting event was one evening we had a bear cub in our backyard fruit trees, and we boys chased it out to a small, heavily wooded plot near our house. Again, we boys, with brains of mush, decided that whoever could pull the bear cub's tail was the winner. We all, including my brother Kent, searched for the cub. Finally, Kent hollered, "I found him, and I am going to pull his tail!"

Unfortunately, the cub whose tail he was pulled was a skunk, and Kent got a full load of wonderful skunk spray. Kent staggered out of the woods, and we hurried him home a block or two away. I hollered for Mom and she came out, told Kent to strip, and washed him down with the hose. Then she poured a can of tomato juice on him and made him sit outside for a couple of additional hosing's and scrub-downs, and he slept on the back porch that night! We stopped chasing bear cubs!

Occasionally, we—Mom and my brothers and me—would return to Wichita for a short period, living with our grandparents until Dad could find a place for us to live at his new FBI assignment. We were a real vagabond family, but it certainly didn't create long-range problems for the Howard boys; we continued to grow and accomplish our goals—if we knew what they were!

MOVING TO MUNCIE, INDIANA, 1946-1954

When the FBI assigned Dad to Muncie right after the war, Kent and I lived with our Uncle Eddie Howard (Dad's brother) his wife Aunt Idris, and their daughters Lynn and Karen in Wichita. Meanwhile, Mom and Dad searched for a house in Muncie. Later, I learned that J. Edgar Hoover had decided that his "shooters" should be put in Indiana, sort of the center of the US, for rapid response. Since Dad was, I believe, one of the shooters, it worked out for him. Or he may have first been sent there because he screwed up, in J. Edgar's eyes. When Dad was assigned to the Kansas City office, he and another agent were chasing the Number Eight Most Wanted, ran him off the road, and chased him into the woods. There, the bad guy shot Dad's partner in the butt with a shotgun. Dad had the choice of taking his partner to the hospital or letting him bleed to death while he pursued the bad guy.

Dad of course took his partner to the hospital—*bad*, in J. Edgar's eyes, since Number 8 got away and therefore Harry screwed up. Later, I do remember Dad frequently being gone on cases where a "shooter" was needed. I sure wish I had asked him about the things he did in the FBI. I am sure I did, but he seldom would talk about it. But my dad—being a strong, silent type—rarely talked about anything from the past. I do remember when he worked with the now famous G. Gordon Liddy, also assigned to Indiana because he was also a Hoover *shooter*. Occasionally, he had dinner at our house, and was that interesting! What fun that was! And G. Gordon never stopped talking and expressing his beliefs! I believe he had hair then, and, thankfully, his ideas agreed with mine!

Moving to Muncie, possibly as a result of the Kansas City event, was memorable for many reasons. I attended Garfield Elementary in the sixth grade and immediately became a Safety Patrol Officer who helped students cross a very busy the street that ran in front of Garfield, South Madison Street. Probably because of Dad, as sometimes happened, I won the award as Safety Patrol Officer of the year and got to go to a summer camp, Crosby, for free. Garfield was a really special school, on the south side of the tracks but loved by the students. We won the City Touch Football Championship. Of course, we had to locate our star fullback, who may have been in jail before the game. Another of our stars was "L. only M. only, Sims," or, as we called him, *Lonely Moanly*, but we did win the city Championship. However, when our school burned during Christmas vacation, instead of being happy as most students would be if their school burned during Christmas, I remember how sad we all were, because we truly loved Garfield, and it was a wonderful and fine school!

I will never forget the first Indiana high school basketball game my dad took me to, the Officer on the door just let us in, as we had no tickets. Wow, we were on the playing floor near the north end of the court! It was during the Indiana sectionals in the Muncie Bearcat gym that was built in 1936, which seated 9,723 and was sold out with season tickets. And, as with the Green Bay Packers, there was a waiting list for tickets! What a madhouse: the Bearcats were playing, and the place was crazy! Oh, if you didn't get to experience Indiana high school basketball in the '50s, you haven't lived! Back then, all of schools were not class separated, and thus all played in the same state tournament. Sometime later, Muncie Central was beaten by a very small school, Milan, with fewer than fifty boys in the school, in the final game for the Championship of the state of Indiana. While this was devastating to Muncie folks, a great motion picture resulted!

After the batboy jobs in Muncie and Wichita, I moved into babysitting, where I made considerable money, probably because I was the oldest brother, and I was considered very responsible. I guess I was pretty good at changing diapers, but later in life, my wife never thought I was good at it (smart, huh?).

The next venture that I tackled was a paper route, which paid very well—but don't think I enjoyed it much! I believe it was quite profitable, but collecting the payments wasn't much fun, and it started to become apparent that dealing in money is not one of my strong suites!

After the newspaper business lost my interest, I ventured in to the grocery business. I became a stock boy at Standard Food Market on South Madison Street in Muncie. This was while I attended Wilson Junior High, a very proud south-side-of-the-tracks school. We lived at 2002 South Walnut, about three blocks from the school. While I was at Wilson Junior High, and with much of my personal involvement, we started a radio station. I was fortunate enough to be one of the first announcers, and I still remember saying, "Wilson Junior High, school city of Muncie," which was how we opened our radio program.

At Standard Foods, my initial job was to sack groceries for the customers. I am still offended today when grocery sackers do a poor job when they sack our groceries! My mother loved to tell about finding me in my room at night, shortly after I started at the Standard Food Market, stuffing the sheets into a pillow case, sound asleep. Later, I moved to the produce area, and I think I was asked to become the produce manager during the summer, as I was working full-time because school was out.

Probably since my father was my hero, my major concentration in high school, along with classes and clubs, were sports. I had converted our garage, which was obviously an "add-on" to our rented house, to a sort of indoor (but very restricted in size) basketball court. Since I was new to Indiana, basketball was a new sport to me. The court, which was in constant use, resulted in my shooting ability being pretty good but my slowness didn't make the coaches' eyes light up! Of course in Muncie, sports dominated, especially basketball. The Muncie Bearcats basketball team was feared throughout the state. I did learn to play "Indiana" basketball and was a decent shot when I played on the Walnut Street Baptist basketball team. However, high school Coach Art Beckner cut me, stating that my future wasn't in Central HS basketball. He did say I was a great shot but so slow that I couldn't offer the team—it was nicknamed "the Purple Hurricane"—anything. I did really want to also play football, probably because I had indications that my Dad had been so good.

Unfortunately, I was a very skinny young man who couldn't have gained weight if I had wanted to. Dairy Queen had just surfaced in Muncie, and I had a milk shake every day, to no avail. During two summers, I even went to Colorado to work on a wheat ranch, hoping to gain weight so that I could play football. While in Colorado, I learned the meaning of hard work: up before sunrise and plowing until it was very dark. Those summers were instrumental in my maturing and development in addressing challenging problems that surfaced in everyday life.

I learned to drive while there. Unfortunately, I also probably burned up an older '39 Ford engine as I tried to mastered the challenges of a manual stick shift. I got stuck in the mud and, not too smart, as a beginning driver, overheated the engine. My very understanding cousins who ran the wheat ranch, Richard and

Wirt Goodloe, besides forgiving me for the engine, taught me to work, drive, and repair many different farm items and even how to milk cows—which I hated! We did rebuild the Ford's engine, so I learned another skill that served me well in later life.

Feeding the chickens wasn't much fun either, but wringing their necks so that their heads popped off wasn't bad, however! We did that a lot, because we ate lots of chicken. Of course the daily lunches on the ranch were wonderful, but I didn't gain a damned pound! Usually the daily lunch contained fried chicken, sausage, beef, pork, vegetables, and tons of mashed potatoes with great gravy!

My two primary jobs while on the wheat ranch were plowing using two enormous John Deere Model D tractors hooked together with a homemade rig and pulling a thirty-two-foot sweep plow, and driving a wheat truck during the harvest. My cousin Betty Goodloe, Wirt's wife, really a very beautiful lady, was a magnificent cook and household manager. She used to tell about hearing me driving a tractor in my sleep, peeking in and seeing me sitting there bouncing away, driving my tractors in my sleep.

The first year, because I wasn't quite tall enough for backing the truck, I occasionally fell out of the truck as I backed up, attempting or trying to see the auger box location into which I would dump the wheat. Because the truck was so heavy and was in lower compound gear, it stopped when I fell, as I leaned out. While I didn't gain any weight of note, I matured somewhat and gained a great deal of personal confidence. The money was eye-watering too!

My final job before the going to the Academy was a summer job on the railroad as a *Gandy dancer*. I did gain a few pounds, hardened my body a bit, and learned to operate in the adult blue-collar world. My railroad professors were Old Tony, who immigrated to America as an eleven- or twelve-year-old from Italy, alone, unable to speak English, and Big Mike, who could use a spike maul one one-handed and was as tough as nails. Big Mike taught me the tricks of how to use the maul with the least effort too. My mother used to tell the story of hearing me driving spikes as I slept. Tony and Mike taught me to work like a man, and many of the ways of their world. I think of it fondly, often! Toward the end of the summer, I could drive a railroad spike with the best of them, and, in fact, the railroad asked me to stay with them as a fore-man, because Old Tony and Big Mike recommended me, since I had been the acting foreman for a few weeks. It seems that I was able to detect or find faulty ties or loose joints while inspecting the track better than most—another great confidence builder!

My athletic world wasn't a great success: I made the high school baseball team—not sure I played much—and played center and defensive linebacker on the football team. Again, I wasn't a star, but I think I might have helped block an extra point when we won the state championship. I also tackled the Indiana, Mr. Football, when he broke loose for what he and others though would be a sure touchdown. I must have had an angle on him, because I was exceedingly slow, and surely I didn't chase him down!

About this time several young ladies who were really special and probably, unknown to me, created my inner desire to achieve, entered my life. Sherry Pierpont was the first girl or young lady I had a real interest in, because she was so smart and such a challenge to me in the classroom. I could beat her in math and some of the science classes, but she always won in English. We had several very hot petting sessions, some of which were on her front porch with her father just inside the house. I think—no, I know—I was a little afraid of her father, a former Marine! From her, I learned that redheads were all right and damned exciting. Sherry was one of the few women who I communicated with in a deeper way and whose opinion I truly respected. She had the ability to offer serious thoughts, which were seldom driven by emotions.

Mary Giles was the first girl I think I subconsciously wanted for a girlfriend, but either I was afraid of her, or I knew she wasn't interested in a tall, skinny, big-eared kid with buck teeth. She was a very beautiful, slender young woman whom I occasionally dated and with whom I had some wonderful necking sessions. I attended a prom or two with beautiful Mary at the Naval Academy especially the important Ring Dance. Once we were exchanging a few kisses in a hammock in her backyard when we noticed someone walk by us straight to her bedroom window, where the light was on. I thought he was going to the window to peek, but as he got to her window, Mary said, "Halt, who goes there?"

Before I could grab him, he took off running until he hit the clothesline. I can still see him running with his head hanging on the clothesline and his feet churning through the air. He hit the ground hard but was quickly up and running and I was laughing so hard at him hanging on the clothesline, that I couldn't catch him.

Mary was a very special lady who was the only lady in my life, that I knew, who wasn't afraid of my Dad and called him an "old softy and a sweetheart." I took Mary to a Naval Academy class 50th reunion; before it was over, she knew more folks than I did, and they were my classmates. I tried to develop a serious relationship with Mary, but with her being good Catholic and with bunches of really neat grandchildren, I wasn't able to convince her to come west. Unfortunately, Mary lost her husband fairly early in their life together.

Sue Hiatt, a tall, beautiful blonde, was my first serious long-term girlfriend. She was younger than me, and I guess I was the dominating member of the relationship. She had wonderful parents who trusted me and, I think they, liked me. Her little sister, whose nickname was Sunny, was very special to me. Sue and I grew up together as high school boyfriend and girlfriend. Again, as the prude I was, our relationship involved lots of heavy petting and very passionate but pure episodes. I can remember a few very embarrassing times when the male in me forced me to go home. What a wonderful and pure time that was! Today, as I think about it, I am very proud because many of my friends, at the time, were well into "all the way" with their girlfriends. Why I was proud is that I probably could have been "all the way," but I knew it was wrong and stuck to my principles and even acknowledged it to some friends.

Peer pressure was never a very strong force on me. I didn't go all the way, smoke, or even drink until later in life. I was, however, very unfair to Sue when we broke up, and it was a very traumatic event, and it didn't speak well of me. Sue will always be my first girl and when I think about her, I have some very pleasant thoughts. Sue later married a man who I had always thought was a pretty neat guy. Sunny was the little sister I never had and I missed probably more than Sue after we broke up. Sunny married one of my dad's "sons" or former deputies who later went into the FBI.

Sandy Maldaner was my very serious high school junior-and senior-year girlfriend whom I instantly fell madly in love with at some social event in the Muncie Central HS cafeteria. She was movie-star beautiful, really smart, with dark red hair (auburn?) and a Mona Lisa smile that I can still remember striking my heart. At the time I was going with Sue Hiatt, and I quickly, and probably without much consideration, broke up with her!

Sandy and I had a mad, passionate relationship during which time we both suffered from the famous "kissing disease," mononucleosis. I can remember sneaking to her bedroom window and us talking through her window screen just so that we could be together. As close as we were, I was still a prude and believed that sex was for marriage.

Sandy and I traveled with my family to Kansas to meet my grandmothers, who were extremely impressed with her. In fact my grandmother Claire Fletcher (Dad's mother) who was very outspoken, made the statement, "I expected some blonde floozy, but Sandy is just plain a wonderful beautiful young lady."

It was a very passionate relationship, but it ended, probably because of my childish jealously while she was at Purdue. I was jealous of her social life at Purdue and got my nose out of joint—really dumb! Sandy and I had planned to go to Purdue together, but I accepted the Naval Academy, having rejected the NROTC scholarship to Purdue or Notre Dame. Sandy was truly someone special, and today she is still a striking beauty who has had an extremely challenging and demanding life because of a special-needs daughter.

Harriet Hamlin was a very sexy and nice person who really got my juices flowing. She was sort of a secret girlfriend who I saw occasionally while I was going with Sandy. Harriet was an artist, and we conspired to borrow a trellis from an abandoned yard for the Senior Ball. It required a hacksaw and a dark night to "borrow" it. Unfortunately, the dark night caused a definite stirring, and we had a very passionate petting session under the stars, where we were eaten by mosquitoes. While it was extremely passionate but later damned painful!

After my relationship with Sandy terminated, Jeri Trusty was a short-lived intense girlfriend while I was at the Naval Academy. She was a fun and very exciting person who was a thrill to be with. Unfortunately, she may have had some problems at home that seemed to impact her. She is one of those girlfriends who I have always had some conscience attacks over. I did not treat her fairly. She also was a real sweetheart, and I again had some embarrassing petting events, since I was still prudish! I believe she was at USNA for part of my graduation, and for that I am ashamed because I am certain I was unfair to her (and Little Napoleon told me so, along with giving me holy hell for sleeping during President Eisenhower's graduation speech)!

A 4 ship combat mission with our Squadron Commander, Lt Col. Vern Covalt (a Super leader), myself, Little Barry (middle of front row), with a former Willie student of mine on his left.

Family picture with Mr. Nibbs, our $500 white toed fence jumper walking off to find a rabbit.

A young Mom 'Little Napoleon,' and Dad 'Handsome Harry,' at the Blue Moon in Wichita, KS.

Grandma Hattie McIntyre, better known as 'Hop-a-long Hattie, for her constant travel by bus.

The very young Night Captain, about 23, of the Wichita Police Department in his motorcycle attire with baby Barry.

30

My high school picture.

Sandy Maldaner and I at the Muncie
Central High School Senior Prom.

My plebe year
picture. Already
mature a bit!

Muncie Reds, a minor league team of the
Cincinnati Reds organization. Mike Blazo
is standing on the right.

The late Admiral Guillermo
Allegra Zariquiey, former Chief
of Peruvian Naval Operations
(NO) and his beautiful family.

Barry, Charlie Pinkham and
Terry Priebe. Terry was the
stroke, I was #7 and Charlie
was the Coxswain of the
Varsity Light weight boat.

Barry, Zeke and Bob at the Class
of 1958 50th Reunion.

Mary Giles and I at the Ring Dance for the Christening of my Naval Academy Ring in the waters of the 7 Seas.

I was the Royal Contribine for the NEPTUNUS REX COURT, for those who needed to be accepted into the Royal Order of the Deep. This is my card admitting me into the Royal Order of the Deep.

DRAW NEAR AND KEEP SILENT
ALL YE WHO MAY SAIL THE HIGH SEAS WILL
SHOW DUE RESPECT AND HOMAGE AS YE ARE IN THE
AWE-INSPIRING PRESENCE OF

A TRUSTY SHELLBACK

WHO DID ON 25 JUNE 1957 WHILE ON BOARD THE
U.S.S. NORTHAMPTON CLC-1 ENTER INTO THE
KINGDOM OF NEPTUNUS REX AT LATITUDE 00°00'
LONGITUDE 39°15'W AND DID APPEAR BEFORE HIS
ROYAL COURT AND WAS DULY INITIATED WITH FULL
ANCIENT HONORS AND WAS MYSTICALLY ACCEPTED
INTO THE ROYAL ORDER OF THE DEEP

NEPTUNUS REX
Ruler of the Raging Main
BY HIS SERVANT

H. A. RENKEN, COMMANDING

Mr. Ralph Wiles and his students at Marianna, FL. Ralph was my hero and final T-37 instructor who saved me from being eliminated from the flying program.

My new wife, Dorlyne Bailey, Electra, TX, in her Tanabada Dancer's outfit.

Flying a C-130 and stepping off aircraft 524 after a mission.

This is the aircraft that I had a little accident in India landing at Leh airfield, Ladakh, India at 10,500 ft. altitude.

We are building a party room for relaxation, telling lies and learning tactics, and maybe a little drinking, no, a lot!

Being congratulated by the Wing Vice Cmdr., Nick Ferris and the Cmdr. Brig. General Bevan after my last mission.

Hugs and Kisses from the pretty ladies after my last mission.

Little Barry filled in for Marv Bishop who went home, and Big Barry. Little Barry obtained the Black Panther for the 13 TFS, also named 'Barry.'

Dorlyne subtly encouraging me to return home and cancel my extension!

General 'Fat' Fred Haeffner, Col. Odonnell Escorting my Mother and friends to mobile to watch fighter aircraft landing. I landed with an emergency and had to take the cable.

Standing in front of my 311 TFS F-4

FOR COLLEGE 1950-1954

I am not sure when I decided that I wanted to attend West Point, but I think it was sometime during my sophomore or junior year in high school in Muncie, Indiana. I really wanted to go to West Point, and I started writing letters to anyone who I thought could help. My knowledge of entry into the Point, in general, was very limited. My Mother and Dad seemed to be very pleased that I wanted to go to an academy. I assumed, although we never talked about it, that because my dad had been in government service all his life, he was very pleased that I wanted to follow in his footsteps.

At that time in Muncie, a trust fund left by a Mr. Storer had surfaced that was going to send many of us to college on very good scholarships, and I was told that a college scholarship was assured. I had taken the naval ROTC test and had earned an NROTC scholarship to either Notre Dame or Purdue.

Also, I had joined the Indiana Army National Guard because I read that there was a procedure to get into West Point through the National Guard. I may have cheated on my age a bit to get in the Guard, but a few years later, I was told that the Guard was "thrilled" to get the FBI agent's son in the Guard. I suppose they bent a few rules to accomplish that! I truly enjoyed the Guard experience and quickly made corporal. Probably the only element of the Guard I really remember is studying for corporal and getting lots of help from the "old heads." Later I had an assigned job or an MOS for a .30/.50 cal. machine gunner. Our summer camp deployment was fun and certainly a learning experience. After the summer deployment, there wasn't any doubt that I enjoyed the military, and the academy was for me. Strangely, I never attempted to try to gain admittance to the Point through the Guard. Of this I am sure: the National Guard experience in many ways prepared me for attending the academy in a real world way. Also, since I spent eighteen months in the Guard, it counted for my military pay in the Air Force, so I got a little extra and, when I retired, even more. So my venture as a sixteen-year-old paid off in many ways!

Dad suggested that if I wanted to get an appointment, then, I should meet with Congressman Ralph Harvey, Indiana Fifth District, US House of Representatives. I first wrote him a letter, and then I visited with him on his farm near Newcastle. I got to his farm by hitchhiking. The congressman advised me that his academy appointments were competitive, and I would test along with the others who wanted an appointment. I started a study program, but I was flying blind as to what to study. Basically I studied similarly to how one would study for the SAT or ACT tests. Unfortunately, or maybe fortunately, the testing days I was very sick and the school nurse, Suzie (Mrs. Suzanne Scott), gave me a shot: she called it vitamin B, which must have helped, because I did fairly well on the tests. I must admit that I remember little about the several tests other than I think it was six hours one day and three the next. I have frequently said that I probably wouldn't have done so well if I hadn't been sick—thank you, Suzie! *Lucky*, again!

I believe that I had to wait several weeks before I received the results of the testing. I was told that I finished second out of twenty-one, and I later learned that the fellow, Wayne Day, who had finished first, had been in Ball State College for two years and was from Muncie Burris, the other high school in Muncie. We commonly referred to Burris as the rich kids' high school. Since I knew little about academy entrance procedures, it had never occurred to me that I might have other options besides West Point. Later I was told that Wayne Day wanted the Point, and there was only one appointment to the Point that year. I was asked if I might be interested in the Naval or the Coast Guard Academy. Having never thought about it before, I immediately visited the library and began a little research on the US Naval Academy. I was impressed about what I read. However, while I had seen several movies on West Point, I had never seen any on Annapolis. I accepted the Naval Academy and even today, I am still very happy I did. The four years at Annapolis for me were extremely tough but fun. *Lucky* again!

While in high school I was a joiner. I joined every club that might offer some education and broadening of my views. As I moved through school to my senior year, I became president of what I considered the two most productive high-school organizations, the Hi- Y Club (male-only club, which managed the concessions at high-school sports events) and the Youth Forum (social-science interests). The Hi-Y Club was basically for the school jocks that were very active to do well for the school, but the club was somewhat bigoted about who was allowed to join. We actually had a blackball membership procedure. As president, I was determined to broaden the membership base. Fortunately, I was familiar with Robert's Rules and few others were, so I was able to convince the membership by cheating the process. My first and very successful effort was to select for membership a fellow, Jan Etchison, who I had known for some time and who

I knew would be a great addition to the club. I won't deny that I cheated like hell by saying I was using Robert's Rules and forcing several votes.

Finally, after the blackballers got tired and wanted to go home, Jan became a member. Immediately he took over popcorn sales and in a few months doubled the profit and frankly watered the eyes of the jocks. As an aside, later in life, Jan became a friend of all the jocks, and he became a prime mover for our high school alumni association. Getting him into Hi-Y and the long-term results is something of which I am very proud. Jan was also extremely successful in various businesses, and I will always believe that his membership in the Hi-Y contributed to his successes.

For one of his businesses he needed some cash, which I lent him: $10,000, interest-free. Much later I needed the money, so I told him that I needed the money, which he sent me. A few months later, he sold the business, and Jan sometimes yanks my chain by telling me that if I had waited a few months, my $10,000 would have been worth approximately $147,000. "Jan, it is really not nice to mention that!"

Membership in Youth Forum, of which I was president, consisted of those who were going to college and would be considered as the school's deep thinkers but not nerds. The members were easier to keep on track and there were few battles over those who wanted to join Youth Forum. Members usually recruited new members, and no one was ever refused membership. I do think I was the only member who wasn't in Honor Society! I have to admit that I really enjoyed our meetings, which were designed to address a specific topic. For example, one meeting was on communism. A member would be designated as discussion leader, and the other members would select and read applicable sources about the topic.

This particular topic caused a minor explosion in my house! That meeting was very dynamic and extremely educational but somewhat naive. After the meeting, old big-mouth, me, said to the local FBI agent, my Father, that true communism probably was a good idea if done properly. Neither my brothers, my Mother, nor I had ever seen Dad hit the ceiling and start screaming like he did after my naive little statement. He sat me down and gave me what I assume was the standard FBI lecture on communism. Also, I believe that night he actually called J. Edgar Hoover, the Director of the FBI, and asked him to send a copy of his book, *Masters of Deceit*, to me. A few days later I received by the fastest mail possible at that time, a signed copy that I still have. Additionally, later my father arranged, through one of his informants, for me to attend a "secret communist cell meeting," which gave me a real shock. Using a phony name, I may have attended a few more meetings, and it became clear to me that their allegiance was not to the USA but to the Soviet Union. Of course, always the professional, Dad made me provide him a written report of the meetings. I never knew if he actually filed them with the FBI.

HOW ACHIEVED THE ACADEMY, 1951-1954

As I said earlier, sometime around my sophomore or junior year in Muncie Central High School, I decided that I wanted to attend West Point Academy for my college. I mapped out a plan as to how to accomplish that goal after studying West Point at the library. First I joined the Indiana Army National Guard as a sixteen-year-old, year old, fibbing about my age because I had learned that the Guard had West Point slots. The Guard was pleased to get me, probably because I was the son of the local FBI agent and I was somewhat of a big fish in the small pond of Muncie Central High School.

I took the tests set-up by the Congressman, which lasted one and a half days in the post office, which was next door to my high school. As a result of the testing, I was offered either the US Naval or the Coast Guard Academy since I came in second in the testing. I quickly studied about the Naval Academy and agreed to accept the nomination to Annapolis.

I was then sent to the Great Lakes Naval base for my physical. My Dad traveled with me. I did eat seven pounds of bananas to make the minimum listed on the physical weight standards.

The doctor who examined me told me that I really didn't have to eat all those bananas. It was a long time before I ate bananas again.

The administration of my high school, my folks, and others were very pleased, and maybe only Sandy, my girlfriend, was disappointed, as we had planned to go to Purdue together. Of course I had to wait to be accepted by the Academy, but it was sure nice knowing that I knew where I was going! At our high school graduation ceremony, they made a big deal of my appointment to Annapolis, and I know my folks and the National Guard were proud.

Now, more than fifty years later, I am still extremely pleased and proud that I attended the US Naval Academy, graduating in the class of 1958 with a regular commission in the USAF. I simply say I was one of the 899 who graduated, never having failed or bilged a course or having to retake a bilged exam. Our class had started with 1237 members ranging in age from seventeen to twenty-two. I certainly wasn't a star student, but I did stand higher than my friend and classmate, Johnny McCain, who eventually ran for president of the United States. Sometime after I graduated, they stopped giving Academy graduates regular commissions, which I think was a mistake. I suspect many chose to leave the service after they complete their required time in service: five years. I think having the regular commission kept me and others like me in for a full career, even though the airlines, with greater benefits and considerably more pay, really wanted our bodies! But, to me, that life, being a bus driver, couldn't have been as fulfilling or as much fun as an Air Force career, first as an intelligence officer, then as a C-130 trash-hauling pilot in Europe, pilot training instructor (T-37), an instructor pilot and a maintenance test pilot (T-37, T-38, F-5 and F-4s), an F-4 combat fighter pilot, three times a squadron commander, and twice a Wing Commander in the Pacific!

The year I graduated from Muncie Central, as I said earlier, a very successful local gentleman, John Storer, through his estate established a very lucrative group of scholarships for graduates from Muncie Central or Burris High. I was disappointed that I did not receive an honorary scholarship, as many of my friends actually received a full scholarship, especially those I competed with and beat in high school. However, years later I learned that one of my classmates whom I seriously cared for, Mary Giles, did not receive a *Storer Scholarship*. Mary should have been the very first at both schools to earned a Storer, according to the established criteria, which she exceeded enormously by her demonstrated leadership efforts in high school and her extremely serious need. Mary was the three-year class secretary (class of over four hundred) and the President of the only women's very large social organization, the Violet Club. Additionally, she was an officer in most other high school organizations to which she belonged. Finally, of all who received one of the scholarships, she was the neediest, in that she was a daughter of a single parent with a very sick bed ridden brother. In fact, she had to work a year after high school to have the money before she could attend the local college, then Ball State Teacher's College. I learned that Mary didn't get a Storer only a few years ago, and I was terribly embarrassed and felt damned foolish that I had been disappointed that I foolishly wanted an honorary scholarship, and she received nothing from the Storer committee. Had I known that she did not get a scholarship, I know I would have battled for her. Unfortunately, I left for the Academy just a few days after we graduated, when the Storer awardees were announced, and I didn't realize until many years later that she was treated so unfairly. I am still shocked that she was so unfairly treated. It was a disgrace to the entire *Storer Scholarship* program!

I now realize that graduating from Muncie Central High School was a tremendous arrow in my quiver of life, and it gave me a real preparation for the future. We graduated at a unique time, when the teachers and the school leadership were still respected and probably feared a bit! I wasn't a *Goody Two-shoes*, but I did not smoke and did not drink, although most of my friends did, but not to any serious degree.

OFF TO THE ACADEMY, 6/6/1954-6/6/1958

I received my appointment to Annapolis, and my orders told me to be there early on June 6, 1954. When that day in June, 1954, arrived for me to go to the US Naval Academy, my Dad escorted me to the Academy for my joining of the Brigade of Midshipman and my swearing into the military. At that time, being in the Brigade meant we were under Uniform Code of Military Justice (UCMJ). This meant, if I screwed up, I was under Federal laws that my Dad as an FBI agent was concerned about or responsible for enforcing.

It was a very impressive swearing-in as a midshipman by Admiral C. Turner Joy, the Superintendent who conducted the ceremony. He was an impressive and distinguished man; unfortunately, it was apparent that he was a very sick man. Later that day, I said good-bye to Dad, and the fun began.

One of the very first events that occurred and has had a constant and deep impact on me throughout my military career was our visit to "Shorty" at the Jack Stays, to which the Admiral actually took a bunch of us. While Shorty, and truly a shorty, was an enlisted Master Chief, it was very apparent to me that the

Admiral looked up to him with very special feelings and respect along with an acknowledgement that Shorty had special skills that made him invaluable to the Admiral or most anyone in the Navy. Shorty's "job" was to teach us how to tie Navy knots—useful to us as Navy men—but it was very clear, Shorty's institutional group was very much more important than tying knots for us in the future. It was not unlike how a young, successful person would look up to a mentor, but with even more respect. It was a lesson that was so impressed on me, creating a strong and continual respect for senior enlisted men and later women of the Air Force. Surprisingly, not many other Air Force officers shared—or *demonstrated* might be a better word—my very deep respect for senior Air Force enlisted personnel. Possibly the Air Force, early on, didn't properly demonstrate to the young officers or acknowledgement of the contribution they made.

Many years later, the Air Force finally established the senior Chief's position, similar to Shorty's position in the Navy. Unfortunately, we initially established the position and selected those Chiefs' based primarily on testing grades, rather than the more important "whole-man leadership" ability. At the time I was Air Base Wing Commander at Yokota AB, Japan and the Air Force Chief of Staff and someone I truly respected, Gen. Charles Gabriel made a visit to Yokota and the 5th Air Force.

The 5th Air Force was commanded by Lt. Gen. Chuck Donnelly, who was, some say, my sponsor, and who I respected like a father. We played golf at the famous Tama Hills Golf Course, which belonged to our base. This was about the time that rubber-spiked golf shoes were starting to be worn, and I wore them as they were very cheap in Korea where I was before Yokota. Gen. Donnelly being an old school golf type, constantly harassed me about my "rubber shoes." Since Gen. Gabriel and Donnelly had an extra-long meeting with Japanese political leadership, they arrived at the course a bit late, by helicopter. I met them as they landed. I was to play as a partner with Gen. Gabriel and Gen. Donnelly who was not a great player but was a super "better," had another partner, probably the course Pro! As they got off the chopper, I noticed that General Gabriel had the same golf shoes on that I wore, which, of course, I quickly pointed out to General Donnelly. "Amateurs," he said!

As we played, Gen. Gabriel discussed how disappointed he was with the new Air Force Chiefs and indicated that he was considering eliminating the position and asked for our opinion. When it was my turn to weigh-in, I told him the story about Shorty at the Jack Stays at the Naval Academy and that the Chiefs must be selected for leadership ability, not just test scores. Since General Gabriel was a West Point graduate, I reminded him of the special status of the Army's "Sgt. Major's Position." I told him that I had a Wing Chief who was a leader and he made my life easier, the base more professional, and gave the enlisted folks a champion and someone who knew and thought as they did. One of the tasks I was given when I took over the Wing (I replaced an unsuccessful commander who had busted an ORI) was to stop the homesteading at Yokota. Many enlisted, and some officers had spent ten to eighteen years at Yokota, because it was such a wonderful location. Great facilities, best golf course in the Air Force and the ability to catch a *hop* home to the States, almost at will. The second challenge I had was to "fire" the hospital Commander because of some flagrant breaking of Air Force rules according to a letter submitted to the Base IG.

With my Chief, we established a "no multiply extension" policy for the enlisted and many officers. Actually, our Wing Chief had an extension submitted, but he insisted that I disapprove it, saying he and I needed to set the example!

Regarding the Hospital, the Chief found that the culprit was not the Hospital Commander but his hospital Administrator, who seemed to break almost every rule for his personal benefit. While

I am sure I could have reached the same decisions that the Chief led me to, it probably would have taken considerably more time, and I might not have been as successful. Of course as I told Gen. Gabriel these stories and Gen. Donnelly quickly confirmed them.

Gen. Gabriel did not eliminate the Chief Position but he did reestablish the criteria emphasizing leadership, and today in the Air Force, the Chief's position is in concrete and certainly is a key position, as it should be! Sometime later, Gen. Gabriel told me that I had made a key contribution to keeping the position, of which I am very proud.

AT THE US NAVAL ACADEMY, 6/1954-6/1958

I quickly learned that I was in a special and somewhat distinguished group of folks, many with some college or prep school, a bit older, most in the very top portion of their high-school class; most were class officers, and many were successful high-school athletes. Suddenly, this big fish from Muncie, Indiana, was now a very little fish in a big pond with some very sharp and experienced fish in the pond of a demanding institution.

As an example, there were four of us in our plebe summer room, and only two of us made it through the plebe year and later graduated. The first few days at Annapolis were a blur, and only snapshots do I remember. I was assigned to a room with three other new plebe midshipmen. We, to some degree, tried to march to other events, briefings, or meetings required to become established as functioning plebes.

The standard military haircut was part of the beginning. I will never forget when someone who later became a friend and was a former California beach boy, Walt Ryan, got his haircut. He had extremely long hair, and he seemed to want to tear up a bit as it was rapidly removed from his head.

During this period we were issued tons of clothing, on much of which we had to stencil our names and our midshipman number, mine being 3947. We were fed pretty good food, had a medical physical, as we all stood in line buck naked. Several shots, a chance to cough once or twice, and a fickle finger of fate were part of the naked line. During one of my coughing periods, the doc examined my jewels and exclaimed in a very loud voice— "Man, you have three balls!" Needless to say, this announcement gave me a bit of false status, but it was simply a small item that is fairly common—but it served me well.

Later, for some unknown reason, I and a few others in our plebe class were selected to receive a Yawl Handler's certification, which meant that we could check out and take out a *big* sailboat (larger than twenty-five feet) for a trip in the bay! First, of course, we had an extensive training period. I assume they picked folks who had no previous experience sailing, since I was one of them. It was a great opportunity and certainly fun. But, since I used the certificate only one time, it was probably a waste of resources. However, whoever previously had the yawl that I checked out had left a six-pack of beer. It was greatly appreciated! I did prove that I was a sailor at heart and could sail and did it pretty well.

Before the summer was over, as I previously said, two of the four in our room had resigned or departed for some reason. Our room was located next to the entrance to the rotunda, on the first deck, 2nd wing, which was near the famed Naval Academy Memorial Hall where John Paul Jones' flag of **"Don't Give Up the Ship"** resides. One of the plebes in our room who departed was a giant Southern lad who I am sure the football coach wanted badly, but really he seemed to be a bit of a wimp! The other one was a super troop from Arkansas who eventually became a big man in Coca-Cola.

We, the new plebe class of 1958, learned to tie knots, sail boats, fire weapons, and a host of other things, including how to march and those associated movements with marching with a nine pound M-1 Garand rifle in military parades. However, this small fish in a very big and challenging pond did survive plebe year when many didn't!

Recent Naval Academy graduates had been assigned to manage, educate, or harass us, and trying to shape us up. It seemed all of them had one thing in common, a very loud and demanding voice.

After those summer months of being disciplined into acceptable midshipmen plebes, we were assigned to our Midshipman companies, of which there were twenty-four at that time. I was to be in the 4th Fourth Company in the First Battalion, which was in the northeast front of the large Bancroft Hall facility. Bancroft Hall housed all twenty-four companies, including a snack bar, a kitchen/dining room that could feed the entire Brigade of over four thousand Midshipmen and the Officers responsible for them. Also in the building were a barbershop, cleaners, a small but well-stocked store, good medical and dental facility, and a wonderful Naval Museum entrance to the building.

My new roommates, or "wives," as we called them, were Bob Green, a wrestler for Hilo, Hawaii, and Guillermo Allegro Zariquiey from Lima, Peru, who later became an all-American soccer player. He quickly was named Zeke by some up classman. The three of us lived together for our entire four years, which was a bit unique, because midshipmen had the opportunity to change roommates (wives) twice a year. We were very compatible.

We plebes were individually assigned to a "Firstie" (senior classman) as our mentor, or someone who would show us the ropes. Mine was Dave Dunn who, when he graduated, joined the Marine Corps. Long after Dave graduated he was selected as a highly prized Distinguished Graduate. Unlike many Firsties, Dave was never very close to me, and, because of his efforts concerning a 2nd Classman, Roger Lyle, I damn near got run out of the Academy, but more about this later.

MY "WIVES", GUILLERMO "ZEKE" ZARIQUIEY and ROBERT "BOB" GREEN, 6/1954-6/1958

When my roommate Guillermo Zariquiey from Lima, Peru, and I graduated from the Naval Academy, we both received a call from Mr. J. Edgar Hoover, Director of the FBI, during graduation. Mr. Hoover said to me, "Your Dad, Harry, and I are very proud of you, congratulations." Mr. Hoover astutely also called my "wife" Guillermo (Zeke) at graduation to congratulate him for graduating from the Naval Academy. Zeke of course was thrilled with the phone call, and he told everyone about it. Mr. Hoover's foresight paid off many years later. Zeke moved rapidly through the ranks of the Peruvian Navy, being the Naval Attaché twice in Washington, DC, and subsequently the Chief of Naval Operations or Boss of the Peruvian Navy. Not only did Zeke rise in the Navy, but also his family grew!

When a Naval ship of any country ports in a foreign city, their country arranges with the host country for the representative from the ship to receive local money from a local bank to be used for paying the crew, so that they will have local money when they go on liberty. One time in England, Zeke, as a very young officer, was selected as his destroyer representative to pick up the money for the ship's crew. The bank made a terrible mistake, giving him way too much money, and he, being a Naval Academy graduate, naturally returned the overage to the English bank. The bank later said they had made a similar mistake some years ago but never got the money back.

Zeke had many key jobs with the Peruvian Navy, including Chief Communications and Security officer. When Peru captured the leaders of the Shining Path terrorists, including a young American lady, he was given the job of establishing their incarceration location. He built them a nice facility on a small, isolated, sand-covered island with no contact with the outside world. Later, one of the Shining Path terrorists took a shot at him; the bullet was stopped by his bulletproof vest. He later wore the bullet on a chain around his neck until he died.

As my friend continued to move through the ranks, he finally became the top man in the Peruvian Navy, the Chief of Naval Operations in Peru. While Zeke was in that key job, he received a call from a Deputy Director of the FBI, headquartered in Washington, DC. The Deputy then asked if he could come visit him in Peru. Of course Guillermo welcomed him, and the Deputy asked the Admiral if he remembered Mr. Hoover's telephone call, which, of course, he did. The Deputy then told my Admiral friend that several Peruvian Generals and Admirals had embezzled money from the U.S.AID program when they were assigned as Attachés to the embassy in Washington, DC.

Guillermo mentioned that he was Naval Attaché twice in Washington, and the Deputy acknowledged that and said "It was the only time that there was no embezzling going on!" Admiral Zariquiey had to bring charges against more than ten flag officers from the Army and Navy, just before he retired.

After my friend retired, he came to live with us in Florida, since he was fairly certain that his life was probably in danger.

This was because he had also been instrumental in arresting and incarcerating the key members of the *Shining Path* terrorists in Peru and also several senior Peruvian Military Officers whom he brought charge against. So, in fact, he was hiding from both the bad and the good guys!

My other roommate (wife) was Bob Green from Hilo, Hawaii, a wrestler and the son of a Portuguese sugar-plantation foreman. Bob wrestled the entire time he was at the Academy and several of my classmates and I visited him in Hawaii during our 2nd Class summer. Bob fairly quickly met a very beautiful Annapolis girl, Bette, whose father was part of the Academy staff. Upon Bob's graduation, he and Bette were married, and Bob also went into the Air Force. Bob and Bette eventually had a large family, and we were stationed together in France and at Williams AFB in Arizona. The last time we got together was at our 50th reunion, and we had aged well. Unfortunately, after the reunion, Zeke had a heart attack and passed away, and, after some serious administrative runaround, we were able to get him buried in the Academy cemetery on the hill.

Life as a plebe was very challenging, and we had to learn how to memorize tons of information such as items of naval history, the movies being shown in town, the next meal menu, Officers of the day, and many other important or very useless items. When as plebes traveling around inside Bancroft Hall, we marched very stiffly in the center of the hallways, looking straight head, without talking, either at a rapid pace or we could run, if necessary. Any upperclassman could stop a plebe and demand answers from them of the items memorized or something they might think important.

Of course our lives were controlled by a bell (actually a buzzer) that told us to get up, fall in for a meal formation, fall in to go to class, when to go to bed, and when to turn the lights out. Plebes, during the week, could not be in their beds or as we call it "the sack or the blue trampoline" unless they had medical permission. We faced a lot of mental and some physical harassment with pushups or being hit with a wood shower shoe.

As a lead-in to the next chapter, I need to add a few words about the harassment and physical abuse or the corporal punishment that I took as a plebe at the Academy. Frankly, I wish it was still part of the Academy life because it certainly prepared an individual for later life and especially the challenges of combat. Life always has challenges and heartbreaks and my life as a plebe, gave me an insight on what I could mentally and physically endure. While painful, it prepared me for the future for the ups and downs of life. While I was probably harassed more than most, it did not hurt me and it certainly strengthened me for the future. Once I became an upperclassman I did not harass or pick on the plebes but I will always believe that my plebe year was beneficial.

I will add that I have every intention of punching out my tormentor when I saw him after the Academy. At one of our class of 1958 reunions, at the football game some of my friends had seated him in front of me knowing that I said I would punch him out when I saw him next! But by then he was such a jerk that I realized he wasn't worth punching but I did tell him that my class expected me to hit him. He just laughed and said, "Ho Ho, Barry you always were a joker, it is good to see you."

ROGER LYLE, 1954-1956

My plebe year started out as many others did, and my First Classman, Dave Dunn, gave me hints about plebe year, but he was somewhat reserved, and we didn't spend much time together. Unfortunately, after a while, a 2nd Classman (college junior) named Roger Lyle began to seriously harass me. At first, he said it was because I wouldn't fix him up with the lady I fixed my "wife," Bob Green, with: Mary Giles. However, later I learned that there was a more serious reason. It seems my First Classman, Dave Dunn, had given Roger a Class A punishment for being drunk. Frequently such an offense can get you kicked out of the Academy, and this almost got him kicked out of the Academy. Lyle, in his tiny little mind, was getting even with my first classman by punishing me—what an ass! I never told my first classman, Dave Dunn, about what Lyle was doing, because, as a plebe, I just assumed I deserved the harassment, including the physical part of it.

We still had corporal punishment to plebes at that time, and old Roger hit me a lot with a wooden shower shoe (besides being an ass, he had damn big feet) when he wanted to or I screwed up with some information he wanted. Finally, it got so bad that I decided I was going to beat the crap out of him; I wrote my folks a letter saying I was going to get kicked out because I was going to beat the hell out of an upperclassman, and mailed it to them. After dropping the letter in the mail chute, I chopped (ran) to Roger's room and kicked the door open, but neither he nor his roommates were there. I then positioned myself so that when he entered the room, I could attack him! There I remained for a couple of hours until the bell warning that bedtime was approaching. Naturally, since I was a plebe, now trained to respond to the bells, I departed Lyle's room and marched back to my room and to bed. The next day I cooled off a bit and I had to call my folks to tell them I wasn't getting kicked out of the Academy for striking an upperclassman.

When I went home for Christmas leave as a plebe, I had decided I wasn't going back because of Lyle. Fortunately, Dad knew the Ball Hospital Administrator, a retired Naval Admiral and a Naval Academy graduate who gave me a pep talk. He took me to lunch and convinced me that I should return to the Academy, as Lyle was just a bump in the road that would pass. And he was correct! I will never know if this Admiral had any involvement in what happened when I got back to the Academy.

Fortunately for me, in the room across the hall from our room was a great football player, pulling guard, Len Benzi, also from Hawaii. Len was a classmate of Lyle and was a great—really great—football player who had been a star in our Cotton Bowl Victory. Len, to get Lyle off of me, chose an established tradition by betting Roger that I could eat seven cannonballs desserts (apple dumplings with hard sauce on them, and they were about the size of a large softball). If I should accomplish this feat, Roger would then have to spoon me (shake my hand) and quit picking on me. Of course, to do that, I would have to eat a normal and complete evening meal. The cannonballs arrived, and seven were selected for me to eat. I began eating them; they initially tasted pretty good! But, I quickly filled up, and I was trying hard to finish the sixth cannonball, and I was really slowing down. I believe it was Sunday night, and we were in our class-A blue uniforms (our very best uniform). Len realized that I wasn't going to make it, so he had someone distract my enemy, Roger, and while Roger was looking away, Len, *bless his Hawaiian heart*, reached out and grabbed most of cannonball number seven and stuffed it in his class-A uniform pocket. As I finished up what was left, a cheer from all those around went up, and Len firmly grabbed Roger's arm and steered him to me, forcing him to shake my hand. *Free at last!*

I am certain that I would have never graduated but for Len's help. Additionally, stuffing the material from the seventh cannonball probably ruined his best uniform! Once again, *lucky*; thank you, Len!

While a plebe, I became an associate of the famed Class of 1958 Nebraska mafia, although I was really from Kansas, and through them, I met Johnny McCain and Teddy Smedberg. Both had Admirals for fathers, and, like me, they were a bit academically challenged. As a result, for the rest of the time I was at the Academy, as long as I believed I knew as much or more than they did, I would pass and make it through the Academy. However, my friend Johnny did expose me twice to serious problems, not that I truly blamed him; (must be some Democrat in me) for trying to blame him for my occasional transgressions!

This all came out when Johnny's father, Admiral McCain, then the Commander of the Pacific, pinned my Silver Star on me at Udorn AB, Thailand. After the ceremony, I had earlier asked everyone to leave after the ceremony, so that I could talk to the Admiral. His son and my longtime friend, Johnny, had been recently shot down over North Vietnam and now was a prisoner. As all left, the Admiral, who I doubt was taller than five foot six, lit a cigar (a big Churchill). I said, "Your son Johnny is a long-time friend from our time at the Academy. Is he OK, or have you heard anything?" He took a puff on his cigar and said, "I told the dumb SOB not to get shot down, but I haven't heard anything." Then he said, "Barry Howard, Barry Howard…. You almost got arrested with him at the Circle Inn Tavern near Annapolis, Maryland, and also in Jacksonville, Florida." Somewhat shocked, I said, "Admiral, please don't tell my bosses!" He just laughed and shook my hand, put his arm around me, and said, "Be careful flying over North Vietnam, Barry!" I still get teary-eyed thinking about how he did that!

The Johnny I knew would have made a superb and tough President, à la Ronald Reagan, but it appears that his many serious lifetime challenges obviously had changed him; he had terrible—no, horrible and ill-informed—senior consultants who I had tangled with during the 2000 campaign. As a result, he ran a horrible campaign against Obama. Johnny was one tough SOB when we were at the Academy, and he just couldn't allow himself to be beaten in anything he did! I was standing next to him when we found our final class standing; I'll never forget what he said, "Damn, if I had known I was so close to being the Goat [the last last-place grad who always receives some recognition], I wouldn't have tried so hard!"

Hell, while he was a naval student pilot, he was able to fight his way out of an aircraft that had turned upside down when it crashed in the Kingsville Bay. No one who saw the accident expected him to make it out! The future Senator and Presidential candidate, apparently with his very heavy aircraft upside down in the bay, put his back on his seat and raised the aircraft enough so he could get out. I think his already-greying hair did turn solid white that day from his accident! I had driven over from Laredo, Texas, for our promotion party to our next rank. We were celebrating us Air Force guys getting promoted to First Lieutenant and Lieutenant Junior Grade for the naval troops. I believe we partied very well that night as we were all, Navy and Air Force, being promoted to the next rank. My good friend and fellow rowing crew member, Marty "Fado" McCullough, gave me a ride to the party. Unfortunately, Fado had his broken right leg in a cast, but we got to the party safely. However, that night as we were going back to the BOQ (Bachelor Officer's Quarters), the car got in fight with a telephone pole and lost, and I gained a broken jaw and a short stay in the Naval Hospital, but more on this later!

As I continued "enjoying" plebe year, I did have some pleasant times with my many classmates: at football games and especially with my new sport, crew, which I became deeply involved with and learned about that year.

How did I get involved in crew? I was walking toward the area for baseball practice, which I had hoped to play at the Academy. I had to cross a long, wooden bridge next to the baseball dressing area and the crew Boat House. The Boat House was where those who rowed crew dressed, worked out, and climbed into their shells to do their practice rowing. As I crossed the bridge, an older gentleman in a car shouted at me, "Frank, what are you doing here?"

Being a well-drilled plebe, I said, "Sir, my name is Midshipman Barry Howard, 4th Company, *sir!*" Rusty Calloway, the varsity crew coach, said, "Oh, I thought you were Frank Shakespeare of our Olympic Gold Medal crew team; you look *just like him!*" Needless-to-say, I suddenly had a serious interest in rowing crew—whatever that was! Good-bye baseball, hello crew! I began rowing crew and I fell in love with the sport, because eight rowers and a coxswain did well only when they became a team of one, in total sync! What a wonderful feeling when the shell of eight rowers and the coxswain are working as one and the boat or shell just seems to explode with each stroke, simply gliding along on the water. Even more fun was when the coxswain decides to take the stroke up and increases the rate of strokes being taken and the boat virtually jumps forward. Crew became my sport and gaining weight became a constant goal, as I was always in the first heavyweight boat, until I lost weight down to 160 pounds, then I had the choice of the second heavyweight boat or the first lightweight boat. I always took the first boat, wherever it was! Crew was a year-round sport, so my commitment to crew continued the entire time I was at the Academy.

After Roger Lyle was removed from my life, plebe year seemed OK, and we all hit the books, suffered as plebes do, and prayed that we would beat Army in football so that our plebe harassment would end. Unfortunately, that was the era of Lenny Dawkins, the *lonesome-end-era*, and we suffered accordingly.

Our plebe summer cruise was great; I was on the *USS Iowa*, a battleship, and we were exposed to the life of an enlisted sailor at sea. We even learned how to holystone the wooden deck of the *Iowa*. You are given a stone with an indention in it, and a wooden stick like a broom handle, and you line up next to several other plebes and in unison you slide the stone back and forth, removing the outer layer of the wooden deck. Of course the Deck Chief would say, "OK, back and forth," and after a few strokes he would command, "Shift!" and we would move the stone forward the width of the stone. Today, I doubt if there are any wooden decks left in the Navy!

On this cruise we visited Spain and England, and our trip home was interrupted by our President Eisenhower's trip across the ocean for a meeting. We then cruised in circles until he passed overhead. I didn't think you could recognize parts of an ocean, but it seems like you could, if you passed over it enough! On board, the emergency rations consisted of mostly ham, and I swear it was reconstituted ham and I had seen it before, several times!

Visiting Spain was great part of the cruise, but having lived in the sterile American environment, eating in Spain gave most of us a chance to experience *Montezuma's revenge*! Of course we had to wear our uniforms ashore, and you might see a Midshipman walking at a rapid pace down a street with a strained look on his face. Then he might start running for a bit, then his expression changed to a sad and embarrassed look, as he started walking as if he had something in his underwear, which he did! Good old *Montezuma* got him, and few of us missed the opportunity to meet that guy! When we had a meal in the room, we received a bottle of wine with it; some of us collected the bottles of wine and filled a bathtub with them resulting in a wine bath!

Going eastward, we crossed the International Date Line, and we suffered the initiation of all pollywogs under auspices of **neptunus rex**, Ruler of the Raging Main—thus becoming, "A Trusty Shellback!" Returning, I, now being a Trusty Shellback, was selected as the Royal Contribine (see picture) for those who flew to Spain and to join us. They were still pollywogs and had to be initiated for **neptunus rex**. Unfortunately, this time honored and fun exercise has now been banned and slowly the Trusty Shellbacks' of **NEPTUNUS REX** are dying off. I would comment that each initiation was dependent on the genius of those organizing it and it was all designed in good fun but occasionally someone got hurt or got *even* with someone. I am personally sorry that the PC world saw fit to ban it as it was a great moral builder and a very special Naval traditional which also decreased the stress of being at sea.

After our summer cruise, we had almost a month off. And Muncie sure looked good to me! It was pretty obvious, that I had matured and had a broader experience stem than my high school classmates and the girls seemed to be very impressed with me which I enjoyed. I did tell a few exciting war stories like firing the 16" guns on the Iowa and some tales from Spain and England.

After plebe year, I became a typical third-class midshipman, rowing crew and hitting the books to stay in my class. With no one placing challenging demands on me as they did during plebe year, life was good and quiet! Finals were always a challenge to me, but, fortunately, I made it through the Academy without bilging (failing) any classes or final exams, but I came damn close a few times. One thing an Academy education establishes in a graduate is the ability to face the challenge of any type of exam or keeping up your grades so that you can stay with your classmates. I did manage to graduate without failing a single final exam and graduating with my classmates!

I have to admit I did not give plebes a hard time, as my life as a plebe had been too miserable, and I really tried to help them. One of the terrible events that happened during the third-class year was that a plebe who lived across the hall from us, Joe Demasi, one night went to the "head" (bathroom) and had a normal sitting performance, read a magazine for a bit, folded his robe and placed it on the floor with the magazine on top of it. He then took his bathrobe tie cord and hung himself using the hook on the back of his toilet stall. Another plebe heard him and saw his arms drop below the stall door in front of his legs but said, "He thought he was praying!" But later, the plebe that saw his hands drop had to leave the Academy, as it truly affected him mentally. What was so heartbreaking was that Joe was a Star student, Captain of his plebe soccer team, and had a really nice girlfriend. Having been very close to other suicides during my life, much as I try, I will never understand them.

Our second-class year, which is the same level as being a junior in a college, was exciting but nothing of note other than, now I sat on the "fat boys" table in the dining area eating extremely high-caloric meals, with ice cream at every meal, so that I could gain weight for crew season. I would get up to 175 pounds, but after a few weeks of spring rowing, I dropped to around 160 pounds, which obviously resulted in less strength, and I dropped from the first heavyweight crew boat to the second boat. Naturally, the lightweight crew coach offered me the first boat on the lightweight crew team, which I accepted, and I went from bow in the heavyweights to number seven rowing position behind my friend, Terry Priebe, who was the stroke of the lightweight first boat. The lightweight team can have someone who weighs 159 pounds, which I claimed! This bouncing between heavyweight crew and lightweight crew continued through my years as a rower or—oarsman (say it fast and it sounds dirty!).

I did, when we marched to class, carry notes, which I dropped to good-looking ladies and which said, "Help! I am being held against my will; please write me at [my address] or call me at this number (Can't remember the number as it was a bank of phone where someone would take a message) during the hours of [such and such.]" A few times it worked well, and I would hear from a lovely lady, and we would have a few dates. The only young lady in the area of Annapolis, which included Washington, DC, that I really had an interest in was named, Joan Lofgren, who I met in Washington, DC. Joan was the beautiful daughter of the wine taster for Taylor's Wines, a New York upstate winery. She would frequently bring a great bottle of wine when we had a date.

Dating at Annapolis was somewhat unique. Normally the young lady would get to Annapolis on her own, and her midshipman would have arranged a place for her to stay, possibly a hotel, but normally at a "drag house." A drag house was a big older house in the city of Annapolis. It was usually run by a Navy widow. The house would have a few TVs strategically located, surrounded by several couches and several bedrooms with two or more single beds in each room. The couches were for the midshipmen and the beautiful young ladies so that they could snuggle a bit and maybe even kiss! However, public display of affection (holding hands, kissing, or hugging) outside the drag house was strictly forbidden and if caught doing it, you would have the opportunity to spend a few hours marching on Saturday with other who had also receive demerits!

Two unique events occurred while I was a senior midshipman or Firstie that were somewhat different from most other happenings at the Academy. A couple of us bought a '49 Studebaker that we kept in the junkyard since owning a car at Annapolis, at that time, was illegal. It was a functioning car, pretty fast, but it loved oil and damn near used as much oil as it did gas, and the heater had died long ago! One time a classmate from Indiana, Tony Miller, and I drove it home to Indiana for Christmas break; the weather was cold and the heater had died and been buried long ago! I remember stopping one very late night on the Pennsylvania Turnpike, to eat and to get warm. We had our collars turned up, hats down, hands in our pockets—the lady at the register, put her hands up, thinking we were going to rob her! We assured her that we didn't want to rob her, but we were just riding in a very cold car and wanted to warm up for the next leg of the trip. I'm not even sure what happened to the old Studebaker.

Always staying on the edge of legality, several of us got together and rented an apartment our first-class (senior) year: TVs, beds for lady friends, kitchen for snacks, and a refrig. for beer, (probably National Bohemian or Gunthers) the cheapest available that we could have delivered, since we couldn't be seen carrying beer.

I do need to digress a bit here and mention our honor code, which was unlike West Point's and, later, that of the Air Force Academy (West Pointers built Zoomie-land!). I think ours was more realistic in that you were only on your honor at certain times, such as exams, when you signed your name, or when someone challenged you with, "On your honor, did you cheat on the daily test" or "Did you shine your shoes?" Thus we were able to play "cops and robbers" a bit and not do receive Honor violations for minor things. Once I was in the Air Force and had worked with West Pointers and later Zoomies (Air Force Academy cadets), I was shocked how they could work their speech to avoid lying yet still appear to me to be lying by "sea-lawyering" around a statement.

In our apartment we did consume some beer; in fact, we even wallpapered a wall in the living room with empty beer cans. On one occasion a friend had a young lady visit that apparently had a contagious disease. Shortly after that, at the Sunday evening meal, it was announced that she might have contaminated some in the Brigade and, if needed, sickbay would be open after chow! There was a long line that night at sickbay! Not for me, however!

In any case, the apartment was a real success and kept many of us a bit broke but out of serious trouble. We kept out lady friends there, drank some beer, watched football games, and told lots of lies! It was great preparation for becoming the world's greatest fighter pilot (WGFP)!

On one of our midshipman summer cruises, we were taken on flights off a carrier, and some of us got to also recover or landing on the carrier—yes! Taking the hook and all! I was one of the lucky ones, and I flew with a Marine Squadron. The majority of the Marine pilots had a betting pool about who could get the most midshipmen airsick. Fortunately, the pilot I flew with was Lt. Col. John Glen, who was later an astronaut, and then a US senator. He said, "I will not try to make you sick; I want to sell you on aviation," which he did, convincing me more than I was already convinced! He let me fly the aircraft and actually tried to teach me a bit. I was thrilled and of course I didn't get sick, so I could give my classmates a bit of grief about their getting sick!

Life at the Academy continued, and I was able to maintain satisfactory grades and passed or did not bilge any final exams and graduate. I can't say I didn't push or challenge the system while there, but I won and I did graduate in 1958, with the class I started back on June 6, 1954.

I was also the 4th Company illegal barber; actually, I began barbering as a plebe after Christmas vacation and continued for most of my time at the Academy. When I got my hair cut during my plebe Christmas break at home, my barber said he started cutting hair in the Navy and he gave me a set of clippers. The midshipmen's barbershop had changed the rules, and we plebes were at a disadvantage concerning getting haircuts, so I started cutting other plebes hair for a quarter a cut. Big income for a plebe! The first one I did was Johnny Pinto, a very light-skinned Italian with black hair and a very white scalp. Did I butcher him! But practice makes perfect, and pretty soon I had lots of customers. On one cruise I even cut the hair of a Navy Admiral who was on board for a visit.

I think by the time I graduated I had four sets of clippers. For one year, our company TAC officer was Major George Patton Jr., son of "The General Patton." Each year one of our company officers at Annapolis was a West Point graduate, normally a Major in rank. Preceding Patton was Alexander Haig, whose company won the Colors, which meant that they won the competition of the twenty-four midshipmen companies.

Patton was our ramrod-straight Company Officer during my second-class year. One day he called me to his office; of course I saluted and maybe clicked my heels in front of his desk and reported as, "Midshipman Howard, Sir!" He said, "Sit down, Barry; we need to talk about your business of cutting hair." I maintained silence because this started off like I might be marching off punishments soon! I had been *busted* several times for cutting hair, which had resulted in several marching punishments! With his opening statement, he reached down and opened his bottom drawer and motioned me around his desk. He pointed to my clippers that had been previously confiscated and were in his drawer. Those clippers had resulted in a bit of Saturday marching! He said, "Should you ever need any of these, just help yourself. I always want our troops to look good!" Naturally I said, "Yes sir!" And his next words were, "Dismissed, Barry; you are doing a good job."

The summer before he arrived, I had started drinking, and I got in a bit of trouble with a Marine Major who was married to a Miss America, and he had "chitted" me. A chit is a form that is filled out on a midshipman who does well or badly and becomes part of his military aptitude grade at the Academy. I think I told him one night at a bar at on a marine base after several adult beverages as we were talking that, "He was a pretty good guy and only half as big a pussy as his troops said he was!"

As a result, Maj. Patton had a counseling session with me about drinking, but it wasn't nasty; in fact, it was a good session, and I have to admit, I began to really like and respect George Patton Jr. He simple said, "Drinking is a normal part of the military and one must control it or not drink and he preferred to drink!"

I did use a beer opener or church key that I kept in my desk drawer to simply open my "so-important" can of black shoe polish. During a room inspection, when we were gone to class, he found the church key and wrote on my desk blotter in big red letters: *What's a matter, Barry, can't stop drinking?* And he drew a line to the church key lying there. Later, I explained to him that "Chit was a one-time event" and once again he said, "Remember, drinking is part of our military life; learn to control it, or don't drink!"

Patton loved to visit us during our study periods, as it took him five years to complete the four-year course at West Point. So he really monitored our studying habits, and I think—no, I know that he knew everyone's most troublesome academic subject, and he constant asked the individual about it when he saw him. He would occasionally, after some sort of party requiring a formal uniform and some adult beverages; he would pull surprise visits to us in his cape and sword. He hit our room one night, and, after hitting the door with his sword as he came in, walked around the room and saw that we were studying, said as he walked out, he said, "Carry on, and hit those books!"

He really smelled *goooood*!

Once he walked out, one of us said, "Wonder where his horse is?" Suddenly there was another loud knock at the door and in he walked again! He said, "I left my horse at home!" He then simply walked out; but I think I saw a smile on his lips!

I'll never forget how our 4th Company was robbed of being the Color Company. The award went to our sister company, the 3rd Company, run by US Marine Corps Maj. "Bonzo" Parrish. Parrish was a true Marine, who needed a shave immediately after he had just completed shaving. In any case, the competition for the Colors was tied going into the final event, which was Company Marching. Now, there is no way the 4th Company could lose the marching competition. We had a Midshipman Company Commander, Fritz Warren, a former (and truly a picture of a) Marine Drill Sargent.

When Fritz commanded, "March!" I have seen trees on the parade field try to march; he looked like, shouted like, and was in fact a real former Marine Corps Drill Sergeant. I watched the final marching event from my shell on the river, and when Fritz said or shouted to the Company, "Attention!" my body automatically came to rigid attention in the shell, and, of course, my teammates really laughed at me!

In any case, unfortunately the year before, the winning Color Company had a guy named Alexander Haig as their Company Officer, another Army Officer? That day, as I watched from my shell, to me, it seemed the 4th Company won it hands down. Unfortunately, maybe, there was a bit of politics at the Naval Academy in that they didn't want the Army Representative to win the Colors twice in a row. In any case, apparently the Majors, Bonzo and George Jr. had a bet that the winner would win a dinner at the Officer's Club, with unlimited adult beverages accompanying the food!

Since I was a second-classman, I happened to be the mate of the, *First Deck, first wing* the morning after the bet was paid off at the Officers' Club. Maj. Patton's office was on the First Deck of the first wing. A Mate has an elevated small desk where he can stand, with a phone behind him to receive messages concerning actions for the Brigade, which he will announce. He also monitors and records events that occur in his area. That morning I looked up from recording something and saw Maj. Patton walking toward me. I sensed something wrong, but I quickly chopped (hurried) up to him and said my mate's spiel, "Midshipman Howard, Mate of the first deck, first wing, Sir!" He said, "Shut up, Howard," and then I noticed old ramrod-straight Patton was actually a bit—no, actually seriously bent over! He went into his office and very *quietly* shut the door. Next thing I heard was, "Mate, Mate, Goddamn it, Mate, get in here!" Naturally I ran to his office, and I stood in front of the closed door and started to give my spiel when he said, "Mate, get your ass in here, right now!"

I quickly moved in front of his desk and saluted, but I realized that silence was a virtue now. He flipped me a fifty cent piece and said go down and get *us* ten cokes. The coke machine was in the basement one deck down, and of course I was not allowed to leave my floor on duty. I started to say, "Sir, I can't leave the—"

"Get your ass down and get *us* ten cokes!" the Cokes came in cups; they were a nickel each at that time. He did hand me a tray to put them on, and off I hurried. I returned with the ten cokes, and he simply said, "Shut the damn door and sit down." With that he opened a desk drawer and pulled out a bottle of bourbon. He then poured a shot in each coke, separated four of them toward me, and said, "Those four are yours, and these are mine." I started to say something, and he just shook his head, and said, "It is bad to drink alone!" and I shut up. Since I knew, he knew that I couldn't drink, *but* I did as directed by the really hung-over loser, who was also really pissed. However, we just talked about many things, not about losing or anything important, but I slept well that night! Patton was always my hero, and I tried to model myself after him: duty came first, stupid regulations were stupid, he absolutely cared about his troops, and he included his wife in his life.

Another time, he arrived when the Officer of the Day, a Lt.Junior Grade Naval Officer who was on duty and was visiting our room, possibly trying to catch me cutting hair. Patton said to the Naval Officer, "What are you doing in one of my rooms?" He then angrily motioned him out of the room. After they left, we quickly moved to the door to listen to Patton say in a very strong, authoritative voice, "You, Sir, are not welcome in my company; I take complete care of all of my troops, and I never want to see you here again; do you understand?"

I truly loved George Patton Jr., and I even went to visit him in Vietnam, but he had been air-evacuated a few hours before I arrived with a battlefield wound. I am sure that his daddy was proud of him!

During my second-class year, I was part of the Brigade Activities Committee (BAC), and in that capacity we were instrumental in pushing Navy sports, primarily football. That year we played Notre Dame at Notre Dame, and since I had planned to go to Notre Dame before I received my Academy appointment, I was familiar with the terrible disadvantage that teams face playing at Notre Dame! Since I knew that only a few of us would travel to Notre Dame, I proposed, and it was accepted, that we locate very large speakers and place them on the sidelines at Notre Dame. We then had the Brigade together in the gym producing cheers and noise to drown out the crowd, especially the sound of the beads that one attending the game could see being used by the Notre Dame fans!

We accomplished our plan, and I was at Notre Dame managing the event. Actually the next year the NCAA made it illegal to do what we did, *but we did beat Notre Dame!* After the game, our coach, Eddie Ederlatz, grabbed me, and, with tears streaming down his face, stuck a hundred-dollar bill in my pocket and said, "Thank you; I am Catholic, and to beat Notre Dame at home is a dream come true and you did it for me; from the bottom of my heart, thank you!"

Sadly, that exciting weekend was personally sad for me, because my cousin and longtime buddy Lynn Howard was killed in Colorado. My father immediately went to Colorado to investigate the tragic event at the scene. Unfortunately, Dad and Lynn's father—my father's brother, my uncle Eddie—had lost their brother, who was shot and killed in a "hunting" accident by a fellow who, I had been told, owed him $10,000, and this was in the 1920s or so. As a result, Uncle Eddie really encouraged his family to be very afraid of guns.

Lynn was going with a guy who frankly was a real nut case, and we all had encouraged her to get rid of him. He later said that he had taken her out to teach her how to shoot his pistol. Apparently, according to the boy who shot her, he had pointed the gun at her after she told him they were through, and she panicked and tried to hit the gun away, and he said it went off. The bastard then left her where she died, and went to town and saw a movie. Later he or someone reported her missing, and he said he left her where they were shooting, "as she was mad at him." Of course then they found her body.

Dad got the shooter to tell him the actual story of what happened, but he was the son of a very wealthy man in Colorado. Unfortunately, Lynn was found about a hundred yards outside the county of Dad's longtime friend, the county Sheriff. The Sheriff of that county where she died would not cooperate. He may have been influenced somehow by the boy's father. I think not being able to officially get the truth officially out really affected my Dad forever.

Several of my friends had met Lynn earlier. When they graduated from the Academy, and they were assigned to Colorado upon graduation, they ran into the shooter at several parties, and each time they loudly mentioned that he had murdered my cousin. The last I heard about him is that he had flipped out and had been kicked out of several Colorado colleges and just disappeared. My Daughter, Barrie Lynn, is named after my cousin Lynn.

That success at Notre Dame may have led to an elevation of the BAC! Later at the Army/Navy game in Philly, we members of the BAC were there a day or two early to set up our program. I believe there were three or four of us to a room in the hotel, and I think Teddy Smedberg, the Superintendent's son, was one of us. We all had lady friends there with us, and after a hard day of work, we were in the room with our lady friends; hell, I can't even remember who I was with! Anyhow, we were taking a nap, preparing for the night's events, and our lady friends were in bed with us, *but* a sheet separated the men and ladies, honest! We were officers and gentlemen, remember! Anyhow, there was a knock at the door, and since it was left unlocked, someone shouted, "Come in, it's unlocked!"

Guess who? The Superintendent, Admiral Smedberg, stopped by to see his son, Teddy. Oops, or aw shit! All the good we did at Notre Dame died that weekend. I don't think the BAC was part of the halftime performance at next year's Army/Navy game, but honest, there was a sheet between the men and women, *really*! Officers and gentlemen we were!

I normally always had fun, whatever I would do, and at the Academy I continued enjoying myself, except for some of the major challenges of academics. At our famous Ring Dance, after dipping our class rings into water from the seven seas, we could wear them. I proudly escorted Mary Giles, the truly first love of my early life.

Finally, graduation was approaching, and I had already had a date for the event with Jeri Trusty, from Muncie, but I think we were both losing interest in each other. She did come for half of it, and Joan Lofgren was there for the second week of graduation week. Little Napoleon was furious with me about that, and because I may have slept through General Eisenhower's graduation speech. Also I believe Mom was also unhappy, because she thought I was kicked out of one parade because my friends thought I might have had something to drink; not true: I hated to march, and I think I had a sore leg.

As I said earlier, an extremely beautiful and wonderful young lady entered my life while at the Academy: Joan Lofgren. Joan was a lady I met in Washington, DC, at a Sunday afternoon party when I was a first-classman or a senior at the Academy. She was striking, not only in beauty, but also with a very black eye, which she swore was a result of tangling with a light pole. She was attending a famous cooking school in DC. Also, she was a recent Catholic convert who was unable to think about raising children without having a strictly Catholic upbringing. We even met with a priest about it, who told me to just hang on and she would, over time, be more understanding. We went to Princeton's graduation together (I was made an honorary by members of the graduating class from the Naval ROTC graduates). While there, I had a long, serious drinking session with Secretary of State John Foster Dulles. Sure wish I could remember all the wonderful advice he gave me or I probably tried to give him!

Joan was one of the most beautiful people I ever dated, and it would have been an exciting long-term relationship if the really minor Catholic problem hadn't existed. I suspect our problems were in my hard head, and I just wanted a reason to not be seriously committed, yet.

When I graduated, up to 25 percent of us could go to the Air Force, since the next year, the first class from the Air Force Academy graduated. I chose the Air Force because the Air Force Representative at the Academy told me that as soon as I qualified for flying, I could attend pilot training. The Navy said, "You must go to sea for three years first"! Unfortunately, the Air Force Representative failed to tell the Air Force personnel system, but more about that later! Subsequently, as the years have passed and the Air Force Academy turned out graduates, only a very few from the Naval Academy now can go to the Air Force.

FIRST AIR FORCE ASSIGNMENT, SHEPPARD AFB, TEXAS, 9/1958-2/1959

Upon graduation from the Naval Academy, I first participated as a member of the wedding parties for several weddings as many of my friends were married quickly after graduation. I was given several months off before I had to report to Sheppard AFB Intelligence School at Wichita Falls, Texas, in September 1958.

To fill the time I had, I was offered an engineer's job with Perfect Circle Piston Rings, in New Castle, Indiana. It was an enjoyable few months, and I was able to be productive for them in that, based on my Naval Academy education, I designed a smoke stack smoke suppressor which was used for many years after I left. The design was similar to what Naval Ships have to suppress smoke in combat. I was pretty proud of it, too. I know that the company believed that effort made my employment worthwhile, but I suspect I was hired because of my Dad.

One of my major disappointments is that I never *succeeded* in grilling my Dad about his experiences in the FBI, especially during the war. *This is probably one of the main reasons the reason I have written this book.*

One of his tales he did tell me, later in life, was that when he was in Muncie, he had suggested that a string of bank robberies were made by an individual, but others in the FBI *ho-hummed* his suggestion about the individual. Later, when the robber was caught because of Dad's efforts, J. Edgar personally got involved. J. Edgar was truly a hands-on leader, and, after the robber was caught, he confessed to all the robberies that Dad had said he had done. As a result, I believe that J. Edgar gave Dad a large bonus; I think it was near $10,000, which was a great deal of money in the 1950s.

Another of Dad's stories I learned from the black plant union leader (UL), also a Mr. Howard, who was in charge of the union at Perfect Circle Piston Rings Company, New Castle, Indiana. I had worked there for ninety days after I graduated from Annapolis. In any case, Mr. Howard (the union leader) one day he asked me if my Dad had ever talked about how Dad broke the strike at Perfect Circle. He hadn't, so Mr. Howard the union leader, told me.

I must digress for a moment about shooting Dad's .38 special pistol. Under Hoover, each agent had to shoot a box of ammunition a month. Dad frequently took me along, and, as a result, I am a fair point-and-shoot gunner. Always, if we were in the woods someplace at the end of shooting, Dad would find a stump and stick his always-lit cigarette in it. He would then try to shoot off the lit end by ducking down and firing between his legs at about twenty-five to thirty-five feet. I would also try, but neither of us ever hit it.

In any case, the union's Mr. Howard had my Dad say to him, "Mr. Howard, let's go for a ride." They stopped in a field with stumps, and Dad walked out to one of the stumps and stuck his lit cigarette in it. He walked a short distance away, bent over, put his gun between his legs, shot the end of the lit cigarette.

Mr. Howard and his union ended the strike that day. Dad never told me about it, and I didn't ask, even after Mr. Howard told me about it!

After working at Perfect Circle Piston Rings for ninety days, I departed Muncie in early September in my 1958 light cornflower blue 1958 Chevrolet convertible without power steering (what a dummy I was; I didn't get power steering, so no woman would drive it!). I was to attend a Photo-Intelligence Officer's course at Sheppard AFB, Wichita Falls, Texas.

I'll never forget the drive to Sheppard, as it seemed each hundred miles, as I drove toward Texas, the temperature increased ten degrees. I believe it was 120 degrees when I got to Wichita Falls.

When we Naval Academy graduates arrived at Sheppard Air Force Base, several of us rented a house together (Harry Brown, Stu Craig, Howard Hall, Don Norkin, and I). Several nurses had previously rented the home we rented. They were not the best housekeepers! We did a navy scrub-down of the house and then hit the road to meet Texas women. We of the Texas Snake Ranch then cut a wide path concerning the ladies of Wichita Falls. The house was near the local college, Midwestern University. About the time we arrived, the fall session was about to begin, so the college had a mixer for new students. Old Barry and another of his roommates took a card table, two chairs, and a pad of paper and several pens. We had a sign that said we were from the yearbook and new students should sign up with name, address, and telephone number. We simple put a check mark by those young ladies' names we considered worthy of recent Naval Academy graduates! We were a bit over-enamored about ourselves!

There was one lady, who was extremely beautiful, there with what appeared to be with a very drunk cowboy. She did not sign up, however. Her name was Dorlyne Bailey. Dorlyne, or Sinky, as she was called by her father, since she was the number-five daughter, and in Spanish *cinco* is five, thus in Texian, Sinky! She later was my marvelous wife, an officer's wife, mother, home-maker, and five times, an extremely hardworking Commander's wife. She was a great mother and certainly raised our children wonderfully.

Also at Sheppard with us were Jack and Dotty Cresko and the famed Jim Hocker, world-renowned *smiler*! Everyone loved Dotty, while we tolerated old Jack and Jim Hocker always cre-ated a happy scene when he was around!

After arriving at Sheppard AFB, almost immediately I went to the flight Surgeon's office for a flight physical so that I could apply for pilot training, which I passed except for the eyes. A Flight Surgeon is a doctor specially trained to administer to aircrew members. I repeated my visit to the Flight Surgeon's office each month for a couple of months, always passing all but the eye test. Later, at the Officer Club, I did meet the base Ophthalmologist, Corky Williamson, from Kokomo, Indiana. Corky was a basketball all-American at Indiana Uni-versity who played under Bobby Knight. We became good friends, along with his roommate, a little All-American foot-ball player at DePaul University, Dr. Bob Kesling, who was an Oral Surgeon.

Every month on the second or third day of the month, I visited the Flight Surgeon's office for a flight physical, for which I regu-larly failed the eye test but was otherwise found to be healthy. I spent a lot of time with Corky and Bob; in fact, Bob let me *scrub in* on several operations! It is amazing what can be done to the human body, and since I have spent considerable time on the operating table later in my life, those operations I observed served me well for my challenges later.

One day, as I was approaching the end of my Intelligence Officer's course, Corky called me at home and said that he had left a book he needed on the table by the front door in the house they rented, and, "Would I pick it up for him? "Of course I will," I said.

It was a book filled with all eye charts used by the Air Force. Needless to say, I stopped at a copy store and made copies of the eye charts I recognized. I spent all my free time studying the eye charts, and after I felt confident, I took another flight physical. Corky refused to check my eyes, but had someone else do it. *I passed!* To say I partied after passing the test is an understatement. Corky did give me a pair of glasses to fly with, just in case, but he assured me that I fairly passed the test! More on the glasses and flying later!

Finally, one of the Intelligence school's secretaries fixed me up with *the* Dorlyne Bailey, and we became a regular team. I met all of her friends and family, and, after a while, I could understand most things she said in her beautiful Texican. She had a way of charming everyone, and, of course, when they asked her where she was from, she would say, "Brooklyn!"

While at Sheppard, I began hunting quail with one of our instructors, Tony Anthony, who was later our best man. One day we were looking for some birds, and we found them in an isolated area and began hunting. Oops—suddenly, someone who looked very official and with a gun on his hip showed up and asked for our permit to hunt on Carter McGregor's land. Naturally we had no permit, so we were taken to see "Mac" McGregor. We quickly apologized for hunting on his land without a permit, me mentioning that I was not from Texas and I was "an out-of-state" who didn't know the rules. When he learned that I was in the Air Force, a Naval Academy graduate, he told the man that had picked us up to write us a permit. It was obvious that he was a patriot, and he may have mentioned that his father flew in WW II. Since my grandfather, Harry Burns Howard, considered himself a Texan, with his six-gun under his pillow and his constant gambling, smoking, and drinking like in the cowboy movies, Carter McGregor's enhanced my love of Texas!

But at the time, there were some elements of Wichita Falls who weren't happy with Sheppard Air Base and the men and women there. Some of our younger enlisted troops were being attacked in town, and, for a while, we junior officers traveled around at night looking to protect our enlisted troops. I believe that I went to see the Base Commander and suggested that what the Navy had done in a similar situation in a town that wasn't happy about the naval base being there. They paid the entire force with only two-dollar bills—nothing but two-dollar bills. Suddenly, the local folks realized how much the base folks put into the economy, and the trouble stopped! Not sure we could do that today, since most military folks have their pay sent to a bank but it sure worked at Sheppard!

I don't know how high in the intelligence class I graduated, but, again, I *luckily* got to choose Barksdale AFB, Shreveport, Louisiana, which I considered was the best assignment we had.

BARKSDALE AFB, LOUISIANA, 3/1959-5/1959

I departed Sheppard with an approved Flight Physical and a completed application for pilot training and headed for my new assignment, the 2nd Recce Tech, Barksdale AFB, Louisiana. I checked in at Barksdale in March of 1959, and I was assigned to a house on the golf course with several other young lieutenants. On my first trip to the 2nd Recce Tech facility, I was taken into a conference room, and the Commander walked in the room with a bunch of papers in his hand. He was extremely friendly and seemed happy to have me there. As we talked, he became very serious and said, "I am going to give you three pieces of papers, one of which you should sign." He then pushed what I realized was an application for pilot training, and I think another one was for navigator training, and finally a letter of resignation. Fortunately, I had my briefcase with me, and I quickly pulled out my fully filled-out application for Pilot Training with attached flight physical, *passed*! He immediately and happily signed it for me.

My next stop was personnel where I was told that I had a three-year directed duty to Intelligence! What a shock! The Air Force representative at the Naval Academy told all of us when we were sworn in that if we were not qualified for aviation at graduation, when we did qualify, we could immediately go to pilot or navigator training. Naturally I told the personnel person that, but he then showed me the regulation, which clearly gave one a "directed tour of duty" after attending any class that lasted as long as my Intelligence course had lasted. I made a call to the Air Force Rep at the Naval Academy, but he had been reassigned. I have to say, it was truly the low point in my beginning Air Force career.

Trying to get out of my directed tour of duty, I started a letter-writing effort, and my Squadron Commander not only supported me but also helped me fight the system. I, first, started a letter campaign to Personnel about what I was told at the Naval Academy by the Air Force Representative, "That I could go to pilot training as soon as I was qualified." After many letters to AF Personnel and my Congressman, Ralph Harvey, someone approved that I could go to Pilot Training once a slot was available. I am sure that Congressman Harvey made it happen! The next challenge was to get a slot, which became a major roadblock.

One afternoon at the Barksdale Officers' Club (OC), I met Maj. Bill Frasca, a US Naval Academy graduate and who was the Aide to Gen. McConnell, the Commander of the 2nd Air Force. It was a Wednesday evening at the Officer's Club bar. After hearing my tale of woe, Maj. Bill told me to come by his office in the morning at 0800, and we would work to get me a slot for pilot training. Of course I was waiting in his office when he came in the next morning; his General was on a trip. Bill picked up the phone and called Personnel. I'll never forget his conversation: "This is Maj. Frasca, Gen. McConnell's aide." The person on the other end obviously asked, "What can I do for you, Major?" The Major, then putting the phone on speaker, bless his heart, said, "We have a lieutenant here, Barry Howard, that we (meaning he and I) need a Pilot Training slot for, ASAP." It was Thursday morning, and the personnel troop said, "Could he make it to Marianna AB, Florida, to start class Monday morning?" Bill had him on speaker, and I violently shook my head in the affirmative! Bill said, "He'll be there or I will kick his ass!" *And I was! Lucky* again!

I was jumping for joy, but Maj. Bill slowed me down, saying that clearing the base would be a challenge in such a short period of time. I assured him I could do it, which I did by noon Friday.

Unfortunately, at Friday night beer call at the Officers' Club, I was one happy and eventually a very drunk second lieutenant, buying lots of drinks for others and myself. That night in the main dining room, General McConnell had a formal Dining-Out which involve those attending wearing their formal uniforms and the ladies of course dressed to the nines! I have to admit, I don't remember much about that night. However, early the next morning, Saturday, when I heard a pounding on our front door, I sensed something was wrong. Answering the door I saw my 1958 Chevrolet convertible parked perpendicular rather than parallel as it should be in the driveway.

It was an Air Policeman and he said, "If you are Lt. Howard, you are to report to General McConnell's office in your Class-A uniform at 0900." Uh-oh! I knew I was in big trouble, and my Class-As were packed away in my car! They also needed ironing badly. The Air Policeman even mentioned that it was a strange parking attempt on my pretty Chevy convertible!

I arrived at General McConnell's office and was quickly marched into his office! Several other officers were already in there. I stood at attention in front of his desk, saluting and sweating like a pig! "Lt. Barry J. Howard, reporting as directed, *SIR*!" The General said, "Lieutenant, you nearly ruined my Dining-Out Saturday night at the Club" I immediately apologized, and someone said, "The lieutenant was celebrating his starting in pilot training Monday, Sir"

The General looked me up and down, very solemnly, and said, "Lieutenant, I think maybe by your performance Saturday night that someday you will make a great fighter pilot, but you must learn to control your consumption. Now I want you off this base by noon, do you understand?" "Yes *SIR*, thank you, and I will do better in the future!" I saluted and got the hell out of there! I was off the base well before noon on the way to Florida!

Many years later, I was assigned to the Pentagon in Operations in the basement near the purple water fountain and I, of course, got my hair cut in the Pentagon barbershop. One time I recognized a retired General McConnell getting his hair cut in the chair next to me. As he was leaving, he said, "Same time next month?" Of course the barber said, "Yes sir!" After he left, I asked the barber if he was sure that he would be there; he said, "He always calls in, but he'll be there!"

The next time he was in the chair, I was sitting across from him in my full Colonel's class-A uniform with all my ribbons on, with my fighter-pilot boots bright and shiny. I stood up and saluted him and said in a very loud voice, "General, you may not remember me, but I was the Lt. Barry Howard, who almost ruined your Dining-Out at Barksdale!" He looked me up and down like he had that Saturday morning long ago, and said, "Looking at your many ribbons, it appears that I made a right decision that morning; are you a fighter pilot?" In a very loud voice, I said, "Affirmative, *sir!*" He reached out and shook my hand and said, "Good luck in the future, Barry!" I saluted him, and I did my sharpest about-face and marched out of there. I think everyone in the barbershop was clapping as I marched out! Unfortunately, he died a few weeks later, but I was sure proud that I had redeemed myself with him.

The short time I was at Barksdale, I did get deeply involved in the Photo-Intelligence business, and I was learning like a man drinking out of a fire hydrant. The 2nd Recce Tech is one of the major facilities that received inputs from the U-2 and later the SR-71. Knowing that I had a Commander who had eventually helped me to get into pilot training, I was determined to pay him back by working hard for him, and it is always fun to learn new things and skills. The skills I learned at the 2nd Recce Tech later really paid off during the Vietnam War when I was stationed at Udorn, Thailand and developed the FAST FAC F-4 program.

PILOT TRAINING, MARIANNA AB, FLORIDA, 6/1959-11/1959

My arrival at Marianna AB, Florida, in June 1959 was without note, except I was in a class with several more senior officers— real captains! Fortunately, in a class ahead of me were a friend and his wife, Mike and Joan Stevens. Mike was from the USNA Class of 1959, and he was the stroke on the first heavyweight crew shell, which, at the start of each season, I was normally in as the bow oarsman. The Stevens made my introduction to Marianna easy, and they became lifelong friends, and later my wife and children became their friends also.

After my quick entry into Pilot Training thanks to Maj. Bill Frasca, I arrived at Mariana Sunday, before class started on Monday. I was very fortunate, because it was obviously a class full of some experienced Air Force officers along with some cadets and junior officers. In the class there were two officers who really stood out and have remained lifelong friends: Bill Douglas (Snake One, with me being Snake Two at the Officers' Club) and Ken Gardner. Ken and Bill had been operational B-66 navigators, which meant they had tons of stick time and lots of flying experience. They were initially my tablemates with our civilian instructor, *old man* Marv Paine.

Because Ken and Bill were so experienced, they made me look like the flying dummy that I probably was, because I was new to the flying game. Our instructor was older than most, and probably should have been retired, as he did after our class departed. He wasn't mean or unreasonable; he just couldn't separate an inexperienced pilot, as I was, from Ken and Bill, who had several years flying in the B-66, where they learned flying and had lots of stick time. Of course they quickly soloed, and I took a bit longer and I really never measured up to Bill or Ken.

I will admit my experience at Mariana paid off when I became a basic flying instructor pilot and especially for my pilot training students when I instructed at Williams AFB, Arizona. I had great empathy for young students because of my suffering and almost being eliminated from pilot training, possibly primarily because of Marv Paine. At least he was never a screamer, like some! Probably, he just was simply an old *fuddy duddy* who was past his prime and should not have been teaching.

I finally soloed and at the time was dating a young lady from Dothan, Georgia. While on my initial solo, I located her house and did a bit of acrobatics—or what I thought was acrobatics— over her house. Needless-to-say, dummy as a solo pilot, Barry, screwed up and got into a spin. Of course our instructors had shown us spins, but I was not sure I knew how to get out of one, but I tried! Naturally I panicked a bit as the T-34 descended in the spin. I pulled the canopy back to bail out, but, as I did it, I let go of the controls, and before I could jump out, the aircraft started flying! *Major Lesson number one: let God have the aircraft when you screw- up, and He will probably save you.* Throughout my flying career, this lesson paid off several times. After I recovered the aircraft, I flew straight and level back to Marianna, *but* I forgot to close the canopy and pull my dark visor in my flying helmet down to hide my glasses!

Now enters another challenge to my flying career. When I had finally passed the Flight Physical, the Optometrist, Corky Williamson, the Indiana high school basketball all-star and who also played for Bobby Knight at Indiana University, made me promise that I would wear the glasses he had made for me. When I arrived back at the field, it had clouded over, and I had my visor up so that Mobile Control could see my glasses that I had promised to wear! When I got back to the flight room, there was a note for me to report to the Flight Surgeon.

I could not imagine why I needed to go to the Flight Surgeon, and when I walked into his office, he took me to the eye-chart room and asked me to read the 20-20 line. I, of course, missed a few of letters, but he said, "Man, you have good eyes: 20-10!" Needless-to-say, I quickly departed the Flight Surgeon's office, knowing that I had just been given another *lucky* break by the Flight Surgeon, Dole Sharp!

While at Marianna, I had a real clash with one of the permanently assigned officers, Lt. Larry Hadley, when he inspected my room in the BOQ and wrote it up. I reminded him that I was a lieutenant like him, and I didn't appreciate him going into my BOQ room. If he had a problem with the condition of the room, talk to the BOQ maid! The training report I got from him wasn't very nice; something about being *adamant*! I remember playing him in a basketball game, and it was a very bloody affair, but I think I had my revenge! He did, however, shoot down a MIG fighter in Vietnam, so he was a good fighter pilot, besides being a pain in the rear to me in pilot training!

Fortunately for me, the leadership of the civilian flying organization in which I was flying or learning to fly, probably along with prodding from Bill and Ken, realized that I was being treated somewhat unfairly and scheduled me for an elimination ride, with a Mr. Ralph Wiles, who should have been a fighter pilot! He was a ball!

I, at the previous Friday night at the Officers' Club, had promised our Flight Surgeon, Dole Sharp, who was being reassigned, that I would pick up his girlfriend after he departed from the Fort Rucker Army helicopter base located a couple of hours away. At one of Dole's last nights at the O'Club, he had mentioned that Corky Williamson and he went through Air Force medical indoctrination together, and they had been good friends. Corky had told him about me and my eyes—again, aren't I *lucky*? The lady he asked me to pick up was a former Miss Florida and absolutely beautiful and a real sweetheart! Unfortunately, I was scheduled the next morning to take my elimination ride with Mr. Wiles.

I had agreed to meet Dole Sharp's girlfriend at the Fort Rucker Army Officer's Club. When I arrived, she was sitting at the bar with a drink, and beside her were two or three drinks that she said were mine. The officers around the bar were buying her drinks and every time she had someone buy her a drink, she got one for me, which she had sitting next to her! Talk about feeling like a real stud—this absolutely magnificent lady was waiting for me, with drinks. The Army officers obviously hated me, and I just smiled! I have to admit, being greeted with a hug and kissed by such a beautiful lady in front of a bunch of jealous grunts was great! They, the grunts, kept buying us drinks, and we had a bunch. We had several drinks and dinner and started back. On the way back, she went to sleep, and I stopped to sleep some too—wish we had done more, but I was an Officer and a gentleman on that trip. I was more than a bit concerned about my elimination ride the next morning! After a couple of hours of sleep and I was ready to return to the base with the sleeping beauty, but I did put the top down to help me burn out the earlier intake!

Unfortunately, I simply was a taxi driver on that trip. Later I had a few dates with her, but she had terrible and unhappy problems and frankly scared me off. I learned sometime after I graduated and I had departed Marianna that she committed suicide; she was that very unhappy, ravishing beauty who really suffered her beauty!

Arriving back at Marianna with the convertible top down and with this beautiful lady asleep on my shoulder, I drove into the base around 0600! Unknown to me, Ralph Wiles, who was to give me my elimination ride, followed me into the base and observed me with the top down on my light blue Chevrolet convertible and a *really* beautiful honey asleep on my shoulder.

Later that morning, after I briefed him about the flight and made the walk around of the T-37 side-by-side jet, we climbed into the jet. I had made a very good walk-around of the aircraft and even found something wrong that the crew chief could fix which impressed Ralph. Ralph was his usual bubbly self, cracking jokes and saying, "Come on, let's see if we can eliminate you, big boy!"

On takeoff, as we broke ground, Ralph pulled off his mask and lit a cigarette, which meant to me, maybe, just maybe, I might pass the ride, because what he did was really illegal! As a result, I flew the best I had ever flown, and Ralph made it a check ride instead of an elimination ride, and if it wasn't the highest in the class, it was close to it! I frequently, as my Air Force career continued to improve, said a little thank you prayer to Ralph Wiles, my hero!

After the check flight, he became my permanent instructor, and was he fun! He was going to an airline, and I was going to be his last student. He told me at my graduation from Marianna that he had followed me into the base the morning of the check ride. Seeing me with the "Honey" asleep on my shoulder, he said he was sure I would make a great fighter pilot. I need to add, when I agreed to pick her up, I did not know that I was up for a very serious elimination ride the next day. However, because I promised,

I couldn't or wouldn't back out! In any case, arriving at the base, I headed for my BOQ room, put the Honey in my bed, and headed for the flight line and my elimination ride!

Since Ralph had a future job with an airline, he had a little act he loved to put on. In preparation for his airline career, he would walk around patting an "imaginary Stew walking beside him on the bottom" saying, "That's OK, Honey, we can have dinner together tonight!" My kind of guy! Once again, damn *lucky*! Completing training at Marianna, I was sent to Laredo AFB, TX for advance training in T-33 jets.

LAREDO AFB, TEXAS, ADVANCED TNG (T-33s), 12/1959-9/1960

I arrived at Laredo in December 1959, but I had to wait for my class to start in an unassigned status. I even had time to run up to Electra, Texas, to marry Dorlyne Bailey. We were married in Electra and had the party at the Sheppard AFB Officer's Club. My friend Charlie, the club manager, arranged a great party for over a hundred folks, and I think I paid very little!

During the marriage ceremony, when the preacher came to the bit about, "If anyone believes this marriage should not occur, please speak now or forever remain silent or hold you peace." Corky and Dr. Bob at that time did a lot of coughing and clearing their throats. Dorlyne was petrified! However, they never said anything.

I'll never forget when Dr. Bob pulled a couple of Dorlyne's impacted wisdom teeth, possibly illegally, shortly before we were married, of course, she had dry sockets and required further treatment. Again, I had to sneak Dorlyne into Bob's office for treatment.

Our marriage was great, and, because of her inputs and help, my career blossomed, and I even received a couple of early promotions. Dorlyne stayed in Electra for a few days after our marriage ceremony, settling things and leaving her job.

Returning to Laredo, I learned of a Naval Academy Class of 1958 promotion party at NAS Kingsville, Texas, about fifty miles from Corpus Christi, Texas. Kingsville was an advanced naval flight training base, and some of my classmates were there. It was one hell of a party, with many Academy classmates were there. My friend Marty "Fado" McCullough, who had a broken right leg set in a full-length cast, drove us to and from the party. We were promoted to First Lieutenant in the Air Force or Lt. Junior Grade in the Navy. On the way home, with Marty at the steering wheel, damned if a wooden telephone pole didn't attack us. And it won, big-time!

I awoke with a very attractive redheaded Navy nurse calling my name, and I realized something was wrong with my mouth. My mouth was wired shut because it was broken.

After a few days in the Navy Hospital at Kingsville, I was allowed to return to Laredo, where I was awaiting the start of my advanced pilot training class. Because of the accident, I was moved back a class, from class 60-H to 61-A.

At Laredo, Dorlyne and I found an apartment in a former GI barracks that had been converted into apartments and located off the base. Nearly everyone in the apartments was military; Mike and Joan Stevens lived upstairs, and "Sugar" and Tom Johnson lived across the hall from us. When Tom would leave for flying, Sugar would hug him and in her sweet Louisiana voice would say, "Sugar, fly well"; hell it made me want to do well too! Of course, we named her Sugar, forgetting her actual name was Jean!

Dorlyne became the Mother of our two children, Barrie Lynn and Michael Scott, and was my wife for thirty-two years. She was forced to live an almost vagabond life, living with or because of me in Laredo, Texas; Muncie, Indiana; Electra, Texas; Evreux, France; Chandler, Arizona; Williams AFB, Arizona; Homestead AFB, Florida; Wichita Falls, Texas; Shaw AFB, South Carolina; Langley AFB, Virginia; Goodyear, Arizona; Woodbridge, Virginia; Montgomery, Alabama; Oklahoma City for Tinker AFB, Oklahoma; Osan AFB, Korea; Yokota AFB, Japan; Osan AFB, Korea (twice); Clark Field, Philippines; Austin, Texas; and Lubbock, Texas.

While I worked for Neil Eddins at Langley and later at Tinker, she gained two special nicknames: *Lois Lipchitz* and *The Wicked Witch of the West*; Dorlyne was truly loved by all I worked for, with or Commanded!

Unfortunately, we were actually separated for a few of our last years of our marriage. I certainly gave her reason for a divorce early in our marriage, but I believed I had "straightened out" after Vietnam and always was a good father, family man, and sincere husband.

When we were in Japan and Korea, where we had no social services assigned to our Wing. We, therefore, she and I, were often officially involved in serious martial or family problems of those assigned to our wing. She functioned as a perfect Commander's wife and was involved in more, much more, than any other wife I had seen in similar positions. My not getting promoted to General probably hurt her more than it hurt me, because she had worked so hard. However, I knew where I had screwed up in the past, so I wasn't so shocked! She was a great mother and certainly raised our children wonderfully.

Back to Laredo, the Flight Surgeon finally released me to fly with my jaw still wired shut, giving me some medical scissors to wear around my neck to cut the rubber bands that held my jaws together, should I get airsick. He did it really unhappily, but because of my seeing or bugging him every day for at least a month, he finally gave up and gave in to my desires. It is amazing what you can get done if you bug the medical folks enough! I can still say "Falcon 58 [my call sign], gear check, full stop" with my jaws held tightly together! The broken jaw forced me back a class, so, instead of the more-senior and experienced students I had been with at Marianna, I was now the most senior in our class and became our class Commander. The class consisted of mostly recent academy graduates from Annapolis, a few from West Point, and many of the very first Air Force Academy class.

I need to digress a bit here and mention that after my plebe year at the Naval Academy, my Congressman Ralph Harvey called me and said he had no one qualified for the Air Force Academy and would I like to be his appointment to the Air Force Academy. The Congressman did not realize how tough my Plebe Year had been, but I graciously declined the opportunity! Once again, a *lucky* decision! However, commanding the class also gave me a flavor of whom I would be dealing with later.

At last, I had a Command, in charge of a flight of student pilots, and, although a very minor Command, it still demonstrated to me that I like to be in charge! Of equal importance, I suspect that it was decisive in my having Maj. Barry R. Butler as my instructor, which was a really wonderful break! He was a proven warrior with four-and-a-half kills in P-38 in WWII and home from the war at age nineteen! Not only did he teach me to fly jets, but also he showed me what a Senior Officer ought to be like. We frequently debriefed over vodka tonics at his house with his wife Maxine, Dorlyne, and his three sons, Peter, Jim, and Little Barry! I was doing fine in the T-33 jet program because of Maj. Barry.

I had really blossomed under his instruction, and for many weeks I was leading the class in academic grades and flying and might have graduated number one in the class. However, on my final instrument check, I let my past successes go to my head, and I truly fell flat on my face, busting the instrument check ride. Unfortunately, when I hit the instrument phase of flying, I met a challenging instructor, who thought that I had no idea what I was doing, and he was partially right. At the same time, instead of studying flying, I had been concentrating on trying to solve some serious Congressional problems in the class, as Class Commander, generated by simple immature jealousy among Academy graduates. After eliminating the serious Congressional problems and much work, I, of course, subsequently passed the recheck, but it caused me to fall from close to first in the class to eighth.

In fact, it may have been God-sent for me! Had I graduated first, I would have gone to fighters, since we had seven fighter assignments. I then would have had the false belief that I knew how to fly better than most, and might have killed myself, as many did who went initially to fighters. By taking Barry Butler's advice and going to C-130s at Evreux AB, France, I slowly, truly learned more deeply about flying, especially instruments. I even became an instructor pilot (IP) in the C-130! Once again, really *lucky*!

STEAD, AIR FORCE SURVIVAL SCHOOL, 9 /1960

En route to Evreux, I was sent to Stead AB, Nevada, to attend Survival and Evasion training school in September 1960. We were to receive the two-week course of survival training, which included a night trek trying to evade a trained enemy force. Once caught, you were placed in a concentration camp, where you are treated poorly and interrogated by the "enemy." Water-boarding was not unheard of, and later in the program I am told that all pilots or aircrew members were given a taste of it. I would add that while we were at Stead, we were all tortured, probably as badly as any Muslim terrorist was ever tortured by our CIA!

In preparation for the internment, I had several garlic buds, which I gave to my friends and we then ate them. The *enemy* seemed to avoid us a bit more than the others, and several comments by the *enemy* indicated that the garlic worked. At the end of the program, another night trek over a longer distance was part of the curriculum where the young and dumb of us including myself, raced each other to finish first. I did stop long enough to pull out a city boy from NYC caught in a fence that crossed a stream, and he had damned near drowned from being stuck in the fence! I completed the trek in the first bunch and quickly hit the sack, as I was worn out.

Later that night, my friend Jim Blackwell, also destined to C-130s at Evreux, awoke me and said, "Barry you have a new daughter!" However, in the morning he did not remember telling me about the daughter, but many around us that night acknowledged that he had told me that wonderful news! And it was true, and my wonderful daughter, Barrie Lynn, was born, which was confirmed later by a call to the camp from my Dad in Muncie.

That night in the casinos, my friends would tell the dealers that I was a new father, and I won a real pile of money. The dealers, after I won a bit at their table, would tell me to move to another table, where I would win again. Those dealers are very patriotic!

I rode back to Muncie with some friends, and we stopped to eat on the border of Nevada and as we were departing the state. I dropped a silver dollar in a slot machine and won the exact number of silver dollars as the number of inches Barrie Lynn was long. Barrie Lynn Howard entered my life, and what a life she has had. But, more on this later.

EVREUX AB, FRANCE, C-130s, 10/1960-4/1964

After attending Air Force Survival Training at Stead AFB, Nevada, I was on to Evreux AB, France, in October 1960. I received all my C-130 training at Evreux rather than attending the C-130 training in the States, as most did. I arrived at Evreux fresh from pilot training in T-37s and T-33, with a short stop at Stead AB for survival training. I left my wife and new baby daughter back in the States, and they traveled between Muncie, Indiana (my home where Barrie was born), to Electra, Texas (Dorlyne's home). Actually, it gave me a chance to concentrate on becoming a C-130 pilot. Fortunately, the squadron I was assigned to, the 39 Troop Carrier Squadron (TCS) was loaded with folks who knew how to make dummies like me into a functional and fully qualified C-130 copilot and, more importantly, took pride in it.

Then I *lucked* out and became Jack Fremont's copilot. Jack was the grandson of John C. Fremont of early exploration and leadership of California fame. Jack had tons of combat aviation experience in the SA-16 seaplane in Korea, so he knew the real world! Later, I flew with Dave Sutherland, who was an old head in the C-130 world, and, through his training and his friends, who constantly worked me pretty hard, I was fairly quickly upgraded to instructor pilot (IP). Of course, the old heads of the 39th such as Phil Reid, John Sedlak, Ted Miles, and especially the Squadron Commander, John Paul Jones, started the ball rolling. The "old heads" of the 39th started my training, and the former members of the famed Four Horsemen (Mills, Sutherland, Chaney, Coleman, Boudreau, and Santucci) and their friends from the "Trash Hauler" world or the C-130 world, finished it. The Four Horsemen was a formation of four C-130s that flew as a demonstration team for several years before they were cancelled, possibly because they challenged the Thunderbirds fighter acrobatic team in demands to perform.

Experiences I gained in the C-130 world were fantastic: cracking near-zero conditions, approaches that were unique and probably only marginally approved and worldwide travel where spoken English was an effort or not at all.

After I became an aircraft commander, I also became a part of one of a few crews trained to work with the Special Ops folks. The Special Ops folks were highly trained ground warriors composed of small teams who were assigned and trained operated behind enemy lines to take out key targets or just drove the enemy nuts! Special Ops today are called Special Forces. At that time in Europe it included the Special Ops center at Bad Tolz, Germany. They used us for training their folks on night low-levels insertions and always provided great training and very challenging deliveries for us on the C-130s. Bad Tolz was the location of US European Special Ops training, and they were wonderful to work with. Also, working with the Berlin Brigade, also a Special Ops group, who mostly spoke English, was always fun. Frequently they would ask us to drop them in the trees so that they wouldn't have to carry home their parachutes.

I applied for some time to attend Bad Tolz parachute training. It was a long, drawn-out battle, but I finally won—just when I had hurt my back and the Flight Surgeon refused to let me go. Maj. Jack Fremont replaced me, but he also got hurt during the training and never completed the course.

I was also a member of a special crew designated to penetrate the Berlin corridor when the Russians through the East Germans said we couldn't use the corridor. The corridors were established after the war to ensure the Western Powers had access to their enclaves in Berlin, as the Russians had control of East Germany. We frequently flew with several enemy MIGs (Russian /East German fighter aircraft) on our wing. I gave them fits by slowing down until they fell off, with the pilots giving us the "single-finger salute" as they struggled and fell off the wing. Who can forget old "Pops" Conley, *loadmaster extraordinary* saying, "Captain, we are surrounded with Russian MIGs!"

After all that fun with the MIGs, we then were frequently challenged with very low weather landing in Berlin between the tall buildings on either side of the approach! But when we landed in Berlin, on our radio we received very deeply felt thanks for arriving and challenging the illegal act of the Russians. What I knew, but few other C-130 pilots knew, was that there were USAF fighters, flying caps (combat air patrol), ready to assist us should the Russians seriously challenge us. They were many of my friends from pilot training who I had run into in Europe or down at Wheelus, Libya. They promised me that, "if they got me, they would get them!" Really made you feel good, knowing that the bad guys would pay! (*Not!*)

Later in my C-130 career another really interesting mission was flying with and participating at Toulouse, Southern France, with the French Air Force at their Flight Testing Center. Toulouse was the southern French city that many downed WW II US airmen transited with the assistance of the famed and very effective French underground, the La Resistance Françoise.

While at the Toulouse Test Center there were three major challenges: the flying, the wine-fired luncheons, and the night-life! Thus, many unusual or unique events took place while we were there.

We were able in our C-130 to pitch out (make level turn the aircraft for180-degrees) from an overhead at one thousand feet and landed (documented on film) in forty-three seconds from pitch to touchdown was something that I was never able to beat in any fighter I flew, and I tried many times! During tactical or high-threat operations, to get an aircraft on the ground the quickest with the least exposure to enemy ground fire a pilot would approach the runway to land above the field at a thousand to fifteen hundred feet above the runway. Then the pilot makes a sharp 180-degree turn to a downwind paralleling the runway, where landing gear and flaps may be extended or he may lower them as he performs a descending turn to line up with the run-way for landing.

My opinion of the French flyers was much better than of their ground troops. They were real professionals and were constantly trying to improve their system or try anything that had combat value. At the time, France was being militarily challenged in North Africa by an insurrection.

Flying the C-130 and learning the new LAPSE (Low Altitude Parachute Extraction) deliveries when they first came to Europe and of course practicing normal mass formations and airborne drops were excellent training. In weather, "station keeping" (using radar and normal navigation for station keeping) was certainly a learning experience!

It was not unusual for a C-130 aircraft and crew to be sent to various locations in Africa where normal Air Force support was nonexistent. Being in Africa as an independent aircraft with occasional contact to your Headquarters through single sideband radio (SSB) communications was a great leadership training school. In conditions like that, you, as the Aircraft Commander, made many challenging decisions, and later you would tell Headquarters, "Oh, by the way, we did the following ..."!

Being left at Kindu Airport, Kiev Province, Congo, as the Airport Commander as a young lieutenant with a Blue UN hat on and only a knife on your hip, I learned a lot about leadership. Thank goodness for the Mali UN troops left to guard the airport and myself—but more about this later!

How could I forget sleeping on the C-130 wing with my hand in the refueling hole so I wouldn't fall off as we delivered earthquake relief for Iran and several other countries in the four years I was at Evreux? Additionally, we frequently had weeks or months of deployments to Greece, India, or Saudi Arabia.

Of course one of the piece de résistance in C-130s was having the opportunity to operate in India. I learned to land and operate out of at Leh, Ladakh, probably the highest airfield in the world at 10,500 feet. I experienced a crash landing on my first attempt, because the Indian soldier in the tower placed the handheld anemometer perpendicular to the wind in line with the wind, thus calling the thirty to forty knots of late afternoon tailwinds as light and variable winds instead of a serious tailwind. That made landing especially fun, especially after 1630 hours! Because of the shortness of the field, we never landed with more than ten knots of tailwind. I made a good landing, but I couldn't get it stopped before we hit a rather sharp rise in the PSP (steel sheets that interlocks to make a temporary runway) at the turnaround point on the end of the runway. The nose strut was fully depressed when we hit the rise, with full braking and propellers in reverse, thus putting heavy force on the nose gear, forcing it up and breaking the its support to the aircraft. They fixed the aircraft in two days, and a rule was established: no landing with more than ten knots' tailwind or after 1600. The wind always shifted from downhill to uphill always after 1600.

Thanks to Jack Fremont and especially Dave Sutherland along with Billy "Grover" Mills and Gene Chaney, I learned so much about real-world flying. They taught me so many things that I hadn't learned in flying training, the biggest being humility about my flying ability. On a flight terminating at Cannes, we had a very long and tiring day. Dave Sutherland taught me a great lesson by actually saying to me after he had to make a missed approach at Cannes that he couldn't "hack it" and for me to try. A missed approach occurs when you are making an instrument approach in the weather and you arrive at a position where you cannot land the aircraft because of weather, lack of seeing the runway, or poor flying of the approach. I never asked Dave if he was simply teaching me something, or was he really unable to hack it, because we had had such a long and tough day. Anyhow, I, as copilot, made the approach and landing, which gave me great confidence for the future but with a great deal of humility, because Dave Sutherland was a superb pilot, and when he said that he couldn't hack it, I learned a bunch! What a lesson!

All of them — Jack, Dave, Grover, and Gene — moved me along at a rapid rate to become one of the youngest IPs in the squadron and the wing. I have always been indebted to them for the training, concern, and friendship they gave me and I know I am now a really a very good and deep pilot without the over or false confidence that kills some pilots. Later, when I became a fighter pilot, I truly had an advantage because of my time in the C-130. The experiences I had in the C-130 and the confidence they built up in me were superb. As I said earlier, Dave Sutherland, Billy Mills, and Gene Chaney also had been part of the famous acrobatic C-130 team, the Four Horsemen.

I know the few times I backed the big C-130, like you would back a car, it was always an eye-opener, and the few times I flew in trail with a fighter in the C-130, I watered the eyes of the fighter pilot I flew behind. If the pilot had a mirror where I could see his eyes, I could note a bit of apprehension of those four big propellers ready to chew up their little bitty fighter, and they said so! The fearsome foursome's education continued on the ground and socially too. I experienced many headaches because of their detailed, regular, deep, and frequent barroom training!

I have always been very proud of my C-130 days: the experiences and the training I received. As a young aircraft commander I found myself and my aircraft in the deepest, darkest of Africa with only a marginal Single Side Band (SSB) radio for contact with the outside world. As a result, I quickly learned serious decision-making, planning, and controlling my environment. Frequently, decisions were made without contacting "home plate" or Evreux Command Post, because you knew they might question your decision. So rather than fight it, just do it, and then tell them later, what you did. I would indicate that I couldn't contact them on SSB, which they always accepted, because SSB was not always dependable.

I was blessed to be in the 39th Troop Carrier Squadron because of their professionalism and the Squadron Commander, Lt. Col. John Paul Jones, who taught me how to be a Commander. Additionally, his beautiful wife, June, taught Dorlyne how to be a Commander's wife. As a result, Dorlyne and I always had squadrons or wings that were fun and very professional and extremely prideful! Having such a good-looking Commander's wife like Dorlyne really helped too!

I need to mention how tough on Dorlyne it was coming to France. First she had Barrie Lynn in Muncie at Ball hospital with help from my grandma Mac, Mom, and, of course, Dad trying to find his fedora. Then she traveled to Texas alone to show off Barrie Lynn to her parents. Then she traveled from Electra, Texas, to Paris, France, with a small baby and alone! That was during the days of prop engine aircraft, which took considerably more time than today's jet to get to Paris! It had to be tough for the little Texas gal with baby Barrie Lynn, but she made it without complaining. Little did I know that I could have gone back and escorted them back, which I later found out!

When Dorlyne and Barrie Lynn arrived, we first stayed with the Blackwell's, Jim and Patty. Our second child, Michael Scott, was probably conceived on a metal GI cot in their spare bedroom!

We were blessed at the Evreux AB hospital with having a great pediatrician, Dr. Art Korman, who had trained under Dr. Spock. Evreux has terrible weather: rainy and very little sun. Consequently, Barrie and Mike had their share of sickness and time in the hospital. Mike even developed tetracycline teeth as a result of his many sicknesses.

On top of everything else, Dorlyne brought me a .38 pistol from my Dad for my birthday, unknown to me. Unfortunately, a .38-caliber pistol is not allowed in France, and it was considered a guillotine offense to have one!

Also, when a military child is in the hospital, a parent must stay with the child, and once when Mike was in the hospital, I happened to not be on a trip elsewhere, so I was staying with him in the hospital. I need to add here that each year at Evreux, I was gone an average of 189 days/year! It was time for Dorlyne and me to switch, so she came to the hospital, and I took the car to go home. I arrived home, and I was shocked that the apartment in the center of the town of Evreux was a mess. I called Dorlyne to raise hell, and once I talked to her, I realized that we had been robbed. Stolen were the silver dollars I had won for Barrie Lynn in Nevada, several bottles of very good booze, and, unknown to me at the time, the .38 pistol that had been used in the capture of John Dillinger!

We were in big trouble, but thankfully, the base interpreter, Rene' Damien, whom we knew well, had a plan. It was the time of short skirts, and Dorlyne had a lime green one along with a light green sweater, and she looked like a million dollars in them. Rene recommended that she wear them to see the judge. Dorlyne has a terrific figure and beautiful blonde hair. Also she was learning a bit of French, so she appeared before the male French Judge in the short lime green skirt, green, a bit-tight sweater, blonde hair, and speaking Texas French. After much conversation with the Judge, he declared the case closed after she told him that she had unknowingly brought the pistol over from my father, the FBI agent, and it had been used in the capture of John Dillinger! How could you be upset with a lime green short skirt and beautiful blonde speaking Texian French? Our base interpreter, Rene' Damien, accompanied her to Court. Of course, it was his idea for her to wear her short green skirt and her green sweater, which was a tiny bit tight. With her natural beauty and her blonde hair, along with the outfit she wore, her Texas drawl speaking French to the judge caused him to be very understanding, and he dismissed the case after reviewing her totally, as well as the case. Rene' said that it was the longest time he had ever spent in a courtroom, indicating that the judge really appreciated Dorlyne. He obviously liked blonde Texans in green tight sweaters and short skirts speaking French. It seems I am repeating myself? I can't say I blame him, because that was also my favorite outfit, and Dorlyne looked like a million dollars and certainly a credit to Texas. Her Texas-accented French was exciting and loved by the French we met while there, especially when she told them, if asked where she was from she would reply, "Brooklyn!"

My first challenge at Evreux was to deploy to the Congo, not as a crew member, since my upgrade flying training in the C-130 had not started. However, en route to the Congo, I got to fly as a copilot some on the way to Leopoldville, Congo. When I arrived as a young lieutenant, I was made the Commander at one of the Congo airfields at Kindu, Kivi province. Kindu is where, sometime later, an Italian aircrew was eaten by some of the natives.

This challenge resulted in lots of learning but was a bit scary, since the only protection I had was a UN hat, a hunting knife on my belt, and a Mali Company of UN-designated troops who were defending me and the airport at Kindu. The Mali Company Commander, Lt. Col. Mademba, later became President of his country, but, unfortunately, he was assassinated in office. He was a fine and very professional soldier who I really liked and enjoyed being with, and my learning continued through him. Kindu was the recruit depot of the Congo, where most new army recruits were assigned. Frequently, regular Congolese officers came in to select, from the recruits, men for their units. Unfortunately, in the Congo, many of the senior officers had no allegiance to the National leadership and might be either rebels or going to be rebels.

I had many very serious learning experiences while at Kindu. One day the troops or the recruits decided to rebel and take over the airfield. They were all over the airfield, and we couldn't get aircraft in the air or let them land. I asked Lt. Col. Mademba, "To clear the field so that we could have air operations."

Lt. Col. Mademba had a sergeant who spoke the local language, Swahili. The Lieutenant Colonel told the sergeant to tell them they had thirty minutes to clear the field, and we went to my office to have tea! With five minutes to go, he told the sergeant to tell them they had five minutes to clear the field, but none moved. He then told him to start a countdown for each minute and then the finally sixty seconds. With about two minutes remaining, he said, "Sergeant, if they don't clear the field at the end of the countdown, shoot about a dozen of them." At the end of the countdown, the sergeant charged his automatic machine pistol and did shoot about eleven of them. The field cleared, and we had no more trouble while I was there until the day I left!

One day one of my logisticians came to me and said he had a problem with one of the Belgian whites that wanted to be flown out, as we did for those who wanted to leave. I asked what the problem was, and he asked me to follow him to the aircraft. Sitting beside the aircraft was a 1958 Chevrolet hardtop Impala sitting on its axles, as the shocks were overcome with weight in the car. The owner of the car refused to board the C-130 without the car, because it contained all his possessions! I looked in the car, and it was obvious he had looted many homes, as there were many sets of silverware, guns, electronics, and other valuables. I told the man that the plane was going to leave, with or without him, *but* not the car. He eventually got on the aircraft, and I don't know what happened to the car and its loot! Since I had owned a 1958 Impala, it hurt a bit not to start driving it.

One of my tasks each day was to drive into town in my military jeep and get fresh bread for the troops who were protecting the airfield. I would frequently stop at one of the many bars and have coffee and a sweet roll, talking to the bartenders, who were always very friendly to me, especially after the shooting incident (clearing the field)! One day, I had someone with me, and I jokingly told him, while sitting at the bar, that the Belgian paratroopers were coming to Kindu the next day. It was strictly a joke, because the Congolese were terrified of them. The next day when I went to town, there were sharpened stakes in the ground everywhere, snipers in the trees, machine guns set up and manned, and the town was obviously on full alert for fear of the paratroopers! Another lesson learned: *Commanders must be very careful with what they say, even a young First Lieutenant.*

While I was there, there remained one white Belgian in his job as the village Pay Master, George, who also ran the jails. He was a good fellow, and I spent time with him when I could. One time at the jail, he showed me a package of meat that had been delivered to a prisoner. In the Congo, your family must feed you while in jail, or you simply starve! The piece of meat was obviously a thigh from someone, or "long pig," as they called it.

One day I was with George, at his house, when the local law decided to arrest him for more pay. They were going take him in, and at the time he was barefooted. They started to take him with them, forcefully, with one "policeman" on each arm. He held up his arms and said that, unlike them, he wore shoes, and he needed to put his on, which he made a great show of doing, and then they led him off. I later got him out of jail after he had convinced them he didn't have any additional money. I tried to tell George that he needed to let me smuggle him out, but he refused. I begged and pleaded with him, but he refused to leave. Unfortunately, sometime after I left, he was crucified, and his picture was in the Paris newspaper on a cross—he was dead, of course. A very brave, but too brave a man!

The day I left Kindu, the troops were again in revolt around the airfield and on parts of it. As a few of us, me being in the last group and departing my first Command were going out to where the aircraft was parked and running. The rebels started chasing us, and, as we ran, I said to Clayton Carter, the aircraft navigator running beside me, "I don't think they like us!" Clayton said with all seriousness, "That is right, white boy, we don't like you," but he kept running beside me! I almost collapsed laughing, because Clayton was as black as the rebels were! We made it to the aircraft, and it did take off.

It had been a challenging and serious learning experience for those couple of months at Kindu, again something that never would have happened had I gone to fighters, as I wanted to do! I have always been a very *lucky* guy!

Later, after I checked out as a crewmember (co-pilot) in the C-130, I flew many missions in the Congo. One particular mission almost got me in deep trouble. I had a very strange experience that I will never understand why young Lt. Howard had to correct the problem, as it had been obviously an on-going problem for sometime. As we were unloading unmarked bags of beans, corn, rice, and/or flour from the United States for the starving natives on the ramp at Leopoldville, then the capitol of the Congo, an obviously Russian fellow with a large ink stamp started stamping *CCPR* on the bags—thus indicting that the food came from Russia! When I saw him doing it, I hit the ceiling and asked others what the hell he was doing but received no response! I asked him, the Russian, what he was doing, but it was obvious that he was stamping the bags of food from America, which were foolishly unmarked. He was now marking them as if they were from Russia. He then said, "No speak English!" So I pulled my gun and confronted him. I now advised the Russian to, "Take his stamp and pad and depart the area rapidly," or I would *"stick the stamp where the sun don't shine!"*

He suddenly became English fluent and became an Olympic runner and disappeared. For the time I was there, which was for several weeks and we never saw him again. My boss thanked me for running him off; why the hell hadn't he?

Another time, as we shut down our C-130 at Leopoldville, we noticed a crowd around a jeep, and we strolled over there to see what was going on. We found an Army Warrant Officer with several knife wounds, bleeding badly. Someone said, "We need to take him to the hospital." But no one, especially some bird colonels (full colonels) present, stepped forward to take care of him. I asked if anyone was going to do it, and most folks suddenly started disappearing. I, a simple First Lieutenant, saw a jeep with either a .50- or .30-caliber machine gun mounted on it. I told them to lead the way to the hospital, several miles away. I jumped in the jeep with the wounded Warrant Officer, and off we went. I was applying pressure to the wounds as we drove to stop the bleeding.

Now my second Command was of two jeeps with a seriously wounded soldier. We got him to the hospital unimpeded—probably because of the machine-gun jeep, which cleared the way to the hospital. Later, when I talked to the Warrant, he said he had violated a serious rule in the Congo. If you hit a biker or walker, you *do not stop!* He learned the hard way: having hit a walker, he stopped to help him, and the walker's family attacked him with knives. *Another lesson learned!*

Some months later, when I was a qualified aircrew co-pilot, having received the required training, I was flying to the Congo with the Wing Test Pilot, Bill Volker. He was truly a superb pilot, and I knew could learn much from him. As we were flying over Nigeria in the dark of night, I noticed he was constantly looking at the outside temperature gauge, so I asked him about it. The area we were over flying had no electronic navigation aids, so we were strictly doing time and distance navigation or *dead reckoning*. He said he noticed a large temperature change, indicating that we had gone through a weather front; it was at night, and we probably had a large wind shift. The winds we had been given did not address any frontal activity, since we received our weather information back in France, and there were no weather stations in that part of Africa. He had us correct our heading by twenty degrees into what he thought the winds would be. Later, when we obtained an electronic navigational fix, we were very close to course. Another aircraft trailing us didn't catch the wind shift and ran out of gas and had to land on a dirt strip way to the east of course. Subsequently, we had to fly in many fifty-five-gallon tanks of fuel to get him out of there. Another lesson learned!

During my assignment to the C-130 at Evreux, France, we flew to various locations in Africa, either in association with the UN Congo action, the astronaut program, or other oddball types of support missions. One factor was becoming very clear: wherever the English were, it was obvious that they had a program for upgrading the local folks to the twentieth Century. It was obvious that England had every intention of preparing the countries they were associated with for independence, and they were making great progress.

Unfortunately, America entered the picture, and Bobby Kennedy made his famous and often repeated statement, "Africa is for the Africans," and, as a result, England and other modern countries withdrew from their associated countries in Africa that they had been bringing along into the twentieth Century. Many of those countries today are having great difficulty achieving national development or have reverted to areas under tribal control with no or very weak national leadership. Nigeria was doing so well until "African is for the Africans," and then it broke up into tribal battles, and even today the stability of that country is questionable. While in India, where England had remained, they had developed and progressed because England completed their program of upgrading India from tribal area control before they were forced to leave.

On a mission to Salisbury, Southern Rhodesia, on which I was now the Aircraft Commander, a senior Instructor Pilot went along to give *check rides*, he said (pilots receive regular *check rides* to maintain their status as pilots) to others and me but, if the truth be known, I think he really had a girlfriend near Salisbury that he wanted to see. It turned out that he also had a friend or friends who had an airstrip, and one day he took my aircraft on a local flight with me flying as his copilot. He said he wanted to make a low approach at one of the dirt strips out in the bush. It was where his friends lived, I believe.

Prior to making "a low approach," I noticed that he was not as sharp as he usually was, and later I learned that he had partied late that night. As we were making the low approach, (a low approach is making an almost landing but only going down low to the runway and not touching the aircraft down). I could see some tall trees on the left side of the runway as we approached it. As we were on final, I kept saying, "Go right some" and "Go right some more;" finally I shouted, "Go right a bunch, *damn it!*" in a loud and commanding voice. Then I said "Aw shit, you just hit some trees!" Of course he had signed for the aircraft, but I was really the Aircraft Commander, so I too might be at fault. We lost about six feet of the left wingtip! We made it back to Salisbury, and a team came in to repair the wing by simply capping it off. Once it was repaired, we started back to Evreux. At each stop for fuel, the repair team, our crew, and whoever else was on the aircraft would get off the airplane after landing and walk around the repaired wing tip, staring at it. The senior instructor had been directed to replace me as the aircraft Commander; they thought I had done it!

When we arrived at Evreux, we were met by armed guards and taken to a briefing room, where the UCMJ (Uniform Code of Military Justice) was read to us, and we were told that we were under house arrest and could not fly. Soon it was clear that I was not the cause of the accident and that I had tried to tell the instructor that he was going to hit the trees. It resulted in a chewing out for me and if it happened again I would lose my flying status; but the whole affair took several weeks before I was back on flying status!

As soon as I was back on flying status, I was put on the Alert Crew, which is on "quick standby" for any emergency that should arise. True to form, we were called out late at night and were sent to Ramstein AB, Germany, to support the 417th Tactical Fighter Squadron which was to deploy to Saudi Arabia with six F-100s. Their Squadron Commander was Lt. Col. Woody Roscher, and off we went. Soon we realized it was an important mission, as the support we received everywhere we stopped was superb.

When we got to Saudi, we were met by the Ambassador and an Air Force Major General who briefed us on the mission. The President, John Kennedy, had told the Saudi King that America would support the Saudis, who were being threatened by the country of Yemen. Allegedly, our President had told the King that we (America) would darken the skies with Air Force airplanes. The F-100s started flying over every city, village, and camel train, or wherever folks gathered. However, within a week, all the F-100s were broken. The General and the Ambassador then advised me that I would start buzzing the whole country of Saudi. Now, remember that I had just been part of a court-martial about buzzing, and I told them what I had been told: that if I ever buzzed again, I would lose my wings. The Ambassador said, "I'll take care of that" and got on the phone. A few minutes later, he called me to the phone and said, "The President would like to talk to you."

"*The PRESIDENT?*" I said! I answered the phone at attention and immediately recognized the voice of President John Kennedy. He told me about telling the King that he would darken the skies with American Airplanes, and now I was to do it. He also said I was cleared to do whatever was necessary to convince the King, who I was to put on an air show for tomorrow, so that we were indeed darkening the skies. Also he said, "That I could even class-26 the aircraft if I had to, whatever the hell that meant?" I said, "Sir, class-26 means to totally destroy the aircraft!" He answered, "Just don't get anyone hurt, Barry!"

I need to mention another time I was on the phone listening to another President. I was in Iran as it was collapsing and I happened to be in the same room with the Air Force four Star, I believe a former MAC Commander, sent by President Carter to handle the collapsing Iranian political situation. I am not sure whether the Shah had departed the country or not. The General put a call into the President and when it is important, most Presidents are immediately available especially during emergencies.

The General said,"Barry, get on the extension, I want you to witness or hear this conversation!" Of course I picked up the phone and when the President came on, he said, "President

Carter here." The General said something to the effect that, "Mr. President, the Iranian Military is prepared to Junta with your approval and they will do as we say!" There was a silent pause and then I could hear a click on the phone sounding like someone hung up, namely the President. The General looked at me and it was obvious that the President had refused to answer. Most of those senior Iranian Military leaders were late executed or quickly departed the country and the present troublesome and dangerous government evolved.

Back to Saudi Arabia: The next day, with the Chief of Staff of the Saudi Air Force in the copilot's seat, we went to one of the King's Palaces out in the desert and really worked it over. You could see the King and many others, and they kept telling us to get lower and closer. I really worked the place over, as did the Saudi Chief of Staff. Finally, after the folks on the ground thanked us and wished us luck, we departed. I was suffering a bit from what we later called "Sheikh's revenge" (similar to Montezuma's revenge) from the Aramco firewater I had consumed the night before. My stomach problems continued, so after we leveled off at altitude on the way back to our base of operations, I headed back to the chemical toilet we had in the tail of the aircraft. Of course I was in a flying suit, so to sit on the chemical toilet I had to have the flight suit down around my ankles. As I was sitting there suffering a bit, suddenly there was an explosive rapid decompression, meaning the aircraft pressurization was gone, and we had to put on oxygen masks to breath, since we were at altitude of around twenty-four thousand feet. I immediately looked up, because we all knew that the weakest part of the C-130 aircraft was the tail section, and I assumed that the air show we put on probably had really stressed the tail section. Much to my extreme concern, I could see blue skies above me, so I screamed at the loadmaster (the guy who is in charge of the back end of the aircraft) to give me his headset. I told my copilot, who was sitting in my seat with the Saudi Chief of Staff in the other seat, to slow the aircraft down and start a gentle—repeat, *gentle*—decent. I told him about the hole in the aircraft above my head.

I have to digress a bit here, because the thought going through my mind as I was sitting on that toilet was that the aircraft was going to come apart; I would be found with the flight suit around my ankles and bare-assed. I really thought that we had class-26th the aircraft!

Recovering, I quickly returned to the pilot's seat, and we gently descended and more gently landed the aircraft at the first available field. Inspecting the hole in the aircraft, where we found that one of the top formation lights had blown out, and there really wasn't any damage to the aircraft—an answer to a prayer and *lucky* again! However, another lesson learned: read and know the Dash-1 (technical book about the aircraft) before putting on an air show, even for the King of Saudi Arabia and his royal family!

While in Saudi, I obtained a copy of a book produced by a key engineer working in Saudi for Aramco Oil Company. The title of the book was *Blue Flame*, and it was how to make a still from material that could be obtained mail order from Sears in the States. Since the sale of alcohol was forbidden in Saudi, many Americans had stills in their houses, where they became skilled at producing pretty good firewater for adults. Before this fine book was produced; several homes had burned because of poorly built stills.

It was always exciting to go to a party in Saudi and watch the folks arrive carrying a glass gallon jug full of a clear liquid although some had learned to flavor the liquid, and those had a bit of color in them. One time I met a very attractive young lady at whose house there was a party. We talked and danced, and she then invited me into her bedroom, which was exciting and challenged my married status. She closed and locked the bedroom door and asked me to join her at her closet door. I had all kinds of thoughts about what was happening, such as, "We are going to wear jammies" or something like that. Suddenly she opened the closet door, and, much to my surprise, there was her still! In the closet were two large plastic containers containing mash and the still, which looked really professionally built. All of those evil thoughts disappeared, and we rejoined the party, but I was a bit smarter about Saudi stills.

A year or two later, we were operating in India and the book *Blue Flame* became a very useful and valuable item for my warrior friends in India. We were quietly using our C-130s to support the Indian warriors fighting the Chinese in their eastern mountains on the Chinese/Indian border. I was assigned as acting but unofficial Aide to Gen. Eric Sin, head of the Indian Army, probably because of my intelligence background. While I was in that capacity, his son became very sick with a disease, diphtheria, which most children in America are inoculated against early in their lives. The disease resulted in Gen. Sin's son having a very high temperature, and the hospital in which he was had no air-conditioning, and he suffered horribly. I happened to have a very large jar of the relatively new flavored drink mix in a jar called Tang. It was Orange flavored, which I had in my Jampat hotel room to drink when I did my five BX exercises, which I tried to do regularly. I took it to the hospital for him, and he loved and drank it happily, thus lowering his temperature.

The doctors at the hospital were amazed at the Tang and wanted more of it. We quickly flew in a large amount of the Tang from our commissary in France, and it was really appreciated by the hospital staff, since we simply gave it to them, and it was a very large amount. Another lesson learned: *the man on the spot can cement relationships very cheaply if the system allows him to think and act accordingly.*

I do need to mention that I was religiously doing the five BX exercises in my room, which required lots of time on the floor doing exercises. I soon developed many sores on my chest. Our Flight Surgeon determined that the sores were a result of bites, probably by fleas in the carpet in my room. Ah, the unknown and many challenges of worldly travel!

My former Aircraft Commander Jack Fremont was part of our group. Through Gen. Sin, Jack and I met most of the senior Indian military leadership and Mr. Dotagera, who was Prime Minister Nehru's personal secretary. Jack and I had been assigned to Gen. Sin as his unofficial Air Force representatives, with me, of course, being the spy. Mr. Dotagera traveled in a chauffeured vehicle that soon became our means of travel. Most important to me for future reference, I talked to an Indian General who had been a prisoner of the Chinese for a short period, and he explained to me that the Chinese were unable to be a world threat because they had very little petroleum available.

Our association with the Indian Generals was truly a learning experience, with wonderful military conversations around the frequent dinner table that was often filled with wonderful Northern Indian traditional meals. It seemed many of the Indian warriors had Sikh religious backgrounds, and they preferred spicy foods. Of course Jack and I also liked spicy food! Our contributions to the dinners were the adult beverages: they preferred Johnnie Walkers Black Label and most wines.

Two incidents come to mind that occurred as a result of our relation with Gen. Sin. The General obviously knew I was there not only as an Aide but also to gain intelligence, because frequently one of the senior Indian officers would take me aside and feed me information. I believe that once Gen. Sin acknowledged my intelligence background, he had me flown to the base that had recently received the Russian MIG 21 aircraft. There I received briefings and a ton of complaints about the Russians, their aircraft, and the lack of technical materials provided with the aircraft. They were really unhappy with the Russians, which I was able to pass on to the US Ambassador to India, John Kenneth Galbraith, which also resulted in my spending considerable private time which him. The Ambassador was a great Scotch drinker, and he insisted that anyone with him must keep up with him; many headaches resulted, because he had a great capacity, and the Scotch was free!

The second incident was a discussion with Gen. Sin, who was extremely concerned that his troops in the Himalayas near Ladakh, Leh, India, who were militarily trained by the English and were thus entitled to a ration or tote of alcohol when in combat. Since we Americans were supplying the troops using our C-130s, and, of course, by federal law we were not allowed to carry alcohol on the American aircraft, all requests to take these troops their combat rations were denied. As we talked, I remembered the book in my briefcase, *Blue Flame*, that I had picked up in Saudi Arabia. I gave him the book, and he quickly called in an administrative Aide who took it. I suggested that we could carry the sugar needed for production of the wonderful liquid, sheikh, from the instructions in *Blue Flame*! Later, I was given a bound book with a small paragraph inside the cover thanking me, their American friend, for providing the book *Blue Flame*.

Later, an Air Force General on an Inspection of our operations had private talks with me about the intelligence I had obtained. One of his questions was why had the Indian Army started requesting so much sugar to be hauled to Ladakh. I postulated that possibly it was so cold up there that they probably or maybe they were feeding the troops additional sugar to keep them warm. Of course I had my fingers crossed! He didn't question that explanation, and since I had my fingers crossed, I was in the clear!

In turn, Gen. Sin was greatly appreciative of the sugar, the book, and what was ultimately provided for his warriors in combat, their daily *tote*. I am sure the troops were also very happy to have their *tote* too! As I said earlier the General, as did all the India leaders I associated with, knew I was doing a bit of spying on the India military, since I originally was an intelligence officer. Of course, the India leadership provided me every opportunity to view everything I wanted to "spy on"! The relationship between their military leadership and the US, at that time, was wonderful.

One night during one of the wonderful Northern Indian meals (very spicy and fiery hot in taste) at Gen. Sin's house, and after several adult beverages, I mentioned that the Indian Communist Party Headquarters very near our hotel. Frequently, when their meetings let out, the party members would dance around in their very sculptured rose garden around their flagpole, which flew a Communist flag. The circular rose garden was probably seventy-five to one hundred feet across, with only one sidewalk up to the flagpole, which was opposite from the entrance of their building.

After several more beverages, and much discussion, it was deemed appropriate that we should capture the flag for either my bar or Jack Fremont's bar. We then piled into the official, large car of Nehru's secretary and our friend Dotagera and headed for the Communist Party Headquarters. The plan was for Jack and me to scurry up to the pole, lower the flag, jump into the car, and return to the dinner party. I don't remember who was with us, but we did have some very senior India leadership! As Jack and I got to the pole and were about to lower the flag, the party meeting let out! Out came the screaming members who would then dance around outside of the rose garden very loudly for the benefit of US military staying in the Jampat Hotel next door. They usually shouted, "Death to the Americans!" Jack and I very wisely (actually dumbly) dove into the roses around the pole since they never went up to the flag pole.

Now a lesson for those of you who have never visited India: roses growing in India have developed very long—actually, extremely long—thorns, to defend against the sacred cows that roam freely in India and trying to eat them.

We quickly learned the lessons of the India roses, as we lay impaled on them. Fortunately, the party members did not venture up the single sidewalk toward the flagpole, but stayed on the outer sidewalk that went around the rose garden, shouting, "Death to the Americans!" Finally, after what seemed like weeks, the party members disbanded, and quiet reigned again. Jack and I extracted ourselves from the roses and the damnable thorns and returned to the car to the laughs and humor of the India leadership who had been comfortably watching our misery. We returned to the party, and again consumed many beverages to ease the pain from the very long thorns! We, unfortunately, did not get the flag either.

My time in India confirmed to me that what happened in Africa a few years before would have a long-range and terrible effect on that African continent. Unlike India which had gone through a completed and designed plan toward independence from England. This included top level training in leadership and the peoples being trained and developed for living in democracy. Even today, India is a democratic nation. This slow development of governmental growth and movement of third-world countries who were guided by major European countries into the reign of the advanced nations or countries was suddenly stopped— probably because an America said something like, "Africa is for the Africans!"

How? Again, Bobby Kennedy's statement, "Africa is for the Africans!" Those European countries that were helping develop the various African nations for entrance into the twentieth century suddenly departed Africa before the development plan was finished, as England had done in India! This was so evident in Nigeria, which was, when I was there in the early 1960s, well on its way to being an organized and modernly-led nation. Today, in much of Africa there is deadly turmoil with tribal fighting, and in some countries there is total chaos, disorder, and disaster. Of course, this demonstrated how America opinion is held in high regard throughout the world.

One time during the week before the British Open, we landed our C-130 at the English base near the Open, and of course many of the players visited or may have stayed at the Officers Club. I walked in after dark, still in my flight suit, and stood behind a large wingback chair with a fellow sitting in it. They were all watching the players practice for the Open. It was long ago, with only black-and-white TV, and very dark in the room. The fellow in the chair offered me one of the arms to sit on, which I accepted. He then bought us a Scotch and water. Shortly after the drink arrived, Arnold Palmer was playing on the screen, and of course I was cheering for him: he was my favorite. After he was off the screen, the fellow in the chair said something like, "You really like him?" Of course I just raved about what he had done for golf. He simply laughed, and we had another drink, which I think I bought.

The dim lights were then brightened, and I about fell over: there sat Arnold Palmer, just smiling, and he shook my hand. We talked for a while about flying, since he was also a pilot and had his own aircraft. I don't remember if he won the Open that year, but he had won it recently, and he will always be my champion. Later, when I was at Willie AFB in Arizona, Dorlyne and I went to the Tucson Open, and we followed Arnold as he played. He did say hi to me. I assumed he didn't remember that day in England, but later, after he holed out, he backed up to Dorlyne and gave her his ball, which I believe at the time the PGA, said they shouldn't do. He turned and winked at me, so he did remember! I think Dorlyne almost had an accident, she was so thrilled!

Years later, I was at Homestead AFB, Florida, I was scheduled to fly him in an F-4 (as the Navy had just flown him in an F-4), which really excited the whole base and especially me! Unfortunately, someone in the Air Force canceled the flight. It was too damn early for my Air Force to be Politically Correct, but how stupid could someone be?

Finally, I should note a C-130 mission to Athens, Greece, where I ran into some Naval Academy classmates and had a few (?) booze berries (drinks), as normally happens when old warrior friends run into each other. The next day we departed Athena Airport, and I immediately called the super carrier in the bay, as one of my classmates was Duty Officer (OOD) that day. I asked for a low approach across the deck, and it was approved. We carefully avoided the tower on the right and made a very low approach; some say we touched the deck, but that was so long ago that I don't clearly remember. One of my Naval Academy classmates was OOD that day, later assured me that no one was angry or said anything to the Air Force about our "low approach or possible touch-and and-go!"

My life in the 39th TCS was fun, educational, and I learned so much about being an Air Force officer and leadership. I recently attend a reunion of the 39th and I was able to learn about others from the Squadron who also grew as I did from their time in the 39th. Thank you, John Paul and June Jones, the super 39th Command pair. Of the troops who arrived around the time I did, two of them, Roy Palmer and Ernie Hasselbrink attended the prestigious US Air Force Test Pilots School. Three others of them had a great Air Force careers and then they made big bucks and had a very interesting "after" Air Force life all over the world, including Tom Sparr, Ricky Davidson and my special friend and Little Brother, Connie Hoffman. They had fun and challenging "after" careers flying while making the "big" bucks! Finally, the 39th was blessed with a future Lt.General, who I had the honor of sponsoring when he arrived at Evreux as Major Andy Isoue. Later, as a General, Andy, really made things "happen" for the better in the Air Force.

All of them are blessed with great wives too, Tom and Nancy, Ricky and Linda, Connie and Sandra, Roy and Joyce, Ernie and Gabriele and Andy and his new wife Shirley!

I do need to add that two of us from the C-130 went on to become fighter pilots each having one of the premiere fighter wings to Command, Osan, AB Korea and Soesterberg, AB the Netherlands.

One day on a C-130 mission to England from Evreux, we visited a nightclub called the 105 Club in London. There, we were pushing peanuts on the floor with our noses (a fighter-pilot game) and I met my savior, Ralph Maglione, who worked in the pilot's assignments branch. Later, I learned that one of our navigators, "Jolten" Joe Lacey, all of five foot six but fierce as a tiger, had flown with Maglione in F-101s, and Joe told him that I should be a fighter pilot! *Lucky* again! How this all worked out, I will explain later.

While in the 39th I was assigned as Survival Officer and as such, I was sent to the Royal Air Force Survival School, at Devonshire, England on the southern coast near the white cliffs of Dover. It was a great school and the English know how to work and how to make the work fun.

We also did considerable water training with large life rafts similar to those in the C-130. I noted that their rafts had something unique and after using the rafts *boarding ramps*, I immediately realized that they had a real winner! I consulted with their senior survival folks and told them how wonderful the *boarding ramps* were and I wished we had them in ours! Anyone who has tried to get into a large raft without the boarding ramps knows how difficult it is.

They said "no sweat mate" or something like that and before the week was over, I had a complete set of *boarding ramp* drawings. When I returned to France, I contracted our sea Survival School and sent them the drawings. In less than a year all Air

Force large rafts were modified and I am sure some lives were saved! Anyone who says that the English aren't our best allies just don't know the truth!

During the school we had a bit of a trek event and we were given a live chicken as part of our food supply. After a couple of days, the Blokes approached me and admitted that they had never dealt with a live chicken. They asked me if I could handle it for them. Sure, I asked, "When do they wanted it done" and they said, "Now!"

With that, I grabbed the chicken by the neck and made a rotary swing of my arm and off popped the chicken's head as the body flew 20-30 feet away. Of course the chicken was minus a head and it started its dying run with blood flowing out of where the head used to be. I believe I heard a few comments like, *barbarian, animal or horrible person, etc.* But that night they all admitted that dinner was better than we had previously had!

Of course part of the trek included a night trek associated with the exercise. How did we prepare for the night trek? First we visited a pub, drank several pints of beer and ate a meal and then slept for a few hours before the night exercise! This was a perfect way to prepare for a night exercise. The Blokes are our best friends and truly fellow warriors.

As the Squadron Survival officer, I built small individual survival kits for everyone which fit in a plastic soap dish. One of the items you put in a small kit like that would be condoms as they make wonderful emergency water containers. I went to our exchange facility and to buy several boxes of condoms, actually hundreds of them. As luck would have it, the Wing Commander's wife was in line after me and noticed my boxes of condoms. She said something like, "That is an interesting purchase Lt?" I simply said, "My wife and I have a great sex life and laughed." She didn't laugh but everyone else around us did!

After more than three exciting years with the C-130, I left the best introduction to the actual and real-world aviation a young pilot could have, for the Air Training Command (ATC). There I would become a T-37 basic instructor pilot at Williams "Willie" AFB, Arizona. This was the first step in achieving my goal of becoming a real fighter pilot.

WILLIAMS "WILLIE" AFB, ARIZONA, 5/1964-6/1967

How I received this assignment at Williams AFB, Arizona, is another exciting story. As I mentioned earlier, I was pushing a peanut with my nose on the floor in the 105 Club in London, England, and I met a major named Ralph Maglione. Unknown to me, "Jolten" Joe Lacy, former F-101 WSO (Weapons System Operator or backseater) for Maglione and now a navigator on my crew. He had recommended to "Maggie" that I get into fighters. Maggie was from AF personnel, and he suggested that I apply for ATC (Air Training Command) as an instructor and gave me his card with his address on it. It worked, and the first set of orders I received to ATC, had *Maggie* in pencil on it, near the bottom of the page.

I arrived at Williams (Willie) AFB in May 1964 and quickly was entered into a two-month Instructor's Training course at Willie. I then began instructing at Willie for two years in the T-37 (Tweety-bird) and enjoyed it a great deal. I became a pretty good instructor pilot and certainly continued my aviation education. Teaching, to me, is always fun and challenging (I think I learned that from my

Dad), and I was able to have one of the top graduates in every class after my first class.

In one class I had the two top students, and they were more than fun; they were a ball, and they kept me jumping just to keep them challenged. My guys or students I remembered the most were Bud Hall, Cal Tax, Bill Ricks, Larry Peterson, and Al Thunyan (Saudi Arabia). As I became more experienced, I became the guy that flew with the students who were having trouble and had to determine if they could hack the program. With one exception: all who I evaluated eventually graduated and did reasonably well. The one fellow I did eliminate actually thanked me for failing him, since he hated flying and had been forced there by his father, an AF General.

I learned when I went through pilot training that sometimes you just clash with your instructor. In fact, as I said before, if a fellow named Ralph Wiles had not rescued me from my initial T-37 instructor, I would have never made it through the T-37s at Marianna, Florida. At Willie, I suspect I became known as a Santa Claus, but I knew that good instruction and confidence-building normally will result in most students learning to fly.

I tried to make learning fun, and the students knew I would try to trick them, not in anger but for fun. I frequently might drop-kicked a student who missed something or an item on the "esteemed" *walk around checklist* that each pilot must use to check his aircraft before he starts the aircraft. He then uses it during starting the engines and he also uses the checklist when he flies. I once even allowed a student to miss the clocks, which were placed against the wheels to keep the aircraft from rolling in the wind. In the T-37, the student was supposed to take them out. Later, in the real Air Force or in the T-38 the Crew Chief would remove the chocks. In any case, when the student tried to taxi, the aircraft wouldn't move! He owed me several beers for that! Student pilots are special people and are extremely fun to challenge and teach. They are all very competitive and success-oriented.

I had one student, Bill Ball from Colorado Air National Guard, who arrived with five thousand hours of flying time. Young Bill was a very smart individual, and the first time you would show him a maneuver, he would attempt to fly it as I did, but he would intentionally butcher the maneuver terribly. I would then show him again, and he would do the next one nearly perfectly. He did have a bit of a problem with formation flying, which involves flying very close to another aircraft and holding the position through all maneuvers. However, he was very successful in the program, and I am sure he became a first-rate National Guard pilot back at his Colorado base.

One of my favorite students was a Saudi Prince, Al Thunyan, who was a really good student, fun to teach, a real warrior, and a tough guy. He wasn't nervous about being in the air, and he had a great command of the English language, as he had attended college in England. We frequently had Al to the house to eat, since he was so far from home. On his first visit, Dorlyne, unaware that Muslims do not eat pork, fixed a fine ham for him. Being a gentleman, he ate some, and after I suddenly realized what we had done, I quickly cooked him a steak on the grill.

At the same time Al was a student, another Saudi Prince, Bandar, was at Williams who was very politically involved and considered himself truly royalty, which Al religiously avoided. This Prince regularly wore clothes that indicated that he was from royalty. Al, however, I thought, could outfly him in a heartbeat, but, following Willie, Prince Bandar became a very good F-15 pilot. As Prince Bandar grew older, he became a very visible individual for his government and later was the Saudi Ambassador to America and extremely well-liked by our government officials.

Al was a natural pilot, and he quickly caught on to everything but instrument flying, which involved using only the gauges in the cockpit to control the aircraft rather than outside references. His argument was that there was never any weather in Saudi. Since I had considerable time in Saudi, I knew his argument didn't hold water. One of the keys to flying instruments was being able to determine the heading from one of the needles that referenced the location of the navigational fix you were flying off of. The needle would give you information about the location of the navigational fix. There were some very simple equations that a pilot used such as, "tail of the needle to another forty-five degrees" for the heading to fly. Very simple, but Al refused to figure it out, even though he had attended the school of economics in London, and math was no problem. Since Al was standing very high in the class, I was determined to make him a very good instrument pilot and maybe first in the class. Of course he resisted instruments, and I think he must have told someone in Saudi that he was failing and it got to the US Air Force attaché in Saudi that he was failing.

Late one night my phone rang, and it was the Air Force attaché calling from Saudi. He asked what he could do to assist Al. I assured him that all Al had to do was some simple math; his answer was, "I guess with his millions, he just isn't good in math." I finally solved his instrument problems by using what he later told the Commander of Air Training Command, Gen. Momyer, was the "hit and show" method of training. What I would actually do when I realized he was not watching a particular instrument or gauge that he needed to be watching or reacting to, I would hit him. You sit side-by-side in the Tweetybird, and, after hitting him, I would point to the instrument that I knew he was not watching. Al, being a tough guy, responded to my "hit and show" method, and it worked, and he became a very acceptable and proficient instrument pilot.

Al was always surprising you. One day Al came in and asked me for a dollar. I assumed he had left his money in his room, and

I quickly handed him a buck, assuming that he needed lunch money. He then handed me a title to a T-28 aircraft to sign. We had seen several of them at the auxiliary field making practice landings or "touch-and-goes" during our landing training when we flew there a few days earlier. I had jokingly said as we talked about the T-28s, "We need a T-28 to fly on the weekends." I began to realize how much money he had.

Another time, we were at a Phoenix nightclub called the Millionaires Club, relaxing and partying a bit. I noticed he was having a bit of a confrontation with a waitress when suddenly he asked for the Manager. I also noticed he had his checkbook out. When the manager arrived, Al asked what the price was for the club, because he wanted to buy it!

The manager, somewhat taken aback, asked him why he wanted to buy the club. He said so that he could fire the waitress with whom he was unhappy. The Manager said, "I will take care of that" and led her away. We never saw her again.

Another time Al and I were on a flying cross-country and we stopped at Las Vegas. He had arranged for us to attend the famous Follies. However, we got there late, and the curtain was closed, and no one was to be let in. I mentioned to the man at the door who we were, and he threw open the curtain and announced us: "The Prince of Saudi Arabia" and, in a lower voice, "and Capt. Howard." Someone shouted, "I would like to buy them a drink!" Of course Al ordered milk, and I had a scotch and water! Al leaned over to me and said, because of his religion, he had milk, and winked! Obviously, he had struck a cord in Vegas, because we had first-class treatment! This trip also proved, as in everything else, he had become an exceptional instrument pilot.

When we night-flew the students solo in the T-37, a couple of us instructors would also fly following them around the night route to make sure they didn't get lost. During one of those nights, one of our former German students, T. Sgt. Hans Schmidt from Bavaria, a red-faced young sergeant who had graduated from Willie, was at Luke AFB and was obviously night-flying solo as part of his training in the F-104s. Hans had a distinctive voice, and I heard him transmit on guard, "This is [Hans' call sign; I can't remember it]; I just had a flameout at eighteen thousand feet, and I have restart at fourteen thousand"—silence for a bit— then "I have another flameout, I am trying a restart, I have restart, and then I have another flameout at seven thousand feet!"

I hit guard (emergency frequency that essentially overpowers all radios) on my radio and said in my strongest voice, *"Hans get out of that damn plane, right now!"*

Hans then bailed out and landed near a small county bar somewhere south and west of Luke AFB. Eventually they found him in the bar after his having consumed several adult beverages and being a happy Bavarian; they said he was smiling, unhurt, and later graduated. I attended his graduation at Luke and talked to him after his graduation. When he saw me, he said, "Capt. Howard, your ghost saved my life! I had a flameout in my F-104, and your ghost told me to bail out; I recognized your voice!" I didn't let on that I really had called him, because he was so sure it was "my ghost" and I didn't want to ruin his story. He was and probably still is a really fun person and a pretty good pilot!

Because the flying world in the 1960s was still real flying, when we would take students on cross-countries, we would sometimes fly in good formation and buzz the beaches of California, and some even flew under the San Francisco Bridge or took a tour of the Grand Canyon below both sides of canyon. Then an aviator's life while demanding was fun, exciting, challenging and *very* interesting.

While at Willie, I had some special friends such as my T-37 Squadron Commander, Maj. John Burris, who we affectionately, called "Juan Burro." We had a group of fellow pilots who hunted together, including *Juan Burro*, but he never shot anything! Finally we agreed that one of us would follow him and figure out what he was doing wrong. We sat him on top of a long cliff that we knew the deer eventually would climb up to for the night. We had the other hunters sort of drive the animals toward Juan. I was behind him and saw a deer climbing the cliff, headed straight for him. I know he would get a shot, but, as the deer got closer, he didn't move. I quickly slid down the cliff and worked my way over to him, throwing acorns at him, trying to alert him. When I got closer, I saw that he was sound asleep. I think I shot the deer!

My Naval Academy four-year roommate or "wife," born in Hilo, Hawaii, Bob Green, arrived at Willie also to be a T-37 Instructor Pilot. He and Bette bought a house very close to the base. Bob and his beautiful wife Bette (who looked like Elizabeth Taylor) had several children, and so they bought a house with a larger tract of land. Bob had been at Evreux in one of the C-130 squadrons too. Bob was a details man, and I am not sure he liked teaching students, and soon he was back at professional school and eventually got out of the Air Force and opened a successful computer business.

Another former C-130 pilot arrived at Willie from Evreux, Phil Handley, with his wife Solvojy and their son. Phil was a natural and very good pilot who later received the nickname "Hands" because he was so good at flying an aircraft. He and I arrived at being really good pilots through completely different routes or methods. He was a natural, and I had to work like hell to be good! When I departed Willie, Phil replaced me as Speedy 5. *Speedy* was the call sign of all Maintenance Test Pilots. Later he also had a Fighter Wing and also wrote a book about aviation. I always envied natural pilots like Phil, but by working hard, I may have been a touch better—the explosion you just heard was Phil reading the previous line!

Finally, another of my friends and his wife arrived at Willie: Ron Ellis and his wife Ellen. Ron started with me in the class of 1958 at the Naval Academy, and he was a superb student and an All-American Lacrosse player. I have told the story of Ron's departure from the Academy many times. He probably stood in the top 1–2 percent of the class, but, because he failed Russian, even though he had a 3.8 on a 4.0 basis in other courses, he was discharged from the Academy. In fact, guys like me couldn't even take Russian, as he did, because our grades weren't high enough. I think he was eliminated with a 2.49 final exam, with 2.5 as passing. He reaped his revenge in that he went to Maryland after leaving Annapolis, and he and his Maryland lacrosse team beat Navy several times in lacrosse. He graduated from the University of Maryland through the Air Force ROTC and joined me in the Air Force. Ron and Ellen stayed with us for a while when they came to Willie.

My first serious misbehaving act occurred at Willie. Cherry (Pitts) Hall married Howard Hall, who I lived with at "the Texas snake ranch" in Wichita Falls. We were of course attending USAF Photo-Intelligence School together. Later, when Howard was in Vietnam, my wife Dorlyne strongly suggested I contact his wife, Cherry, in Las Vegas when I next visited there, as I often did as an Instructor Pilot flying students on their cross-country from Williams AFB, Arizona. About twice a month I would take a student to Las Vegas as part of his training. It was a mistake contacting Cherry, because a very exciting relationship occurred (she told me she was divorcing Howard), and it contributed, as it should have, to the tension between my wife and me. Once again I discovered that a redhead was really "exciting." Cherry was a very neat and very beautiful lady with whom I enjoyed visiting in Las Vegas. It is not something I am proud of now.

At Willie there was a tradition called "roof-stomping," where you got on the roof of the person that is well liked or has done something special like getting promoted. The person being *roofed-stomped* is expected to offer you adult beverages. Of course, to wake up the folks, you really *stomped on the roof* and usually there are a bunch of folks stomping! For some reason, I think whenever I missed Friday beer call or went home early from the Officers' Club, our students *roof-stomped* us.

As we were preparing to depart the base for our next assignment, the Base Engineers had started checking the roofs of the base housing, as the houses were very old. Because the units were very old, the engineers were determining if a roof needed to be repaired. I'll never forget the look on the engineer's face when he came out of the crawl space to our roof. He said, "Did you know that every one of your rafters are broken?" Fortunately we were leaving for Homestead AFB, Florida, so they replaced the whole roof.

My military, aviation, and family life while at Willie were truly a dream come true for many reasons. Of course there was an occasional unhappy or really disgraceful event also! But, I learned more about flying while teaching than I had learned in pilot training. I was able to complete several correspondence courses, which broadened my military mind and helped develop my leadership abilities. My family life was fun, generally strong, and I had a chance to spend lots of time with Mike and Barrie! I was able to participate in many aspects of hunting for doves, quail, rabbits, and larger animals like deer. The doves in the area were numerous and really detrimental to our jet aircraft engines.

I learned a lesson that the federal government can be challenged and changed if one is willing to spend the time and effort to get the facts, as was the case concerning extending the dove hunting season in the area, which I was able to do. After many months of effort, I was able to expand the dove-hunting season in the Williams area, which resulted in a drastic decrease in bird strikes at Willie. This resulted in far fewer J-85 engines (from the

T-38 aircraft) being damaged, so that it was less of a threat to the safety of our young flyers. Of equal importance, I learned that written communications with good and valid facts make bureaucrats tremble, and then it forces them to think more logically and intelligently and react accordingly.

Also, I was able, along with my friends, to shoot lots more doves. I can remember sitting a grocery-store brown paper bag, folded down to about a foot high, on the ground and attempting to hit doves so that they fell in the bag. I never accomplished getting one in the bag, but I did hit the bag a few times, and my friend, Ron Ellis, did put one in a bag!

A French 75 New Year's Eve party at a friend's house resulted in an event that could have been—and today, would have been—the end of my military career. After several French 75s, Dorlyne and I decided to depart the party, actually because of an incident where the bathroom door was kicked in. At the time I had a 1959 Chevrolet Impala Convertible that had been a special engineering project of Chevrolet engineering, with a very strong engine that was capable of lots of speed. I wanted to go to the base New Year's Eve party, and my wise wife thought we should go home since I was probably already bombed! I too, obviously realized that I was bombed, because I allowed Dorlyne had driven us home from the French 75 party. When we arrived in front of our rented house in Chandler, Arizona, I said I was going to the Officers' Club because a friend, Gerald Blake, was going to introduce me to a lovely redhead, Nancy Kluck. I had seen her on the golf course several times. Nothing evil about this—I just wanted to meet her, as she was usually playing in a group of friends who I knew, but I didn't know her. She was so pretty that I just had to meet her, and my friend said he would introduce me to her.

My wife foolishly got out of the car in front of our house, putting the keys on the convertible roof of the car on the driver's side, and went into the house. The "village drunk, me" quickly jumped out of the passenger side, found the keys, and departed for the Club; a real dummy was behind the wheel!

Once you were outside the town of Chandler, the road to Willie was as straight as an arrow, with only one stoplight on the road to the base. Being a jet pilot sometimes translates into a speed demon on the road. Since at the time, there was no speed limit in Arizona, I am certain that I was well over 100 mph as I cruised toward the base. I could see in my rearview mirror a vehicle following me with his lights off. I assume or thought *he* was just some drunk, and I needed to outrun him! I even stopped at the one stoplight at the Queen Creek bar intersection and noticed that the car behind me slowed down and didn't try to pass me.

I pressed on to the base, and, as I approached the gate, the vehicle without lights on turned them on and put on his police lights, indicating that he was an officer of the law. As a law-abiding citizen, I of course stopped for his lights and possibly his siren. As he approached the car, I got out; displaying my size (he later said he was nervous about my size). He wrote me a ticket for speeding, under the influence, and unsafe driving. I accepted the ticket, but refused to sign it as was required because, as I said, "He had driven at an unsafe speed with his lights out." I suspect I probably told him my Father was also a Sheriff in Indiana, and I knew he would never let one of his troops run with their lights off. As a result, I was taken to the jail for the night. In retrospect, had I signed the ticket, I might not have gone to jail!

The night in the Chandler *drunk tank* was a real education! They took away my belt and shoelaces, which I didn't understand at the time; but later, in the evening, as I began to think more clearly (sober up?), I understood why. The shame hit me, and I believe that I probably considered suicide, which the shoelaces or belt could be used for! Later both Dorlyne and I worried that our children would see their Daddy picking up garbage, as Chandler had jail inmates pick up garbage! Fortunately, my wonderful squadron Commander, John Burris, got me out of jail, so I didn't make the garbage detail like the rest of the drunks! Another lesson was learned and again, my military career was in real jeopardy. Fortunately, the Wing Director of Operation, at that time was Col. Mike McCarty, who came to my rescue when I appeared in front of the Base Commander. Col. Mike convinced him to not give me a death sentence of twelve points, which would have cost me my license for a year on the base. Col. Mike said that I had just been selected as the ATC Flying Instructor of the Year, and that I was needed on the flight line. He mentioned that an Air Force regulation, which directed that a pilot is, authorized military transportation to and from the aircraft he was assigned to fly. If he grounded me with twelve points, the DO would require a transport to and from the flight line for me, since I was such a good instructor and I flew every day. The Base Commander would have to provide that transportation if he gave me the death sentence of twelve points against my driving record. The Base Commander, after giving me a well-deserved lecture, gave me only eleven points! As a result, we quickly moved onto the base, and the state of Arizona gave me a speeding and reckless driving ticket rather than a DWI—but a lawyer and court costs destroyed our meager savings.

As an aside, I never met Nancy Kluck at Willie, but when I arrived in Albuquerque in 1998 and began swimming at the Kirtland AFB pool, there was Nancy, also swimming and as pretty as ever. Her husband, Bill, and I have become great friends, and we have been swimming together for over thirteen years. The Air Force is a small world!

MAINTENANCE FUNCTIONAL FLIGHT TEST, 5/1966-5/1967

My Evreux C-130 years of operations and training paid off in ATC in that I was selected as the outstanding T-37 instructor of the year, my second year in ATC. Probably contributing to my selection was Al Thunyan's success, as he was debriefed by the ATC Commander, Gen. Momyer. As a result of my selection, I was told that I could have any assignment at Willie that I wanted.

I asked to be a Maintenance Functional Flight Test Pilot (MFFT) because I knew I could then fly the T-38 and possibly the F-5, a tactical fighter. But more importantly, I knew all those in MFFT were real fighter pilots, and I could learn from them. My choice shook up the Director of Operations (DO) who I didn't particularly like, because I had submitted several volunteer requests to go to Vietnam, and he always refused them. He and several other senior officers counseled me against the assignment. I explained that there was a lack of maintenance inputs to the young pilots, and I thought I could rectify that as a test pilot, and we set up a class for the students about maintenance.

I, of course, won the battle and became Speedy 5 in May of 1966: the youngest test pilot and the only one who had not been forced into the job because he wasn't suited to be an instructor. The other Speedies had been sent to the Functional Test section because they preferred not to train students.

For many months, I had tried to be on a path to go to Vietnam in a fighter by submitting various applications to go. I suspect that, to turn off my paper machine for Vietnam, and as a result of my selection as ATC Flying Instructor of the Year, I was offered the chance to change jobs at Willie. Many of the senior leaders thought I would select instructing in the T-38 or to be an academic instructor or both. As I said, I surprised them all and asked to be a Flight Check pilot. It really shocked them, since most in that business were folks who didn't like to—or in some cases couldn't—instruct. Again, I did what I had learned earlier; I developed a logically written paper that suggested that I could also teach a maintenance class to the students about how to write up aircraft. What I didn't say in my paper about becoming a check pilot was that I wanted to get checked out in the T-38 and the *F-5 fighter* to enhance my ultimate goal of becoming an actual fighter pilot. I knew all the check pilots were old-head fighter pilots, and I would get them to teach me and they did!

Having won the battle, I became Speedy 5 check pilot. However, the other Speedies became my *fighter instructor pilots*, since all were really good fighter pilots. Initially, they would wax my butt in air-to-air combat, since I had never been trained in it; after I completed my testing the of aircraft malfunctions in our test area, the "fight" was always on! I got shot down so many times that I felt like Swiss cheese!

Finally I asked Speedy 3, Tom Livingstone, or, as we called him, "Live Rock", to teach me how to be a fighter pilot and especially in air-to-air. He was a great teacher, and pretty soon I was getting better in air-to-air, as he was a Rembrandt of an air-to-air instructor. In fact, soon he had created a fearless air-to-air monster: *me*! The other test pilots stopped announcing that they were in the test area if they knew I was there, because I would be after them and more than likely would win the engagement.

The Test section had a flying area set aside for doing the flight-check operations. Our procedures were to go to a special frequency when entering the area and check-in by making a radio call: "Speedy 5, entering the check area." After Live Rock made me an airborne killer, the other check pilots would enter the area cautiously or not make the required radio call thus not alerting Killer Howard if they knew I was in the area! When in the area, I would often monitor the Mobile Control radio frequency for other Speedies getting airborne, so that I could set up for an attack on them as they arrived in the test area! Mobile Control was the controlling agency for takeoff and landings; thus, I would know when I would have a potential target was heading for the Test area!

Part of the functional flight-check procedures that we performed was flying the aircraft to full stall to make sure that the aircraft was properly rigged and would not do anything strange when departing from normal flight in a stalled condition, which the students should experience during training. As a result, I became very good at operating in what is referred to as flying "On the edge or zero airspeed maneuvering." This later gave me the ability to operate the F-4 in areas that many pilots avoided for fear of losing control of the aircraft. My time in the "Test Section" was wonderful; I amassed considerable flying hours, learned to fly on the edge, and my confidence grew, which prepared me when I finally got into a fighter assignment. More importantly, I spent time with real fighter pilots who enjoyed teaching me, and later we did the same for my friend Phil Handley, who replaced me in the Test Section when I escaped to the F-4 fighter world.

I continued my battle to go to Vietnam, and I had probably really offended the new Wing Director of Operations, Col. Harmon, who it seemed, had become my enemy. This was probably caused by an incident that occurred on a test hop with a T-38 that had had a double engine change, requiring a test hop. As I took off, we Maintenance test pilots normally held it on the ground a bit longer than normal, gaining airspeed above normal takeoff speed, in case we had to immediately land against traffic. As I broke ground, both Fire Lights came on, and Mobile said, "Speedy Five, it looks like you are on fire!" I immediately transmitted on-guard frequency: "Mobile, Speedy Five is going to closed traffic and will land against traffic, as I have two fire lights and can see flames!" Of course I had to speak in a very calm voice, and we test pilots continually worked on that! At the same time, suddenly several folks started giving me advice. I was very busy trying to get it back on the ground rapidly, because I remembered that the T-38 tech order, the pilot's bible of an aircraft, said, "With two engines on fire, you must get it back on the ground immediately [I believe within less than a minute, maybe 38 seconds] as the boat tail [the rear of the aircraft] will burn off"! I didn't need any help, and I was damned busy flying the aircraft because I was close to stall speed trying to get it back to the runway. Finally I said, "Would everyone please shut the f—k up; I have it under control, and I am damn busy!" As I landed with the fire trucks racing after me, I noticed two staff cars chasing me. Fortunately, the first staff car to reach me was the Wing Commander, Brigadier General McNabb, and after had I emergency-egressed from the aircraft after shutting down the engines and hitting my right knee on the canopy rail, hard! The General hugged me and thanked me for saving his aircraft. I could see the DO, Col. Harmon, looking like a bull pawing the ground, wanting to get at me for telling him to shut up. The General put me in his car, and he took me to Maintenance. *Lucky* again and saved by the General!

Having submitted several requests for reassignment to fighters, Col. Harmon first rejected them, and then he threatened to send me to helicopters. The Chief of Maintenance, Stan Wilkinson, stopped that for me, *lucky* again.

Since I had served in the Air Force long enough, I had the option of resigning, and I had contacted several AF National Guard organizations that offered me fighter slots: New Orleans (F-100s), Albuquerque (F-100s), Tucson (F-100s), and the Denver (F-100s). Since I was unable to go to Vietnam, I submitted a resignation from the Air Force so that I could join an Air National Guard fighter squadron. That seemed to do the trick and suddenly, I had an assignment to the 478th Fighter Squadron at Homestead AFB, Florida, as an F-4 student. What I didn't know until later was that good old Ralph Maglione had helped me again. At last on my way to Vietnam, I was elated! My orders had in pencil at the bottom, "Col. Mag"! Col. Maggie was now, or soon to be, Thunderbird Leader, and the "Birds" had visited Willie. When he left, he said the bottle of Scotch in his seat was uncomfortable, but it was damn good Scotch! I suspect the General and Col. Wilkinson also talked to him about me.

I must admit that my time at Willie was not only personally wonderful but also made me a much better pilot and officer, because by and large those at Willie were outstanding examples of professional officers and leaders, especially at the more-senior leadership level.

Sometime during my assignment to Willie, I heard from some friends that the widow of my Naval Academy very close friend who had been killed in a Navy fighter, Don Myers, was having problems in San Diego, California. Carol (Thompson) Myers was also from Annapolis, Maryland, and had been the high school girlfriend of Don Myers. Don was one of my best friends. They were married after graduation, and Don was killed in a fighter crash "going aboard the boat," landing on an aircraft carrier. Carol had a bad session of luck after Don's death and married a jerk, but the marriage was later annulled. I had to get involved to get her Navy benefits returned. Actually, at the grand opening of the new Navy Officer's Club at Navy North Island, near San Diego, I approached the Admiral of North Island Naval Air Station, and I said, "I thought the Navy *took care of their own?*"

With a great deal of anger, he asked me to see him in his office the next day, and Carol's problem was quickly resolved. Carol was also the daughter of the Naval Academy's longtime track coach, Tommy Thompson. After that, I didn't see Carol for many years. She became an owner in a travel agency, and we met in the Cayman Islands when I was running the Southern Cross Club. Later I represented my friend Don in the marriage of his son. My ex-wife probably divorced me primarily over that, and for that, she was wrong! She had, for some reason, determined that she was not invited to the wedding when actually she was and would not go!

F-4 AND HOMESTEAD AFB, FLORIDA, 6/1967-5/1968

The Fighter Training Wing at Homestead was just forming when we arrived in June 1967, and we were able to get on-base housing, since the base was converting from Strategic Air Command (SAC) to Tactical Air Command (TAC). Fortunately, or unfortunately depending on how you looked at it—the house we obtained was just a block away from the Officers' Club, or within crawling distance! The Club where fighter pilots loved to spend evenings learning from the old heads or telling flying lies and occasionally talking about women! I was assigned to the 478th Tactical Fighter Squadron (TFS).

Because the Wing was newly forming, some of the instructors had less flying time than many of us in the first class. These low-flying-time instructors, in most cases, had upgraded from the backseat of the F-4 to the front seat in Southeast Asia (Vietnam or Thailand). While they were low on flying time, they had considerable amounts of real combat experience and were able to teach us "old-head pilots" a great deal! Fortunately, there was a cadre of really experienced or old head fighter IPs who were able to handle us experienced pilots who were in the class. As a result of the strange instructor mix, it was as good as it could get in training. You could beat or outshine the younger instructors, but there were the old heads who could *sock it to you* if you tried to shine too much.

One particular instructor, Ed Hall, who was a Nellis graduate from the famed Fighter Weapons School when it was a real and a unique school, stood out, since he was a consummate fighter pilot. He was extremely proud of his bombing ability, stating that he had never dropped an unscorable bomb. He also seemed to hold back a little when teaching us "studs" (students) the art of bombing! I really tried to fly with him as much as possible, because he was so good. After we graduated, he admitted that he didn't teach us all his tricks! I managed to extract my pound of flesh from him one day when I flew in his backseat during a monthly Turkey Shoot. Fighter outfits try to have regular "Turkey Shoots" which are simply very serious bombing and target shooting competitions to provide as much challenge or stress in the training as possible. In the F-4, the back-seater calls out altitudes so that the front-seater can mentally compute where he wants to release his bombs. Revenge is sweet, and I may have called out the wrong altitudes for him on a few bombs. He then had some unscorable bombs, which are bombs that are outside the scorable range, normally at six o'clock but not dangerous to anyone! He could no longer say that he had never had unscorable bomb; aren't I evil? But Mr. Ed just laughed about it, I think!

In 1968, I was to be part of a flyover of the Super Bowl in Miami, Florida (which was eventually won by Green Bay 33 to 14). The flight was to be out of Homestead AFB. Tom Delashaw was to be in my backseat, and we even practiced the flyover as the Flight Leader. However, on Thursday before the game, we received a call from the Wing Commander, Gen. "Pancho"

Sugera, who called and said, "He was going to fly in our place." Further, and we were going to sit with the Governor of Florida at the game. I quickly mentioned that we had already practiced the flyover, and, because of the sun position, it was a challenge to not hit the light poles at the stadium. Gen. Sugera said that we would have a radio and be in communication with the flight and would keep them from hitting the light poles! Naturally we were disappointed, but Tom and I could have fun doing most anything.

When we arrived at the game and joined the Governor, of course we were in our dress blue uniforms as this Super Bowl was dedicated to the US Military. I noticed that it looked like the Governor had gained weight, and I foolishly mentioned that it looked like he had gained some weight. He said, "Barry, it is my bulletproof vest; obviously yours is better than mine, because yours doesn't make you look heavy." Astonished, Tom and I said together, "Bulletproof vest?" His aide said, "You did get the word that the Governor had a death threat? That is why we all have on bulletproof vests!" Needless to say, we now understood why maybe we weren't flying and Pancho was!

We did look around a bit throughout the game, somewhat nervously, as we were seated on either side of the Governor during the game as this Super Bowl and our presence on either side of the Governor demonstrated that the Military was being honored. The threat to him was obviously a false alarm, but it sure was a bit uncomfortable for several hours!

Our flyover was to be at the halftime, and I was given a radio to stay in contact with the flight. Fortunately, my good friend, Dick Desing, was in the General's backseat and was very alert and always had great situational awareness (pilot talk for knowing what the hell is going on around you). As they approached the field to do the flyover of the game at the right moment during halftime, it was obvious to Tom and me that they were too low. It became pretty obvious as they approached that they were too low and might hit the light poles. I transmitted, "Pull it up, Lead." knowing that he had the afternoon sun in his eyes and probably couldn't see the light poles.

The flight didn't climb as I suggested so again, I transmitted, "pull it up, Lead," but again no movement and the situation was getting critical. So I transmitted, "Damn it, Pancho, pull it up!" which resulted in the flight immediately climbing a couple of hundred feet. It was a beautiful flyover, even though Tom and I weren't leading it!

Tom Delashaw—I called him "the Tummy"—and Tom was actually a famous Air Force F-104 pilot before and after he upgraded in the F-4. He and I did have a good time after the game, and it took only a couple of days for us to get home. I am told that it probably contributed to the Tummy's subsequent divorce. Later, we were able to finally track our elusive after-Super-Bowl trail, while we were there, somewhat, by our credit card bills. For example, we know that each night about midnight we had chili and White Castle hamburgers, lots of them! We did have fun, however!

When we returned to the base, we were invited to the Wing Staff meeting the next week. Of course, everyone was anxious to hear how the Wing Commander, "Pancho" Sugera, responded to my "Damn it, Pancho, pull it up!" I must admit, I too was more than a little nervous about it! As the Staff Meeting progressed, the anticipation built, waiting to hear from Pancho as he had the various staff members report.

Finally, Pancho stood up and walked toward me, which of course made me a bit more uncomfortable. As he got closer, he said, "Ladies and gentlemen, I want to point out a real leader in our midst, Capt. Barry Howard, who probably prevented a real serious embarrassment to the Air Force! He then shook my hand, and maybe he gave me a huge "Cajun-ass hug," but I don't remember! I loved Pancho and I think everyone else that

I knew did too. Unfortunately, the Air Force gave him only one star, which I think was a mistake, because he was the kind of leader that warriors loved to follow into battle!

Our class at Homestead AFB, because of weather, got a bit behind schedule, and, of course, most already had their new assignments in hand with a reporting date. We flew our last mission at night, with many of the students leaving the next day for their assignment to Vietnam traveling on a commercial airliner. Of course, we had a big party that night, and there were a few—no, *many* adult beverages consumed.

One of the back-seater's had a big Torino with the front-end drive, and it weighed a ton. He was departing for Vietnam the next day so he left the party fairly early and headed to his home, off base. He was a bachelor officer, and the next thing we knew, we got a call from someone stating that he had wiped out the back-gate guardhouse, going off the base to his apartment. I jumped in my car and raced out there. The gate shack had been removed, cleanly, and was about ten to twenty feet from its foundation. Fortunately the lad wasn't hurt, and I found him wandering around, very out of it, possibly from his adult beverages. I asked him about the car, and I believe he said, "Forget it!" I grabbed him and took him to where he lived. Fortunately, his bags were packed; we loaded his stuff in my car, and off we went to the airport. I am sure that his flight was several hours away, but I wanted to get him where the Air Police or even the local Police couldn't get to him. By the time we got to the airport, he was fairly sober and realized that he needed to get out of Dodge, fast! I dropped him off, and I suspect he caught an earlier flight. I told him do not answer a page unless it was from me.

As I was going back into the base after dropping him off at the airport, I drove through the moved gate." They were trying to move it back to its foundation. I didn't stop and say hello! The next day I received a call from the Air Police, and I told them that he was on his way to Vietnam. I don't know if anything ever caught up with him, but he had junked his car and made it safely to his new assignment.

The SAC Wing Commander wasn't very happy about the gate movement, but I don't think he knew I was involved, or he would have had me visit his office. He looked just like Rock Hudson in *Gathering of the Eagles*!

He really didn't like me, because I found some obscure regulation that said if a certain number of members of an Officers' Club agreed; a vote can be taken to change a Club rule. The rule at Homestead was, no flight suites in the Officers' Club and the vote was taken, and the rule was changed: we could wear flight suits to the club!

When the rule was changed, the SAC Wing Commander, a Brig.Gen. Hargrove (a Rock Hudson look-alike who later would make Lt. Gen.) called me in and said if any problems developed, I would be held accountable, since I had been the leader of the rule change. Of course the first Friday night, there was a fight in the then "Stag Bar" where flight suits were worn for the first time and of course I was called into the General's office the next morning. The fighters were supposed to be there too. When the General demanded of his Aide where were the fighters, his aide said, "Capt. Howard was one of them, along with Capt. Delashaw" who was standing there with me. I can't remember his words, but they weren't nice!

Just prior to this event, I had been told that I was being held as an Instructor Pilot at Homestead! Talk about being a very unhappy camper—I was furious and probably not nice to be around! I started training students, actually, before I graduated, but I wasn't one who was a happy instructor. Whenever a ferry flight of an F-4 to Southeast Asia came up, I would quickly volunteer. Later, I ferried an F-4 to Da Nang, Vietnam and, when I landed, the Wing Commander, "Buckshot" White, met me. He mentioned that he was short of experienced F-4 pilots so I took the bait and later talked to the Squadron Commander of 35th Tactical Fighter Squadron (TFS) who also met us. I said I would be happy to fly some missions for him, to which he said super, and thanks, and gave me the scheduler's phone number. I called the scheduler immediately, and the next day, and for several days following, I flew Combat Missions for the 35th TFS. Of course I was having a ball, flying combat, then going to the Officer's Club with the other flyers and being a real combat pilot, at long last, a dream fulfilled!

One day as I was rolling out from a landing from a combat mission, and I received a radio call from the Wing Commander, "Buckshot," who normally talked in a very high-pitched voice and said, "Barry Howard, stop by my hooch (cabin), sit at my desk, and wait for me!" I of course followed his direction and sat at his desk in his hooch as directed. I saw on the desk a message with my name written in *Big Red* letters at the top. I read the message, and it was from Tactical Air Command Headquarters Personnel stating, "Capt. Barry J. Howard was AWOL (Absent Without Leave) from Homestead" and asked for any information about Capt. Howard and his whereabouts. At the bottom of the message, again in red pencil, was a note, "C-130 departing at 1530 hours, with a reservation saved!"

Naturally I was on that C-130 heading back to Homestead. When I returned nothing else was said about my being gone, and my wife Dorlyne and Mike and Barrie were happy, because I had presents for them, and I was in a very good mood, since I had finally flown some combat missions, which was every fighter pilot's dream!

UDORN AB, THAILAND 6/1968-7/1969

Shortly after my return in June of 1968 from Da Nang, Gen. Pancho called me into his office and told me that he had released me from Homestead to be reassigned to Udorn, Thailand, and eventually the 13th TFS (Tactical Fighter Squadron). When I PCSed (Permanent Change of Station or moved to Udorn), I ferried an RF-4, a photo reconnaissance aircraft, which, when it would arrive at Udorn, they would install a nose full of cameras. However, the nose was empty for the "high flight," so that I could take all my necessaries in the nose of the aircraft. I also had a Flight Surgeon in the backseat. I tried to teach the Flight Surgeon to fly, but he was not a good student! It was an unusually long flight of 14:30 hours as we over flew a normal stopping base and went on to Udorn, Thailand. We were provided refueling tankers for the whole trip, thus we could overfly the normal stopping bases. I had made several high flights, but never one that long and without an autopilot, which was out, and a Flight Surgeon in the backseat who couldn't fly worth a damn!

When we arrived at Udorn, I turned off at midfield, because I was well below taxi speed at midfield. When we shut down, the Assistant DO (Col. Bob Taylor) met us and, in a rather angry voice, chewed us out for turning off at midfield. I told him we were just ferrying the aircraft, and we were adequately slowed at midfield to turn off there. He said, "No one turns off at midfield at Udorn." Seemed dumb to me, but I said, "Yes, Sir, but I was from Homestead, and it is desired there to turn off midfield there because of taxiing traffic!"

The next day, after I signed into the Wing, I was taken to the Director of Operations' (DO) office and was welcomed by the DO and the ADO. The ADO said, "You sure look familiar." I said, "Yes, sir, we met yesterday, sir!" He then said, "I thought you were from Homestead AFB, Florida?" I said I was, "But today I signed in to this Wing (432nd TW)." I knew that I would have trouble with the ADO but I really liked the DO, Ralph Findley, who, I found out, was a Reconnaissance or Recce Pilot, but a real warrior! He later became my Champion and really supported me, because I was also a warrior. On more than one occasion, he protected me from the ADO. One time after the ADO had called me to report to his office, as he was chewing me out for bombing in the North, and the DO, Col. Findley, walked in as I was getting really chewed out and said, "Capt. Howard, you are dismissed!"

I quickly departed the ADO's office but stayed within hearing range and heard the DO say to the ADO, "Bob, I know you don't like Barry, but he is one of our best young leaders and is a real warrior who we can count on; I would appreciate if you leave him alone!" Many years later, I ran into Col. Bob Taylor, the ADO, after he had retired in Tampa, and it was like I was his long-lost buddy! Bob Taylor was a good guy; I just rubbed him the wrong way!

13th TACTICAL FIGHTER SQUADRON, UDORN, 6/1968-7/1969

Since I was an acknowledged F-4 Instructor Pilot when I arrived at Udorn, Thailand in June of 1968, my checkout was extremely shortened and a modified one. Actually I really had no check-out other than I flew as "tail-end Charlie" on my first day mission way up North, and as a wing man on my next mission at night (I hated nights) the next day. And damn near killed myself and Marv Bishop. Fortunately, Major Marv Bishop, a truly superb Navigator was assigned to take care of the new guy, me! Marv was a super and fearless "fightergator" and steered me through my "new guy" period. He, along with me, is owed a Purple Heart since we earned them but aren't very good administrators of our records.

My first mission shortly after I checked in was way "down-town" (Route Pack 6) as blue 4 (not a proper call sign, but blue is a generic call sign used by most) in the 16-ship formation, meaning I was the tail-end Charlie. I was in a "gaggle" that was led, unknown to me, by the Squadron Commander (since he didn't attend the mass briefing), and it was his last mission! When we arrived in the target area, the sky was filled with exploding flak. I rolled in as the last aircraft (tail-end Charlie) to attack the target, as briefed. I started down the slide toward the target, and I was almost hit by an F-4 coming up from the target, but he shouldn't have been there! I got the tail number of the aircraft as it damn near hit me, and I decided that I would "talk" to the pilot when I got back on the ground! Yes, I was really torqued, because he had obviously rolled in before he should have, probably not wanting to get shot at. Of course he only managed to start angering and really upsetting the enemy gunners on the ground before the rest of us got there!

Old tail-end Charlie, *me*, would really get shot at, and I did, resulting in my getting really low to avoid the gunners over the target! I also had a hung 750-pound bomb after release. I was able to clearly see into one of the rapidly firing gun pits because I was so low, and I saw some of the men running into an area and coming out with ammo. Obviously it was an ammo storage area, so I rolled in again on it and released the hung bomb on it and got enormous and numerous long-lasting secondary explosions.

Without a doubt, there sure were some angry gunners down there, and the sky was filled with flack! When I looked at the gun-camera film, the sky was actually black with exploding flack! One of the leaders of my squadron put me in for a DFC (Distinguished Flying Cross) *on my first combat mission at Udorn*, which I received months later when I was checking out of the base, returning to the States. But I never knew who did it!

When I finally got back on the ground, after refueling on a KC-135 tanker on the way out, I hit the ground running or boiling and asked the Crew Chief where the aircraft tail number that almost hit me, was parked. Fortunately, my flight leader realized that I was after the guy who almost hit me, and he grabbed me and said, "Forget it; that was the Squadron Commander, Slippery, who departs tomorrow, thank goodness!" Fortunately, he and others held me back, and I cooled off, but I sure was happy that Slippery departed. *Lucky* again: I was prevented from slugging my new Squadron Commander!

When I had been in briefed by him the day before as a new guy in the squadron, I had showed him the book my wife had given me. It was a bound book that looked like the real thing but actually was a joke book with a fancy printed title: *What I Know about Flying the F-4 by the International Famous Pilot, Barry J. Howard*. He didn't even smile when he opened it and all pages were blank! What a weird character; how he got the squadron, I will never know.

Shortly afterward, the Squadron Operations Officer, Dudley *"Cuddly Dudley"* Foster, told me that he had assigned me to the 13th, as well as most of those recently assigned to the 13th when he was at the Air Force Personnel Center. He said our new Squadron Commander, Lt. Col. Vern Covalt, was a great leader and person. It didn't take long to realize what a wonderful Commander Lt. Col. Vern Covalt was and how controlling Cuddly Dudley was! I really liked *Cuddly Dudley*, but everything had to be his idea!

One of the first things we did at Udorn for the 13th TFS was to build a very nice Squadron party room. It is amazing what talent exists in most squadrons, and we built a super party room. It kept our folks from getting in trouble in the Officer's Club, and our new guys learned tons information and tricks of combat talking to the old heads.

Much later, I really stepped on *Old Cuddly Dudley's* authority while he was home on leave by starting Udorn's FAST FAC (Jet forward air controller) program with the very strong encouragement of the Wing DO, Ralph Findley. In fact, when *Cuddly Dudley* got back, he was so angry at me that he terminated my leadership of the program and replaced me with another major.

I became Falcon 5 instead of Falcon 1. It hurt a bit, but I had already set up all the procedures with the recce folks, and we were always target-rich thanks to the recce intelligence folks, then Commanded by Col. Brown and his assistant, Maj. Michael Hayden—who later became, Gen. Hayden, and later the head of the CIA.

At Udorn, we had the RF-4C recce birds and the ground intelligence folks who kept a sharp eye on the enemy ground operation. They would develop targets, and normally the targets were then sent to headquarters in Saigon, Vietnam, for dissemination to the fighter units, resulting in a few hours' or days' delay. We Falcons or Laredo's (new Wing Commander changed our name) worked with the intelligence folks, and almost instantly we had "bombs on target," real and current targets. It doesn't take long in the fighter world for the word to get around that Falcons, later Laredos, have real and current targets.

Frequently when we were airborne, flights would ask if a Falcon, or later a Laredo, was around, because they knew we had good targets for them, whether we were in North Vietnam, South Vietnam, or Barrel Roll (Cambodia). It was really nice to be wanted! Being a FAST FAC was, to me, the best mission available with the existing ROE (Rules of Engagement). We worked continually with the Intel folks and thus had valid, timely, and useful targets rather than those that came out of Saigon, which were frequently several hours or days old and were seldom found. Of course, I don't think anyone but the Intel troops knew that early in my Air Force career, I was also a Photo Intel officer or PI at the 2nd Recce Tech at Barksdale AFB, Louisiana. As a result, I am sure the Intel. Officers really provided us with great stuff, since they knew it would be put to good use by a former Intel. Guy: me!

One night I was in the southern part of North Vietnam near the Quang Khe ferry, and I watched Recce RF-4C photograph the river, the underwater bridge, and the ferry area. The flack looked like an oscillating fan of a garden sprinkler chasing the recce bird. After that I talked to a friend, Bob McCann, who was at Willie with me, a West Pointer, and who was a recce pilot. This of course all started in the bar, where these things always start—I wish the Leadership of the Air Force realized that and returned the Officers' Clubs! I said, "You know, I could follow you over on that mission way above you masked in your radar shadow, and, as you start your run, I could roll inverted and head down with Cluster Bomb Units commonly called CBUs and take out those gunners for you!" It seems that the North Vietnamese gunners had spider holes that they dove in when they heard or saw a fighter bomber coming after them. He thought it was a good idea, and we began to brief it to the wing leadership. Of course the DO, Col. Ralph Finley, a Recce Pilot, thought it was a great idea, and he helped us sell it to Saigon.

My backseater, Marv Bishop, had received orders to go home before we finally were scheduled for the mission. Being a real warrior, he extended his tour to fly the mission, because he knew that the mission would work and save some lives. He also knew I needed his help! We, Bob in his RF-4C, and Marv and I in our fighter would meet after working out the details and where we had to be to be in Bob's radar shadow along with the timing. I think we had two actual missions that because of weather didn't go. Finally, with decent weather, we were inbound to the target area in Bob's shadow. He started his run; I rolled inverted—*man*, that was scary, because it was one of those very dark nights with no horizon or moon available—and pulled the nose down to the right dive angle. I then rolled right side up and started to track the targets.

We had the old CBUs. A CBU is a bomb shell full of little bomblets that spread out and covered a large area, and, if released at a predetermined and proper altitude, you will get total coverage of the little bomblets on the ground. As I was going down the slide, we were a tiny bit early, and we were right in the garden spray of the flak; fortunately, I had pulled down my sun visor in my helmet! The flashes from the flak still almost blinded me and really buffeted the aircraft. Good old Marv was calmly calling out altitudes as we bounced around. Suddenly, I could visualize Marv and me getting shot down and in a prison camp doing push-ups and Marv snarling at me and saying, "I should be home with my wife and kids!" I should have released at five thousand feet, but, because of that image of Marv doing push-ups, I released at six thousand feet and got the hell out of that flak! Releasing higher worked out better, as the CBUs had a donut pattern with the bomblets. They covered all or most of the anti-aircraft firing guns. Later, Intel intercepted a message that we had destroyed or disabled seventeen of the thirty-seven MM gun positions firing. After that, I seldom had to buy a drink in the bar at Udorn if there was a Recce guy around!

My tour at Udorn, Thailand, was what every highly trained individual like me dreamed of and sought. All the training, dedication, and experience coalesced into real action and participation. I was now addressing situations using what I had been trained for and had seriously thought about. Yes, I was now doing the things that I had consequently and inconsequently planned for and was constantly thinking about. An individual has a persona apparent to others, but internally we all, as we trained and prepare for combat, wondered if we would perform properly. I have to admit, I was extremely proud of my performance at Udorn. To satisfy one's self, frankly, is the ultimate, and, as I grow older, it is something that makes many of us warriors, especially fighter pilots, almost or truly unbearable, because we know, "We done good and weren't afraid!

There is a part of Udorn that was a serious challenge and an example of poor discretion I displayed. I met a beautiful and smart lady officer, a First Lt. Julie, an Intelligence Officer, who normally briefed us outbound to a combat mission and debriefed us upon return.

Julie was a maddening affair while I was in at Udorn and on and off for a short period afterward. Julie was probably one of the few women who I respected more than most others. Later she worked for me when I was the Wing Commander at Osan, she provided me very strong and unbiased judgment, which I trusted, probably more than that anyone else on my staff except the Catholic Chaplain. Later, when she worked for me at Osan, Korea, she was married, but I still had very strong feelings for her. She was a very special woman who was not only ambitious but also successful. Unfortunately, she suffered the glass ceiling a bit, which I was able to correct at Osan after she had been passed over. She was absolutely dedicated to the Air Force and performed accordingly.

I met her when I was a Capt. at Udorn and, like with Sandy Maldaner, it was instantly an intense and an extremely challenging event. My prudish nature was probably the only thing that kept me from leaving my family for her. We became a quasi–First family of Udorn and extremely visible. In fact, the Wing Commander discussed our relationship with me and my future in the AF.

One day after returning from a combat mission, standing at the bar with Julie and the Catholic Chaplain, the Base Commander made a rude and nasty comment about Julie. I slugged him, and I really decked him. Naturally, he was going to press charges against me, but the Chaplain told him that he would testify for me about what he had said, and the charges were dropped. I believe that someone wrote my wife about Julie. Julie was very special to me and always will be, but we were able to terminate our relationship when I made the decision that my children and Dorlyne were most important to me.

Sometime later the local warriors in Cambodia decided to retake Channel 85 after the bad guys surprisingly took it from our forces. Channel 85 was on a high mountaintop near the North Vietnamese border, where a team of very brave American and Cambodian troops had kept a navigational TACAN operating, so aircraft coming out of far North Vietnam could have a navigation aid to use. A TACAN is a device that will provide the flyer a bearing and distance to the TACAN for navigation. Additionally, getting a position off Channel 85 could tell Rescue forces or locals where a downed aircrew might be located. The leader of the Cambodian forces attempting to retake the mountaintop was a close friend of our 13th Fighter Squadron. Gen. Vang Pao (VP) was leading the attack. Previously, I had been Vang Pao's acting aide for a short period, and I had great respect for him and his bravery. He was always at the front of his troops. It just happened that I was leading the flight that was to support him as he attacked to retake Channel 85.

Unfortunately, I was loaded with AGM 12s (airborne guided missiles). I don't know if you ever fired an AGM 12, but that is what I was loaded with, and they are terrible weapons for accuracy. I had direct communications with Gen. Vang Pao and he had a gun emplacement of a 12.7mm giving him fits. He asked, knowing him, directed or begged me to take it out. As I said, AGM 12s aren't worth a darn and damned hard to control with any decent accuracy primarily because of a lack of practice, but they do make a big bang!

Fortunately, our Squadron had given Gen. VP a couple of light blue flight suits like our 13th TFS party suits (I had them made by Armij the tailor outside the main gate of Udorn), which he loved to wear. We gave them to him so we could see him when we supported him, as he loved to be in the front lines during the attacks. I could see him again leading the attack. Naturally I flinched, not wanting to hit him with my first AGM 12, and it went a tiny bit high and over the gun. VP got on the radio and became a real cheerleader, talking me into firing another one into the gun site. I believe I guided the next one into the gun, and a cheer went up from the ground and especially from VP.

I'm not sure they succeeded in retaking Channel 85 but at least we made it so they could continue the attack by taking out the gun. VP loved to brag about helping me fire the AGM 12 into the gun, and later he even offered me one of his wives. I had to decline, because yak grease, which the women covered themselves with, does not make for good perfume! I think when Gen. VP left Cambodia, he lived in Wyoming, but he recently passed away. A real warrior died an American!

I did much better putting bombs on the site when the bad guys owned it. Also, when we were finally cleared to hit the so-called Chinese Embassy on the Plains of Des Jarres, Wow! Did we get secondary explosions! Obviously the buildings were storage areas for war fighting supplies! I was fortunate enough to lead the first flight that got to hit the alleged Chinese Embassy!

Another very interesting mission developed as I and a wingman were road reccing near the South Vietnam border in Cambodia. A FAC (Forward Air Controllers) crew from a small propeller-driven aircraft was down, and a rescue was under way near Tchepone, Laos. Tchepone historically was a very high threat area, and I had heard that early in the war (1966) almost an aircraft a day was shot down there. I was directed to be the "On Scene" Rescue Commander by ABCCC. ABCCC was the airborne Command and Control function, initially a C-130. The first Jolly Green, a CH 53, going in to get the FACs crew was shot down, with minor injuries to the crew, so his wingman (Jollies normally operated in twos) went in to get the chopper troops from the downed Jolly and the FACs. If I remember correctly, they were successful, and I was tasked to take out or destroy the chopper that had been shot down, so that the bad guys couldn't salvage anything useful off the Chopper. We were out of gas, so before we could destroy the downed Jolly, we had to hit a tanker first to refuel. Of course ABCCC had moved a tanker close, so we just popped up, got fuel, and were returning to blow up the chopper with our Mark 82s (five-hundred-pound bombs). I told my wingman we would come in high and roll in, since we had a good fix on the downed chopper. By rolling in from high up, maybe the bad guys would be on the downed chopper, salvaging parts and equipment. I believe we rolled in from around thirty thousand feet! My bombs hit close but no direct hit, but my trusty wingman, Bill McLeod, had a direct hit, and there was virtually nothing left of the chopper. Our gun-camera's film showed many bad guys around the chopper just before Bill's bombs hit dead center!

I did have one mission that really rendered me unhappy and caused me to probably hurt some innocent folks of the forced labor personnel who were forced to repair the roads for the North Vietnamese. I believe I was operating as a FAST FAC, and there was a fighter pilot down in Mugia Pass hanging in a tree, talking on his emergency radio. I again became the *On Scene Rescue Commander*. I talked to the man, encouraged him, and I actually seemed to become his best friend and knew that he was terri-fied. I sometimes really think he was a former student named Lynn Powell, as he called me Barry all the time that I was Rescue Commander and talking to him. In any case, two of our Jollies along with Spades (A-1 propeller-driven WW II fighters) for pro-tection of the Jollies arrived to attempt to rescue him. I was run-ning out of gas, and I told him that I had to hit a tanker, and he begged me not to leave. I then told ABCCC that I would stay a while longer, and, if I ran out of gas, I would bail out north of my location, and they could get me the next day, in what was called the "Elephant breeding grounds." It was a very densely vege-tated area, where no one was ever seen, good guys or bad, so I could wait for rescue until the next day. As Jolly lead went into a hover over the man, and their PJ (Para-jumper or rescue-trained guy) started down toward the man hanging in a tree. The PJ was on the end of a line from the Jolly riding on a penetrator, which would allow him to strap the pilot to it, and then the Jolly would pull them up. Suddenly the PJ shouted, "Let's get out of here, it is a trap, they just shot him (the man hanging in the parachute)" and the PJ was wounded. The Spades immediately attacked the area with guns and bombs.

I pulled up toward the "Breeding Grounds" to prepare to bail out, when a voice came on the radio saying, "Falcon, if you look at your 12 o'clock high, you will see your friendly Esso station!" Man, did he look beautiful! I quickly told him I might have to "toboggan," because I was just about out of fuel. *Toboggan* means to descend and actually be a glider to get fuel. He smartly descended down toward me, we got a quick hookup, fuel flowed, and I frankly don't remember if I had to toboggan.

Now that I had gas, I did something that I wish I hadn't done. I was loaded again with AGM 12s again, a terrible weapon but good for what I wanted to do. By the time I was back at the scene of the failed rescue, a sufficient time had passed for those folks who had set the trap and killed our man to retreat to one of the big caves south of Mugia Pass, where the Intel folk and I believed they hid from us. I then put two AGM 12s into the cave, and I know that at least one on them went in really deep inside the cave, because the resultant explosion took a while to bellow out and be visible outside the cave. I am sure that many suffered!

A terrible aftermath of the event was that after I put the tanker pilot in for an award, someone tried to court-martial him for what he did, as the tanker was not supposed to be where he rescued me! Fortunately, one of our fighter pilot General's weighed-in and Mr. Stupid, whoever he was, did not hurt *our dyed in the wool hero and warrior* on our Esso tanker! I was told that Mr. Stupid was told to be off the base by sunset! I'm not sure if it was true, but it sure sounded good to those of us who loved the Tanker crews who did so much for us!

Later, I had the opportunity to checkout a new troop, Dick Woods, who had just arrived in the squadron as a FAST FAC. Dick Woods at the time had the most F-4 time of anyone in the Air Force. On the first such mission of upgrading to FAST FAC, a new troop rides in the backseat. We were running around in the Mugia Pass area very low, at about two hundred feet above the ground, so that he could get a good look around. Suddenly several guns opened up on us, and they were really good gunners, tracking us better than I had ever seen before. They forced me to maneuver the aircraft very ham-handedly to avoid the flak. The beloved F-4 decided to depart and suddenly, we were inverted at about one hundred feet! Dick said something really smart like, "Oh shit! I quickly said, "Relax, I've got it, I have been here before! After unloading the aircraft, meaning I relaxed the back stick pressure, and milked it out of the stall, and flying eastward toward North Vietnam, I rolled back right side up and got the hell out of there. Later Dick said, "I thought we had bought it, but you sure can become smooooth when necessary." Once again, I must admit that the spin I experienced on my initial solo in pilot training and the slow flight procedure we used in Flight Test operations at Willie paid off again! As an aside, we were moving so slow that the guns were firing ahead of us rather than at us or behind us. This was a first!

Because of my experience as a Maintenance Flight Test Pilot, my rank, and my combat experience, I was a Wing Maintenance Test Pilot, Flight leader, Mission Commander and night expert— so I was told. The truth is; *I hate night flying*, it is for bats and owls!

I had extended at Udorn but I received from Dorlyne a very unique picture. I do have to admit that Dorlyne accelerated my return from Udorn by sending that wonderful picture of her in a bikini (God, what a body!), my favorite chair, and a bottle of Scotch, simply stating, "If you want these here when you get back, GET HOME!" No dummy here, I cancelled my extension and returned ASAP. However, this has to be said: Man should not enjoy war so much, but I did enjoy being at Udorn and the many aspects of combat that I was involved in, because that is what I trained so long and hard for!

PURPLE HEARTS AT UDORN, THAILAND

While flying combat in Vietnam, I received the Silver Star, Bronze Star, three Distinguished Flying Crosses, and seventeen Air Medals. I was or am a terrible administrator of my military records and failed to ensure that the two Purple Hearts I should have received were put in my records before I left Udorn. A few years ago, I tried to locate the Flight Surgeon who sewed me up in the 13th TFS party room without painkillers but with lots of booze! After the Doc sewed up my forehead, split from a hit to the aircraft over the Quang Khe ferry where the backseater, Marv Bishop, had taken a short nap after also hitting his head, the doc forgot to enter it in our records. The Doc, name unknown, poured Johnnie Walkers Black Label on our wounds, he said to sterilize it. Many of the squadron observed the whole medical event with many appropriate and inappropriate remarks.

I have since talked to many Flight Surgeons who had been at Udorn, and they all knew the story, but I couldn't find the one who sewed us up twice, and he hadn't put it in our records—twice! The second time I was with Little Barry (Eldridge) and he also deserved a Purple Heart. Should the Flight Surgeon who sewed Marv, Little Barry and me up happen to read this please contact me, so I can get my free New Mexico license plates, and, besides, it is a very handsome and deserved medal.

I need to add something about fighter pilots concerning combat! Missions way up North near Hanoi were called by some "doomsday missions," because invariably someone got shot down from the heavy defenses. Did guys shy away from those missions? Are you kidding? Your best friend would lie, cheat, and do anything to get your slot on a doomsday mission.

At Udorn I also flew 40 Falcon FAST FAC missions, probably the most exciting and productive missions I flew, primarily because we had such good and competent Intelligence folks at Udorn. It was not uncommon for us to hear a flight of fighters calling for a Falcon FAC because we had such good targets. A bit of bragging here for "Cuddly Dudley:" where ever he maybe! I started and set up the damn F-4 FAST FAC program at Udorn, first called Falcons and later Laredos. Naturally, I am very proud of the way I set it up, and my Intelligence Photo (PI) training truly paid off!

Over North Vietnam I flew 116 combat missions, which were probably somewhat challenging and most dangerous. I had a total of combat 229 missions in the F-4 and I think I was hit twelve or thirteen times, but after the first five, I decided that I didn't want to know that I was hit if I didn't feel it, so I asked the crew chief to not tell me.

After Marv Bishop returned home to be with his family, my new backseater became Barry Eldridge, a young and very good pilot. In the F-4 we had both; experience navigators or young pilots in the back seat of the F-4. My young Barry was the one who obtained the Black Panther for the 13th Squadron, which was properly named *Barry*! Little Barry and I called our aircraft the "B and B Express"!

One mission I will fondly remember was when I returned from over North Vietnam with some serious battle-damage and again bleeding heads, Little Barry and I. meanwhile at Udorn they were having a fire power demo for the Tactics Conference. Later this organization became the Red River Rats Fighter Pilots Association named initially for those who had been way north in Vietnam where they really didn't like us! Those who attended the Tactics Conference later became Red River Rats. However, at the time it was called "a tactics conference" and we truly shared tactics, and we all learned from other units' fighter pilots' different tactics, methods, or procedures that saved lives! The passing of other units' information ensured that we seldom made similar mistakes.

I was a bit disappointed that I wasn't part of the firepower demo! Anyhow, with the runways lined with watchers of the firepower demo, I landed. Because of my battle damage, I had to take the approach end cable (a cable across the runway that you could engage if you extended your tail hook, and it would quickly stop your aircraft). At the time, both sides of the runway had been dug out about three feet deep to do some stabilization work for the runway. I engaged the barrier, and the aircraft stopped OK. Normally, when you take the barrier, rescue folks will be available beside the runway, but since the sides of the runway were dug out, the fire trucks came down the runway and were facing me on the runway. As I disengaged the cable by raising the hook, suddenly I got "engine auto acceleration," which means that because of the heat of and on the engine, it mechanically changed its configuration and suddenly increased the idle thrust, meaning the F-4 wanted to rapidly move forward and I was facing the fire trucks coming at me down the runway! And, oh, by the way, I also had radio failure and my emergency brakes had failed. I tried very hard to give the fire trucks hand signals, "To get the hell out of my way as the aircraft accelerated down the runway!" But they obviously didn't see my hand signals or understand them. So I had no choice but to steer off the side of the runway. I am not sure I know how I did that, since I had no hydraulic systems, but I did go off the right side of the runway and missed the fire trucks! I think I did it by the way I shut the engines down. Of course I wanted to get out of the aircraft rapidly, because I wasn't sure how much damage or if I had any fire on or in the aircraft. I quickly emergency-evacuated the aircraft and fell over the side. Of course, I hit my right knee getting out again! Once on the ground, I limped around the aircraft to see the damage.

Arriving at the aircraft, the Wing Commander, Brig. Gen. Wendell Bevan, put his arm around me and said, "Thanks for saving the aircraft, Barry, and you can limp all you want, but since you are my only test pilot around, you'll have to fly this bird when it is fixed!" I did fly it the next day on a Test Hop and I believe it was completely repaired; our Maintenance folks were second to none!

MISSIONS UNIQUE OR REALLY DUMB, 6/1968-7/1969

In the 13th TFS, under the new squadron Leadership of Covalt and Foster the procedure was established that pilots new to the squadron were required ten-day sorties prior to a night sortie. We flew for a month at night, then the Triple Nickel, our sister squadron, would fly nights for the next month. If you remember, I managed to get a total of one day-mission in Route Pack VI, prior to night flying of the squadron.

Since I was a very experienced F-4 instructor pilot, it was OK for me to start night flying without the standard ten preparatory combat missions. My second mission in the 13th TFS was my first night mission, and I flew as # 2 with an experienced leader, and our target area was in Vietnam's Route Pack II, just east of Mu Gia Pass. As we entered the target area from the west on this moon lite night, we saw a bunch of trucks heading southbound. We immediately attacked them, with my leader hitting the lead truck and stopping their progress. Hoping to block the rear exit, I attacked the last few trucks. My leader said, "Good bombs # 2, now pull out smartly—you are getting low!" I then lit the afterburners to get some more air speed or *smash*. Suddenly I heard, *"Aw shit! Pull hard # 2; you have set the grass on fire with your afterburners!"* My conversation in the cockpits to Maj. Marv Bishop in the backseat, the highly experienced GIB, was, "Aw shit, my G-suit is unplugged—tell me if we are going up!" Needless to say, this captain dummy learned a night-flying lesson to make sure the G-suit is properly plugged in so you can put some *Gs* on the aircraft without blacking out! Night flying is always a challenge, and later Marv and I, because of our effort at Quang Khe Ferry, became the *alleged* night experts for the wing. Probably it was also because the DO, Col. Ralph Finley, was a recce pilot and really appreciated what Marv and I had done to the gunners at Quang Khe but we still hated night flying!

The wing again used our night expertise (Little Barry had replaced Marv) during a bombing pause arranged by our political leaders (not my favorite folks!) in Washington, DC. We were in a bombing pause, and it seemed that part of the pause included the right of the US to fly RF-4C reconnaissance aircraft over Hanoi and far North Vietnam, escorted by a fighter. Yes, Barry and Barry were selected to escort the Recce Bird.

There are a few things that one needs to know about Recce Birds vs. Fighter Birds of the F-4 variety. First, Recce Pilots are naturally dependent on speed and having their aircraft lights off to become stealthier over enemy territory. Additionally, their RF-4C aircraft has considerable less drag than the fighter F-4 version; thus, it can go faster!

Since the Recce pilot was to lead us over North Vietnam, I thought it proper for him to conduct the flight briefing. This was a bit of a challenge for him, because he normally flew alone, but he was highly experienced and was also an Instructor Pilot. The plan was to enter North Vietnam at the southern end near Dong Hoi and follow the so-called "Route 1" that ran along the coast.

We would travel to the entry point around fifteen thousand feet, descending to one hundred feet prior or as we entered North Vietnam, and of course accelerating as we descended. I reminded him that we had more drag with our MERs (multiple ejector racks) and TERs (triple ejector racks) and our two 370-gallon fuel tanks, so please accelerate slowly. Of course we wanted to be very close to him, since it was night and very hard to see an aircraft without lights on, unless you are damned close.

Prior to takeoff, as we departed our squadron, we were told to leave our personal sidearm, as we were to be unarmed! I think I said something really smart like, "Bullshit, it will be a cold day in hell when I fly without my sidearm!" My sidearm was a .38 Smith & Wesson Combat Master Piece that my Dad had given me. I think my size allowed us to depart with our side arms. I need to add that Van Pao had given me a *folding stock AK-47*, which I normally flew with but gave away before I returned to the States, since they might have been illegal and since my Dad was an FBI agent, I didn't want to cause him trouble. It was a really dumb decision to not bring it home!

When we got to our bird, we noticed that the maintenance crews were still working on our egress seats, and the Crew Chief approached me with a concerned look on his face. I asked him what were they were doing to our seats? He said that they were placing seat packs in the bird that have had the survival guns removed from them. However, his main concern was that the explosive carts had been removed from the wing tanks and the MERs or TERs so we could not get rid of them if we needed to in an emergency! Once again, someone who had probably never flown in combat made these stupid decisions and probably *not a politician* but a military person in higher Headquarters. In any case, we started up and met the RF-4C in the arming area at the departure end of the runway.

Takeoff and join-up (made by Little Barry) was quick and normal. We cruised over to our letdown point, and our Leader called the let-down and acceleration to route speed. It was late at night, on a very dark, no moon night, and frankly scary. Did I ever tell you that "*I hate night flying; it is for bats and owls, not fighter pilots!*"

As we were accelerating, suddenly Lead turned off his lights, and, for a moment, he disappeared. I quickly called him to turn them back on so we could join up closer, which he did. Once we got close enough for him to see us, off went the lights and he was going like a scalded ape. If you even know a Recce Pilot, *you will note that his left arm, his throttle arm, is always straight, thus meaning that his throttles are full forward!* Unfortunately, a fighter F-4 cannot keep up with a RF-4C, and Little Barry and I were in the fighter F-4 on this very dark night and going to travel over the full length of North Vietnam at about one hundred feet above the ground! To keep up, since we knew the route, we would have to cut the recce pilot off by starting our turns early and meeting up with him further up the route. It was absolutely frightening for many reasons, especially because we were at a hundred feet above the ground, and he had no lights on. Little Barry did an excellent job tracking him on radar. As we got nearer to Hanoi and the high-threat areas, our Recce Pilot was able to bend his left arm a bit and pulled off some power so we could keep up with him and keep him is sight! I know his arm resisted pulling off power and knowing what he normally did, we were very appreciative, and I understood how hard it must have been for him to pull the power back a little! Please understand, I think Recce Pilots are extremely brave but this mission was really dumb!

We were able to complete the mission without any midair accidents or much firing at us. However after we debriefed with Intel, I told the Recce Pilot it was the dumbest, most dangerous, and senseless mission I had ever been on! It wasn't his fault, as the mission was laid on from above. As Little Barry and I walked to the squadron, I gave him some money and asked him to go buy a case of beer and meet me at the DO's office. The DO's office was in an elevated part of a building with about twenty steps up to his office. When the case of beer arrived around 0330, Little Barry and I sat outside the door of the DO's office on the top step and began drinking the beer which was in cans. When we finished one, at first we sat them back in the case, but as we consumed more, we started throwing them down the stairs. A few hours later, when the DO kicked his way through the beer cans, we stood up and I greeted him with a, "Sir, that was the dumbest, most dangerous most senseless mission we have ever been on, and it should never be flown again!" I believe the ADO said, "Well, if we [the Air Force] refuse it, the Army will take it." I simply said, "Hopefully, they aren't that dumb!" The mission was never flown again by the Air Force while we were at Udorn.

Another really dumb mission that I am sure wasn't developed by a combat pilot was an attempt to cut the road near a well-known flak trap and the documented and most effective gunners of the enemy at Tchepone, Laos. The ordnance fragged, for the mission was "high-drag five-hundred-pound bombs" that had to be delivered at very low altitude (below one hundred feet and really best at twenty-five feet or lower) to hit the target. High-drag bombs are normal bombs with a special tail added to them that, when released, spread out like a metal parachute and delayed the bomb hitting the ground, but when it did hit, it was nearly vertical and thus made a bigger hole in the ground. The intent was to cut this *dirt* road to slow the traffic south. Needless to say, the road crews were able to fill and repair the holes in the time it took us to hit a tanker and return to where we dropped the bombs. Again, we were selected to test this wonderful procedure.

After we dropped our bombs and actually cut the road, we hit a tanker and then returned to the scene of damage. This of course wasn't part of the "fragged mission," but I added it, because I suspected that the road would be repaired or was being repaired when we returned. Suspicions confirmed: the damn road was nearly repaired, and we could see truck tracks that had rolled across the road. However, there was one successful part of this mission: the gunners really hosed us as we delivered our bombs, so they obviously shot more than a truckload of ammo at us; thus we eliminated at least one truck load of ammo destine for south Vietnam. How about that!

I believe that the genius that designed this mission allowed it to be flown for one more day, and then sanity returned and it was cancelled. It certainly would have been canceled if they had read our detailed and very angry after-action report!

Another mission that we were assigned was to field test a bomb designed with a proximity-actuated fuse. We were assured that it had been well tested in the States before it was sent for field testing. We had one of the bombs on each wing and delivered the first one on what we thought was an enemy gun site, and it worked perfectly. We dropped it from a normal release altitude around five thousand feet or above the small-arms fire. We re-attacked the site with the second bomb, and this time, at release of the bomb with this test fuse, exploded almost immediately after release, and frankly scared the hell out of us. I don't think that fuse was used again in the time I was there. As my tour continued, I had become very adept at writing-up really dumb missions.

Once as Falcon 5 (FAST FAC), I trapped a convoy of trucks in Mu Gia Pass with my .20 mm gun pod, which we carried frequently as FAST FACs. I took out the lead truck, and quickly stopped the last truck also. I called for fighters to take out the trapped trucks, and ABCCC gave me a flight of F-105s, each with two one-ton bombs with extenders on each of them. An extender which is simply a metal tube on the front of the bomb that causes the bomb to go off a few feet above ground where it hits. The Flight Leader naturally dropped first with his two one-ton bombs with extenders. The entire convoy of trucks was vaporized, and I think the only thing remaining was a burning tire up near where the front vehicle had been. Fortunately, a couple of guns opened up on the F-105s and gave us a target for the remaining 2000 pounders.

I do need to add the reason that the early F-4 aircrafts did not have an internal gun and that we had to use the high-drag gun pod. During F-4 aircraft development phase, Air Defense Command (ADC) inputs believed that missiles would replace the gun—another dumb decision that we, the military, did to ourselves. I would add that the Navy agreed with the dumb decision too! Later when I was associated with the test business, we were able to prove the need for an internal gun and, as a result, were able to modify later generations for F-4s with an internal gun as well as other good modifications. I was proud to have been involved in some of those changes!

Another dumb thing we did to ourselves as fighter pilots concerns an optical recording devise for the F-15, initially called a gun camera. I was then the ops guy on the F-15 committee, and we were all pushing for a video recording device. The R&D guy wanted a "gun camera" and only a gun camera! I tried to explain to him that there was a better thing, "a video recording device." Nope, only a gun camera would satisfy him, and, as much as I tried to explain the advantages of a video device, we got an antiquated gun camera, which required a photo lab to support it. A few years later at a great initial expense, the gun camera was replaced by a video recorder about the size of a cigarette pack, and the pilot simple pulled out the recording pack and took it to debriefing, and they had instant review of the flight using a small TV.

Earlier, I mentioned the Purple Hearts that I didn't get because the doc forgot to enter into my record occurred at Dong Hoi. The weather was pretty bad over North Vietnam one day, and so as we operating as a FAST FAC, we went out over the ocean, let down to just above the water, and headed into North Vietnam again at Dong Hoi. To our surprise, there was a fairly large boat unloading supplies to lighters (small flat-bottom boats). We had a couple of tubes of rockets, so we set up to attack the boat. We got some good hits on the first pass, but on the second pass, they opened up on us, and we took a near-hit to our slab (rear flight-control surface), which pushed us down toward the water. I quickly pulled back on the stick, and we lightly struck the water! Later, we learned that we had our wing tanks pulled off, probably by the water.

I hit my head pretty hard, and blood trickled down my face. Fortunately, I had a handkerchief available and stuffed it in the front of my helmet to stop the bleeding. I asked Marv how he was doing and got no answer, but, looking in my mirrors, I could see that he was taking his afternoon nap, as he was a bit older than I was. But he appeared to be OK. Since I assumed that we had some aircraft damage, I headed south for Da Nang, which was much closer than Udorn. I made a call on guard, attempting to find someone who could look us over for damage. An RF-4C responded and closely checked us over, finding no damage. He did mention that we had no wing tanks. Since the aircraft was flying normally, and we did do a controllability check and none of the systems seemed to be malfunctioning, so we (Marv had awakened from his nap) returned to Udorn AB, Thailand, uneventfully.

Because of my background as a photo interpreter, I did review certain areas that we often flew to better understand where our targets might hide. I also found a great target area where I, as an experienced old head who was normally tasked to take VIPs up whom sometimes flew with us. If they had good bombs on my special target, it would normally result in nice explosions or a large burning area! The target area was just east of Mu Gia Pass, which of course everyone, especially VIPs, wanted to see anyway. The target I found was on the south side of the road up high on the karst. It appeared to be either a pump or transfer station, but it would really make the VIP feel like they had contributed to the war effort. I would sometimes hit it on everyday missions, just to confirm my bombing ability, and the target was always there! I recently reviewed a video by someone who in the recent past drove the road near Tchepone and I saw a burned out truck with a 55 gallon tank in the front seat. From film review of some targets we suspected that they put barrels of some sort of flammable fluid in already destroyed targets so that we would keep hitting already destroyed targets. Suspicions confirmed!

One event that occurred for me twice, when I was operating as a FAST FAC tooling around looking for new targets at low altitude, was the sighting of a redheaded fellow gringo (American) playing ping pong in front of a cave a few miles northwest of Tchepone. The first time I saw him, he went wild waving at me, and I made a second pass—not a smart thing to do in the Tchepone area—and I rocked my wings, letting him know I saw him. Of course I immediately reported the sighting, and later I got word to stay away from the cave, indicating that they might try to go in there and rescue the redhead! Sometime later, again, trolling for "pop-up" targets as a FAST FAC, I again saw the redhead playing ping pong. Again I brief Intel on it and made sure that I read the message sent out about it. I never learned if he was rescued or what happened.

Finally, I need to tell the story of Marv Bishop's last mission. Of course we made a four-ship fly over Udorn with us in the lead. When we taxied in, Marv, the navigator, was in the front seat, and he had had a very long (fifty to sixty feet) squadron light blue scarf around his neck, which he threw out, and it trailed past the rear of the aircraft. Unfortunately, with changes of the throttle as the bird was taxied, the scarf was attacked by the engine eyelids, actually pulling the scarf backwards, chocking Marv. I had to pull my survival knife to cut the scarf to keep him from being seriously chocked. After Marv was properly hosed down, consumed some champagne, and was hugged by the pretty ladies, the General said, "I don't want to know when Marv got in the front seat!" For once, I was silent and still am—sorry!

For my last mission, I simply made a nice four-ship pass over Udorn, normal landing, and was congratulated by the Wing Commander, Wendall Bevan, and the Vice Wing Commander, Nick Ferris. I drank some champagne, got a lot of hugs and kisses and then got really drunk. I have on my home office wall a picture of the flyover and a skinny, very drunk fighter pilot in the squadron party room in my party suit, which always reminds me of a very proud part of my past. Unfortunately, my wonderful party suit has seriously shrunk in the closet! (Incidentally, I couldn't have stood in a 100 ft. circle as the night wore on!)

I had extended at Udorn, but I received a picture with a simple message on a Post-it note. "If you want these things here when you get home, you better cancel the extension!" Needless to say, the extension was cancelled, and I was on my way home only a few weeks late.

My time at Udorn was truly the period of my life that created my persona and frankly, as being in combat did to many others, it made me believe I was *bullet proof and, thus, fearless!* It gave me the confidence to do or challenge things that I perceived to be wrong or should be modified. I am afraid that today's Air Force being so *Politically Correct (PC) does not build leaders who attack or are prepared to challenge bad policies or procedures and frankly don't push the envelope as we did back then.* I know they don't have as much fun as we did but they sure have great airplanes to fly!

GOING HOME TO SHAW AFB, SOUTH CAROLINA, 8/1969-7/1970

Returning from Udorn, I was reassigned to the 9th Air Force fighter shop, Shaw AFB, Sumpter, South Carolina. I was assigned a base house at Shaw in August of 1969 and moved the family there immediately, since it was the summer and Barrie and Mike were out of school. I was told when I got back that my son Mike had really acted *as the man of the house* while I was gone, and Dorlyne was very pleased with him.

Fortunately we had friends at Shaw: Jim and Patsy Ketchum from Willie, who we knew previously. Patsy had been Mike's Sunday-School teacher. In fact, I eventually bought a well-used speedboat from Jim Ketchum, as he had been reassigned to the Pentagon. The boat was known affectionately as the *Purple People Eater*! Later this boat was my savior as the only means of escape from constant weekend duties working for Maj. Gen. "Willie P." McBride, the TAC Director of Operations (DO) when I was at TAC Headquarters!

When Patsy was Mike's Sunday Sunday-School teacher, on one Sunday her class was discussing Father's Day. Patsy, to help her students to think about a Father's Day gift, asked them what their father liked to do. My son Mike said, "My dad really likes to go to the Officer's Club stag bar to drink beer and tell tall tales about flying!" Caught again!

The 9th Air Force Director of Operations was a very dedicated Air Force man from my C-130 days and someone I had great respect for, Col. Levy. I assume he had something to do with my being at Shaw. Col. Levy quickly assigned me as the Pilot member of an accident board that involved a mid-air between an F-4 and an F-105F (2 seater) during an Army/Air Force exercise. We had our "in briefing" by the Board Leader. He was tough as nails and a very strong leader, although he was a rare reserve officer put in such a challenging and demanding position. Our first task was to visit the scene, which actually covered a very small area, as the aircraft had collided very low to the ground. It was not a fun event, as we picked up many pieces of the human remains. Some items were immediately identifiable, but many were not. It made for some extremely sleepless nights and a loss of appetite!

Additionally, we helped sort the residue from the two aircraft, which was pretty easy using the following criteria: if you couldn't lift it, it was probably an F-105F aircraft part. F-105s were lovingly called Thuds. Normally, it was not a Thud part if you could lift it; it was an F-4 part. There was one part of the F-4 that really tricked some of the team, which was the F-4 slab or horizontal stabilizer. Since I had done lots of test flights on the F-4, I explained to them that the slab was designed to be very heavy and strong, but it was not a Thud part.

An Air Force Aircraft Accident Board investigates every aspect of an accident to include review of the crew members' records, history of the maintenance on the aircrafts, pre-flight briefings, Leadership briefings for the mission, weather and weather briefings, site weather, and anything that might have remotely contributed to the accident. We also interviewed, under oath, anyone who in any fashion affected or contributed to the flight.

Our Board found that the flight should not have been flying, because the weather and the evidence indicated that the General in charge directed them to fly in spite of the weatherman recommending against it. To top it off, during testimony, the General who was the exercise Director did not appear to tell the truth about several items. His actions were found to be the primary cause of the accident.

The interviews were very revealing and probably weighed heavily on the final outcome. Our findings, which many of us believed would be destroying our future in the Air Force, found the Exercise Leader, a well-known fighter pilot and a Brig. General as primary cause. As the Pilot member, I was the primary briefer of our findings, and I must admit it was a challenge. I am glad I had just returned from combat where I had been shot at most every day, because I had some pretty important people shooting at me as I briefed. The Board findings were totally accepted, and the General retired.

I need to add here that I had been grounded when I returned from Vietnam because of a serious sinus condition that kept me grounded for almost six months. I do need to digress a bit here and state a true flying fact: damn few pilots will ever go to the Flight Surgeon because he or she may ground you and no one wants to be grounded. We are especially bad in combat, because we know that there is always a shortage of crew members, and, if you get sick, someone else has to cover for you or you will miss getting some flying time. Since I was always trying to fly more and learn more, I seldom went to the Flight Surgeon, because they are trained to or may ground you when you visit their office. However, if you meet them in the bar and say something like, "Doc, I have a friend that has such and such a problem, what should he do? Of course the Doc (if he is an experienced Flight Surgeon) knows that the friend is himself but he plays the game and says either, "He really shouldn't fly or give him some advice about how to safely handle it or what he might do to be less affected by the problem when he goes ahead and flies." It is a game that serious pilots and experienced Flight Surgeons play!

While flying combat, toward the end of my time at Udorn, I had lots of pain as I descended the aircraft and frequently bled a little from my nose. Barry Eldridge got used to me giving him the plane as we were returning to Udorn and my doing a loud scream during our descent, which seemed to relieve the sinus pain. As I said earlier, fighter pilots aren't prone to visit the flight surgeon's office when flying combat is available—or, really, any other time when flying hours are available! Because of my seldom visiting the Flight Surgeon, my records don't show why my knees are shot and why I have had such bad COPD. My bad knees are from rapidly getting out of aircraft on the ground after landing with an emergency. Normally when emergency-egressing the aircraft, I hit my right knee pretty hard getting out. My COPD was probably a result of three or more aircraft fires, one in a C-130, one in a T-38, and at least one in an F-4. It has taken me years to finally convince the VA and the Air Force that the deterioration of my body was service related or caused by my failure frequently to see a Flight Surgeon!

My time at Shaw was short and extremely challenging! After the longer than normal Board involvement, I finally had nearly completed our move into our base housing at Shaw on a Sunday and the next day I reported to my new office in the fighter shop. Upon my arrival my new boss asked me to represent the office at a briefing from TAC Headquarters; they didn't know the subject, but indicated that it didn't seem very important.

Wrong, really wrong! The TAC Commander, Gen. Momyer, who had also just returned from running the air war in Southeast Asia from Saigon, introduced the briefing. A representative from Singer Link, one of the Nation's largest simulator builders, gave the briefing. The topic was, "Replacing actual flying with simulation during fighter training program, by about 75 percent going into simulators." As a former and many-faceted fighter instructor pilot, I had to sit on my hands and resisted attacking the briefer. As a new guy sitting on the back row, I was hesitant to say anything. I had listened intently to the briefing, and, since I had taught new and young Air Force folks to learn to fly, been an instructor in C-130s, and instructed in the F-4 fighter training program, I had some very strong opinions about the briefing. I tried to not say anything, since I was really a new guy, but after several senior officers displayed some slightly brown noses and gave high praise to the briefing, I couldn't stand it any longer! I raised my hand, and Gen. Momyer called on me. I stood and said, "General, I hate to be an "against-er" but the briefer really doesn't know what we do today in fighters and fighter training; I suspect he was a Navy torpedo pilot in WW II." The general said, "Major, I missed your name, and where are you from?"

"Sir, I am Maj. Barry Howard from 9th AF fighter shop, and I recently returned from a tour in SEA [Southeast Asia] in F-4s at Udorn, Thailand. Before that I was an instructor at Homestead AFB in the F-4; and, prior to that, I was an IP in ATC pilot training; and before ATC, I was a C-130 Instructor Pilot."

The General then turned to the Briefer and asked what he flew. He said, "A navy torpedo aircraft in World War Two! The General looked at me for a few moments and I thought I was about to get murdered, and he said, "Major, you now have a new assignment; you are coming to TAC Headquarters, and you will be working for me!"

By now I was fearless, and I quickly said, "General, you may be getting both of us killed; I just finished moving into our new house yesterday, and my wife indicated that it would be a long time before we moved again, or that she may kill somebody!" The General laughingly said, "Tell you what; it is the end of July now, and you won't have to be to Langley until after Labor Day! That should give you time to protect us!"

We had just settled in at Shaw and bought a boat from my friends Patsy and Jim Ketchum, who were PCSing and who had introduced us to Shaw and its wonderful opportunities and the Shaw recreation area!

However, we did quickly make a trip to Langley and found a very nice house close to the base. Unlike my Father, who never owned a house, we bought our first of several houses. We also ran into several friends at Langley who had heard of my "invitation" to TAC Headquarters. We packed up and moved to our newly purchased home, met many old friends, and tried to adjust to the Virginia area.

TAC HEADQUARTERS, LANGLEY, VA 9/1970-1/1972

Obviously Dorlyne hadn't *bumped off* either the General or me, and we did move to Langley, Virginia in September 1970, having bought our first house right outside the base. I bought a small motorcycle to travel to work on, and we went to the Pound and got Barrie and Mike a dog, Mr. Nibs, a five-hundred-dollar white-toed fence-jumper! We call Mr. Nibs a five-hundred-dollar dog so he wouldn't know he came from the pound, and he really could jump our eight-to-ten-foot backyard fence, especially when neighbors called him with a steak bone—it was a sight to see!

I didn't realize until I got to Langley what an impression I had made on the General, because I immediately received an open ticket to travel to all the simulators in existence and also to the companies that built them. I was told to travel to all simulator makers that were actually in the free world to see the simulator capabilities and report back to Gen. Momyer. I actually went to only England and Germany and, of course, all over the US. It was quite a learning curve; once again, actually drinking out of a fire hose or hydrant. Fortunately, in TAC Headquarters in the Simulator Shop, there were two senior Sergeants, Jim Englehart and Dallas Butler, who really knew simulators and took me under their wing and were quick to educate me.

Of course to fighter pilots, *simulators* are a nasty word for many reasons. In some cases the simulators just don't realistically simulate, or the use of simulation wasn't done professionally, with, in some cases, non-pilots instructing. Many simulators weren't maintained well, because they weren't funded properly, and, as a result, phony simulation just didn't train flying! The truth about simulation is that modern simulators are just big computer-driven machines, but unfortunately at that time, they were mostly analog (old tube technology). Today's modern-day simulators are now more dependable, more precise, digital, and, in many cases, truly closely replicating actual flying. They are far more realistic, easier to maintain (if properly funded), and are more acceptable to the crews!

On my tour around the simulation world, I found terrible situations. For example, the fairly realistic and modern F-111 simulator in England that had been installed without air-conditioning, to simply save money! Consequently, because of the very wet English climate, it was frequently broken and was unusable because of corrosion from the moisture!

Together, we in the simulator shop, along with the Fighter shop where I also worked, we established a realistic simulator policy which essentially said, as better simulations are developed, we will modify our training, but only a small amount of trade-off simulation exists right now. In fact, in many areas, as time passed, the Air Force would lead the world in enhanced simulation, and the airlines and many flying schools copied much of what we developed. Of course, the National Aeronautics and Space Administration (NASA) really developed and utilized simulations, but they had the funding and an absolute need, since they were addressing future capabilities that actually did not exist and could be trained only in simulation.

When I arrived at TAC Headquarters, I had two hats: one in the fighter shop, where I was wanted by Neil Eddins who was the number-two guy to "Buckshot" White, who was due to leave. Neil Eddins became a good friend and leader, and I was also was assigned to the simulator shop, where I wasn't particularly wanted that badly. The folks in the simulator shop were great, and we did make some real progress toward functional, realistic, and useful simulation.

My longtime friend, Maj. Ron Ellis along with the two terrific Senior Sergeants, Dallas Butler and Jim Englehart, were the backbone of the Simulator Office which included Lt. Col. Rick Lamp. The Office was led by a real fighter pilot, Col. Chuck Maultsby, also a former Thunderbird!

Once we got simulation rolling, I was reassigned only to the TAC Fighter Shop under first *Buckshot*, for whom I had first flown for at DaNang, and he was replaced by Col. Neil Eddins, from Afton, Wyoming. Neil had been the solo and later the leader of the USAF Thunderbirds. I need to also say, because he frequently and happily mentions it regularly, he was a former Aviation Cadet!

My branch boss was Lt. Col. Randy Krumback, a true fighter pilot who could dance and sing and was also our leader on Friday nights at the bar! Working for Neil and Randy was like working for "Fat" Fred Haeffner: exciting, demanding, and just plain fun. My primary responsibility was bringing on board the A-7D and using recent pilot training graduates to be trained in the A-7. Additionally, I backed up Harry Vreeland (who has very close-set eyes!) with the F-4 and improving the production of the training manuals for the training courses. Later, I was on the F-15 committee where I fought for a VIDEO "gun camera" and lost!

Shortly after I became full time in the fighter shop and Neil was now in charge, I heard about a new computer-driven typing system that would make our life easier regarding the training manuals. I ordered it, and it would be the first such devise in TAC. It was the first generation of functional computers or "word processors" that are now useful at the everyday operational or working level, instead of just at a scientific tool. Unfortunately, the device arrived when I was at Davis Monthan AFB, Arizona, concerning and working the A-7D program. It was given to Neil Eddins, well-known computer hater, and he instantly gave it away. Fortunately, I was asked to look at it when I got back, and of course, I knew it was what we wanted and needed. I took a felt-tip pen and wrote my name on the back of it in very big letters and dated it, because I suspected that it would surface again.

Weeks later, Neil came storming back from a Director of Operations staff meeting and grabbed me and said we are going to go up to Standardization and Evaluation (StanEval). They are the folks responsible evaluating our crews for Standardization. We were to see a new device they have for making training manuals. As we arrived, one of the secretaries just raved about the device, saying once the manual was entered into the system, one word, a sentence, a paragraph, a page, or a chapter could be changed instantly without affecting the rest of the manual. When we got there, Neil said, "Barry, get us one of these!"

I said, "Colonel, please turn the damn thing around!" When he did, he saw my name and the date that I had written on it some time ago. I think he said, "Shit!" And we returned silently to our office. I did order us another one, and we lived happily ever after, especially our great secretary, Evey, who dearly loved the "memory machine!"

Fortunately, we fighter pilots had a very good friend, Marylyn Ferguson, in the DO's office who controlled things like the "memory machine," and she had previously sent me the first one, which Thunderbird Leader (Neil) got rid of while I was gone and it found its way to StanEval. When I told her the story, she laughed heartily and got us another one. Neil never mentioned it again!

One project at TAC that I fondly remember was the annual Fighter Pilot symposium at Nellis AFB, Nevada. Jack Petry and I were the organizers or more like the managers of the Symposium, so we went out early to set it up. Because of our challenging positions, they put us in VIP Quarters, and, to our surprise, our room was right above Gen. *Willie P's* suite, the true leader of the Symposium! He frequently used me like an aide, but since I and most other fighter pilots really liked and respected him, I didn't mind. This was to be *Willie P's* last symposium, so we wanted it to be really good.

Jack Petry and I worked very hard to keep the Symposium on track, and we hit the rack early almost every night, but, realizing we were above *Willie P's* room, we knew we had to at least act like we were having a ball after hours, because we knew he expected it. We turned the radio up loud, talked in several different voices, and occasionally made the beds squeak before we went to sleep. We later learned that *Willie P* never stayed in the room at night, so our effort was wasted, and he was staying at a place that had a pool! In fact, we were invited to a party at his friend's house and someone short, stocky, and a bit baldheaded streaked past us into the pool later that night!

The Symposium was a great success, and it was the last one before we started fighter lead-in training at Holloman AFB and Red Flag at Nellis. There was lots of discussion about the future fighter lead-in (my program) and Red Flag, of which my old friend, old fat Moody Sutter, was to be the king. Many claim Red Flag, but it was Moody's idea, and he did most of the building and establishing of Red Flag. However, later some including a few Generals said it was their idea. Wrong! As I clearly remember, Moody first mentioned it long ago, and we lesser guys contributed to the plan that Moody dreamed up, constructed and then sold it to the leadership and built the solid foundation on which it has continued to operate today. It has greatly expanded to include all services, and many of our allies also participate in the Red Flag events. It probably prepares our crew members better for combat than anything else in our training, and fat old Moody was its' Daddy!

Regarding Fighter lead-in, I still have all the papers that were required to develop and establish Fighter Lead-in with either beefed-up T-38s or F-5s; of course F-5s would be preferred. This was simulation that was functional and works, not the dream of some simulator engineer! It took me quite a while to sell it, but it is extremely cost-effective and provides true pilot screening, preparation for more advanced fighters, and a training environment that actually works. I am very proud of Fighter Lead-in!

Almost as soon as *Willie P.* got to Nellis, Mr. Jones of Northrop asked *Willie P* if he had any ideas about how to make the aircraft that Northrop was working on for the Navy safer. Eventually the aircraft would be the F-18. *Willie P* told him he had the best "Behavioral Systems Engineer" in the business, and he could have him go to their plant in California. He then called me in and told me that I was now titled a "Behavioral Systems Engineer" and I was to fly to Northrop in their Gulf Stream tomorrow with Mr. Jones. He repeated, remember, you are a Behavioral Systems Engineer! Yes Sir!" (What the hell is a Behavioral Systems Engineer?)

The next day we flew to the plant, and Mr. Jones said the aircraft we were going to see was for the Navy. They were building it with other companies, and the Navy had lost too many aircraft going aboard the boat (aircraft carrier), and they were looking for a solution. I promised to do what I could. They put me in their recently designed and very realistic simulator cockpit, and I looked around, using their initial checklist. Because of my Navy background and experience, I knew of the problems they were concerned about, since I had lost a couple of friends "going aboard the Boat in fighters!"

After flying a few approaches and landing, I immediately spotted what I thought was the problem and what I had *always* thought was a problem even in the Air Force flying. The radio control head with which you select radio frequencies and volume was down low on the left hand side below and behind the throttles. This meant that the pilot had to probably look and lower his head as he controlled his radio operation during a critical part of the flight, turning final for landing on a carrier. This of course would probably induce vertigo and also be a distraction from looking outside to control the aircraft. I suggested moving it to just below the glare shield at eye level, where they had space in their mock-up.

Mr. Jones directed that they try that, which they did. Today that F-18 aircraft has the best safety record of any Navel aircraft! Mr. Jones told *Willie P.* that I was ten feet tall, and Northrup wanted to hire me as their Behavioral System Engineer. Of course *Willie P.* never told me that until years later at my retirement ceremony at Bergstrom AFB, Austin, Texas! We Behavioral Systems Engineers are really good! I have always wondered if such an engineer really exists. *Willie P.* had a great imagination, constantly thinking up new or better procedures, and it rubbed off on those of us who worked for him.

I mentioned earlier that while at TAC Headquarters I met Marilyn Ferguson, a very special lady, who I dearly loved like a sister, and I think she protected me and many other fighter pilots. Marilyn was a lot like Wanda Welch, also almost a sister and a special friend. She was one of two secretaries for Maj. Gen. *Willie P.* McBride! She was a great lady and would have made someone a wonderful wife. She was great about keeping others, like me, out of trouble with her boss and my hero *Willie P.* and she was someone I respected enormously.

As I said earlier, initially my boss in the Fighter Shop was Col. Buckshot White, but, almost immediately after I got there, Neil Eddins became my boss. To say he was a great boss is an understatement. He eventually made two stars. At one time, he was determined for me to be on or lead *his* Thunderbirds! Several times he asked or tried to submit me for the job. The last time, I think he had all the paperwork filled out, and just asked me to sign it. I was standing in front of him and simply turned around and showed him my shirttail hanging out and said, "Col. Eddins, you know damned well, a sloppy guy like me shouldn't be a Thunderbird!" That ended his efforts to make me a Thunderbird, but I always wonder if I made a mistake declining his sponsorship. I suspect because I had been in C-130s and an Air Training Command instructor, a maintenance test pilot, and an F-4 Instructor, I would have looked good paper wise. I didn't doubt that I could handle the flying; I just didn't think I was pretty or neat enough.

While in the fighter shop, I somehow gained the reputation of being a logical and good writer of policy/position papers. I assumed that Gen. Momyer had been given some heat from the Pentagon about some papers we had previously sent up. To fix the problem, he sent a letter around saying that I was to "chop" on all-important papers that were to go to Air Force Headquarters in the Pentagon. That order made my life more than miserable!

I suspect Gen. *Willie P.* was really responsible for it, since Gen. Momyer, unknown to most, loved and respected *Willie P.* but he sure loved to give him a hard time. It got so bad that my weekends were work weekends, and the only way my family and I could get away was to get in my boat, the *Purple People eater,* and head for an island to dig clams or fish. Later, the Command Post learned that the Coast Guard could find me on the island, so even that wasn't safe!

I must admit that I had a ball at TAC Headquarters, especially Friday nights at the O'Club with Randy Krumback, my immediate boss and Harry Vreeland, a fellow F-4 pilot. We did dance and sing and do Fighter Pilot things, seldom getting home even close to sober and then, very late at night! Fortunately, Randy and I lived close together near the base so one of us was normally able to steer us home! You do know that Air Force Fighter Pilots swear an oath to never grow older than six-and-a-half years old? We did our best to live up to that oath!

Later I became the Ops guy in the development of the F-15, so I was tasked to brief what we referred to as the *Long Knives* or the Air Force three stars. Early on I had learned a trick to wear someone else's nametag when I briefed high-rollers, which always gave me a bit of cover. For the Long Knifes, I was wearing Randy's nametag. I started the briefing, and before long Lt. Gen. Dixon started interrupting me and actually was giving the briefing, as he knew he was destined to be the TAC Commander and was naturally concerned about the future "greatest" fighter in the world. I just quietly stood there, as he talked changing the slides and finally he said, "Maj. Krumback—(he stumbled a bit on *Krumback!*) I thought you were giving this briefing?" I said, "Sir, I thought you wanted to give it, so I just was changing the slides for you."

From the back of the room, a SAC Lt. Gen. Hargrove (my friend /enemy from Homestead) said, "He isn't major Krumback; he is Maj. Barry Howard, who I have known since Homestead!" Fortunately, Lt. Gen. Charles Gabriel spoke up and saved me from getting murdered at the podium by saying, "Barry is one of our many sharp young fighter pilots who we are working to death!" Gen. Gabriel later became our Chief of Staff, and he was a great one!

While at TAC, I was part of the Maj. Gen. Ed. McNeff's Tactical review of TAC training, which was held at Luke AFB, Arizona. The Review produced many products, but one was the institution of the Instructional System Approach to Training or SAT as we called it. As a result of this recommendation, SAT also became my project to manage from TAC Headquarters. Our initial approach was the development of the A-7D training program, which included developing a training program for recent graduates of Undergraduate Pilot Training (UPT) in the single-seated A-7D. The A-7D was a single-seated fighter with a single engine, a program that had lots of attention. TAC hadn't trained recent UPT graduates in a single-seat fighter since the F-100, for which we did have a few two-seaters, (F-100F) but we had no two-seated A-7Ds. The resultant SAT built program for recent UPT graduates was very successful. But just in case, I was in mobile control on the runway at Davis-Monthan AFB, Arizona, when the first A-7D UPT graduates soloed in the aircraft. I had a rental car, and I aimed it south, so, if one of them crashed, I was heading for Mexico.

Along with the A-7D program, we attempted to modify all programs using SAT, which in most cases was done properly. Really, the only hang-ups were when we were using "old heads" to build the program. Occasionally they had difficulty avoiding their ingrained biases rather than using SAT process for program development.

Initially, when we started in SAT, we were learning from the Airlines, but, as we progressed with SAT, our TAC members became the real experts in SAT, and eventually the Army and later the Navy followed TAC's lead along with some airlines. It was personally a challenge to me because it was easy for me to see ingrained biases, probably because of my wide experience stemming being an Airlift Instructor, a UPT Instructor, and an F-4 Instructor, along with being an experienced test pilot. But sometimes it was hard to convince our personnel, especially the more senior ones that their biases were showing!

While at TAC, I received an early promotion to LtCol. Gen. Momyer insisted that I be pinned by him and my wife, Dorlyne. It was a great ceremony, and Dorlyne and I were very proud. All the TAC generals had been invited, along with many Colonels. After the pinning, Gen. Momyer made a short speech about my time at Langley AFB and mentioned that I rode a motorcycle (a really tiny one, and, with me on it, it looked even smaller). He then asked since I was now part of the Air Force leadership, would I get rid of the motorcycle. I hesitated for a minute, and then I said, "General, I am a fighter pilot; I hate riding a desk, and the only time I again feel like a fighter pilot again is when I am riding the cycle!" I was later told by a general friend that he thought the General would rip my new rank off me, but instead he said, "How much does a motorcycle cost?" Later, I offered for him to ride it—which he did!

My time at TAC Headquarters was a very demanding and challenging. Frankly, they worked my skinny little butt off (one of my nicknames in high school was "NB or no butt"). However, I learned a great deal about how things are done in the Air Force and more importantly how to make things happen within the Air Force system. I had great models or mentors from the TAC DO, Maj. General "Willie P." McBride; the Aviation Cadet and my boss, then Col. Neal Eddins; the TAC R&D, then Col. Howard Leaf; and the TAC Commander, General "Spike" Momyer.

LUKE AFB, ARIZONA, 2/1972-7/1975

I escaped from TAC Headquarters in January 1972, and I thought I was going to be stationed at Holloman AFB, New Mexico, and I even had been assigned a base house at Holloman. But I went to Luke AFB, Arizona, to get re-current in the F-4. While at Luke, the Wing Commander, Brig. Gen. Fred Haeffner, grabbed me, and I stayed at Luke, signing in February 1972. Initially, I was the Chief (Commander) of the Instructional Systems Development Training Squadron which had been developed to utilize and develop the Systems Approach to Training (SAT) and develop materials for the resultant programs. This was one of the programs that I steered while at TAC Headquarters.

We developed training devices, modified programs, and oversaw modifications to programs to make sure they reflected the SAT concept. The Air Force is blessed with young, creative, and imaginative pilots who can do almost anything. That is why SAT, which originally began in the Airlines, exploded in the Air Force. Those involved with SAT invented, built, and designed training aids, tools, or programs that were dynamic, unique, and extremely functional. The Air Force went from following the Airlines' lead to being the leader of SAT.

However, we foolishly believed that SAT would protect training programs from arbitrary changes by strong-willed Generals. To some degree it did, but not always when changes caused by major accidents were concerned.

While I commanded the ISDT Squadron, I had the opportunity to put in a very large cost-saving suggestion—for at least $7 million in the F-4 program as a result of SAT—to the White House. The suggestion was approved! I had put my Deputy's name on the suggestion, since he had just been passed over for LtCol and I was certain if it was approved, he would get promoted, and he was. He and his family were invited to Washington, DC, to meet and have dinner with President Nixon. My wife, Dorlyne, was a bit unhappy, since she knew it was really my effort, and that my name should have been on it! Additionally, my Deputy then really let me down, because as soon as he got promoted and could retire, he resigned from the Air Force. We had plans for him to take over SAT and work with the other services to help them develop their SAT programs.

Dorlyne and I decided to have a home built in Litchfield Park, Arizona, by a super builder, Clemmie Arnold. We really liked the house, which had a pool, and we had a prime location, as it was next to the new, famous Wigwam Country Club golf club's Gold Course. I recently return to Litchfield Park for a "Red River Rats Reunion" at the Wigwam Resort, and was shocked to learn that the Litchfield Park road had been moved to the west. It now ran between the house we had built and the golf course, which had also been moved at least three hundred yards west. Fortunately, I had an eight-foot wall built around our house, so the road noise now should be minimal.

Once the house was furnished, the 311th TFTS, an F-4 squadron, had an opening, and I was made the Commander with Clint

Hanna as the Ops.Officer. Sometime later, Clint got the F-104 Squadron down the road from the 311th. Clint was replaced by Rolf Nymo, one of the real old-heads in F-4s. We made a great team, and our A Flight Commander, Mike Ryan, eventually became the Air Force Chief of Staff. Of all the troops I have been blessed to lead, Mike and his really wonderful Irish redheaded wife, Jane, would also have been my pick for Chief of Staff. I can also brag that I helped check Mike out in the front seat of the F-4, *and* I started at least two fights between him and his brother, Jack, at Udorn. All I had to do is de-brief one of the Ryan brothers at the O'Club with the other brother within ear shot and simply say things like, "Those were the best bombs I have ever seen; good job!" Very soon the challenge from the listening brother usually resulted in a fight! Damn, it was fun to train them. Too bad we lost one of them with a *maybe* Saturday morning hangover in a Phantom.

We, the 311th, also had the honor of being the first Fighter Squadron to participate in the superb training exercise program, Red Flag. As I said earlier, along with many other fighter pilots, I had helped with or contributed to my friend, Moody Suter's, development of Red Flag. Red Flag has now grown by leaps and bounds and is now all inclusive of all US military and many foreign forces. No matter how many great leaders claim Red Flag as their idea, it was truly first Moody's idea, and he fought to make it happen!

Unfortunately, my father had died the day after I received the squadron, which put a sad damper on the event, as I had finally achieved my dream to command an actual fighter squadron.

Mom, "Little Napoleon," now alone, frequently visited us and loved to arrive when the truck farms hauled their products to market. She would follow them and pick up the product that fell off the trucks. If I came home from work and there was a tray of veggies with various dips, I knew Mom had been "On the road again, picking up veggies!"

While Mom was visiting us, some of our friends from Muncie, Indiana, visited, and our Gen. Haeffner and his DO, Jack O'Donnell, took them and Mom out to our mobile control unit on the end of the runway to watch landings. About that time thunderstorms moved in, and I was airborne, and it became my duty to concentrate on getting the chicks (students) and all aircraft on the ground before the storm hit. While herding the chicks back to the roost, I had an emergency, losing hydraulics, and other problems. After I got the all chicks back on the ground, I landed, and, because of my emergency, I had to drop my tail hook and take the cable to stop the aircraft. Jack, the DO, drove Mom and our friends to where I was climbing out of the aircraft. Mom walked up and slapped me, saying, "Barry, you big show-off, you shouldn't have taken the cable!" Everyone laughed, because they knew I didn't have a choice with the failures I had, *but Little Napoleon* is always right!

While Commander of the 311th TFTS, I was in heaven, and every day was fun! Teaching or leading young men either as instructors or students to be warriors and fighter pilots was as good as it gets! As I said, our A flight Commander, Mike Ryan, became Chief of Staff and we had several other future generals, and one of them was Tony Tolin, for whom my kids' babysat!

Of course, the Pepsi-aholic, B/ Gen. "Fat Fred" Haeffner, always could stir up something exciting to do. Like the time, at his suggestion, we painted the roof of the largest hanger on Luke in Russian, essentially saying in Cyrillic script, "Screw you, Commies!"

We also had a monthly "Turkey Shoot" and the losing squadron would get to keep the live turkey, foolishly named Barry, until the next Turkey shoot. My guys were really experienced and good fighter pilots, and we always did well for the Turkey Shoots but I always said, "If we ever get that damn turkey, we'll eat it!"

While I naturally wanted to fly in the Turkey Shoots, I believe that my young instructors such as Ted Schwartz, Tony Tolin, or

Frank McCann should get the major portion of training that was available and we old heads didn't need to steal their opportunities to expand their ability. However, after much harassment from those outside the Squadron, I finally led a shoot. I think I was either top performer or the number-two scorer in the shoot. My squadron Weapons Officer and I really thought that I won, but someone jimmied it so I didn't—but it at least shut up the harassers!

A few months later, we lost the "Shoot," and we got the turkey. It was now fall, and we had already planned a hayride for the squadron. We of course invited the wing Director of Operations (DO), Jack O'Donnell, and my mother cooked the turkey-shoot loser's prize, "Barry," unbeknownst to anyone. We had the DO sample the turkey and approve of it before the others got to eat it. Heh heh, the DO approved it—little did he know it was "Barry!"

We had in the squadron (fighter squadrons have tons of untapped talent) a man, who, as a hobby, knew how to preserve skeletons. Barry's bones were assembled in a nice, well-constructed plastic container by a young student fighter pilot for presentation at the end of the next "Turkey Shoot"! It did shock the General and the DO, but the Squadron Commander who lost was thrilled—no damn live turkey to take care of. I know for years it survived at Luke as the booby prize for losers of the "Turkey Shoots"! Recently I ran into a fellow, former student and later IP from Luke, and he said old "Turkey Barry's bones" are still around!

About this time an incident occurred that set me back a bit; Gen. Fred called me and said, "You have been promoted to Colonel below the zone"—*below the zone* is an early promotion, as had happened to me to promote me to lieutenant colonel at TAC Headquarters and we plan to have Senator Goldwater announce it at your Dining-Out; he has been notified." Of course, I said, "Yes, Sir!"

Senator Barry Goldwater was an honorary member of our 311th TFTS and regularly attended our social functions. Of course I have always been a great fan of him and his beliefs and methods, and he was truly what I would call "A real fighter pilot". Additionally, the fact that his wife, Peggy, was from Muncie, Indiana, where I went to Junior and Senior High School was interesting. Of course my wife Dorlyne and my cousin Karen loved to spend time with him at parties, and the senator, being a real fighter pilot, he loved being with them as he did not bring Peggy as she was a bit infirmed at the time!

The day before the Dining-Out, Gen. Haeffner called me and said, "Barry, I am sorry but you were red-lined off the list because your last OER [officer efficiency report] wasn't a "One." Please call Senator Goldwater and tell him that your promotion won't be announced." I said, "General, you must know I am damned disappointed, but I am not going to call Senator Goldwater, because I might tell him who screwed up here at Luke."

Since the new OER system had just started, and I was the junior lieutenant colonel on the base, I did not receive a top-rated number-one OER, thus I was redlined off the Colonel's list. I hadn't expected to be on it, but once I was told I was on it, I wanted it! The General did call him, and Senator Goldwater apologized to me about it at the party. He said I would be on the next list, and I was, but it sure would have been nice to have been on the previous one! What upset me also was that the fellow on base who was promoted below the zone or early did not accept it and got out of the Air Force. He was also the one who beat me out for the first F-15 squadron; of course, someone—I think *Fat Fred*—later said, "He had really screwed up in that regard."

As tradition goes, after my last F-4 flight as the Commander of the 311th Tactical Fighter Training Squadron TFTS, I drank some bubbly and secretly cried, because I thought the fun days were over!

As I departed Luke AFB after commanding both the SAT Squadron and the 311th TFTS, I just knew I was leaving the really fun days and might be on the way to some boring senior leadership jobs. However, I was wrong about the fun days being gone; in fact, I enjoyed the next few years as much as the junior years! Now instead of relying on myself and other fellow young officers who were friends, I now had young captains and lieutenants to depend on, and, *man*, are they good!

Air War College OR THE PENTAGON?
8/1975-6/1978

I had been chosen for Air War College, and, after my fun at Luke leading young fighter pilots, I was off to Air War College, Montgomery, Alabama, for a year of study, relaxation, and friendship! Or so I thought? As I was about to "coast out of Arizona," (a fighter pilot term meaning to leave the state of Arizona) and enter New Mexico. I was stopped by an Arizona State Policeman. Since I knew I wasn't speeding, I asked why I had been stopped; surely I wasn't speeding? The Police officer said, "It wasn't because you are doing anything wrong; it is just that *your* assignment has been changed to the Pentagon" and he gave me a number to call! I said, "How about telling them that I was already out of the state?" He said, "Sorry, I already told them that I had you spotted!"

Later I made the call, and it was confirmed that my Air War College attendance had been delayed, and I was going to the Pentagon to replace a friend who had been relieved in the basement! Damn—and I was almost there!

When I reported into the Pentagon in August 1975, I learned that Gen. Sandy Vandenburg and Gen. Billy Joe. Ellis had both requested me for the simulator shop located in the basement across from the famous "Purple water fountain." Ron Ellis was already there, as were the super Sergeants from Langley AFB, TAC Headquarters. It didn't take long for us to whip the programs in shape, between the others with their brains and my ability to sell what we did. But it certainly wasn't a dream assignment for a fighter pilot.

About that time, I had just been promoted to Colonel and was "pinned" by Dorlyne, Gen. Vandenburg, and the Congressman Ralph Harvey who got me into the Academy.

While I was in the Pentagon, there was an incident at the DMZ in Korea, where the alleged *Korean Peace Talks* took place and which was heavily guarded by the North Korean forces and our US Army specially assigned team, mostly Special Ops types. At the De-Militarize Zone (DMZ) there was a very large tree blocking the US view of the other side, and one of our Army Majors, a black Special Forces troop, was sent in to cut it down. The North Koreans quickly attacked and killed him with their bare hands. We naturally decided to respond in force. A plan was developed that included having our ground troops on full tactical alert, US and Korean fighter aircraft on CAPs (combat air patrols) ready for combat action very close to the DMZ, and B-52s inbound, along with naval ships on station. We were ready for war!

When this all came to a head, our Special Forces Troops would go in and cut down the tree with a chainsaw. A few days before we actually cut down the tree down, we practiced the event. The Pentagon Operational Command Post Staff with Gen. Vandenberg in charge and managing the event. We senior Operational Staff Officers were observers sitting in the Pentagon Command Post as the event was practiced. There was an open mike between the DMZ and our Command Post. As the practice event wound down, Gen. Vandenberg questioned us observers about any faults with the plan. A few suggestions were made, and the General said, "Thank you all for coming, and now for my final question to our new Colonel, Barry Howard: What did we do wrong?" A few hours before, I had been promoted to Colonel by the Gen. Vandenberg. Also, I love to cut firewood with a chainsaw, and I did it frequently. So I quickly said, "I would like to hear the chainsaw started!" On the open mike, we could hear someone cranking the saw several times, and it never did start!

When the actual event took place a few days later and the tree was cut down, before the exercise started, the *Checklist* was run, and the final item on the checklist—I believe it was called the "Barry Howard" item and it said, "Start the chainsaws"! The others and I heard several—probably more than ten—chainsaws started! The tree was cut down, and the North did nothing to stop it.

Soon after we got things organized in simulators, I was moved to Operational Test and Eval which represented the Air Force Operational Test and Eval Component (AFOTEC) at Kirtland AFB, New Mexico, and then Commanded by my friend, Maj. Gen. Howard Leaf. Earlier, I had done a study for then Col. Leaf, when he was the Commander of the fighter wing at MacDill AFB, Florida, and I was debriefing him when his "Hotline" phone rang. He answered and, after a few moments, said, "Yes, Sir, I understand." He then hung up and turned to me and told me, "I have just been fired!" Little did the man who fired him know that then Col. Leaf was highly respected in TAC and the TAC Commander, Gen. "Spike" Momyer, really believed in him? Obviously, he recovered and went on to make three stars and frankly, I know of no one who didn't really like Howard Leaf, a real and proven combat fighter pilot!

I had been the TAC fighter pilot responsibility for the A-7D, which I was very familiar with, and also the A-10 and the F-15.

All three aircraft I had been associated with at TAC on the Operational side of development for training and operations. These aircraft were now in the "test and evaluation" phase of entry into the Air Force, which was handled by AFOTEC at Kirtland and we were their mouth pieces in the Pentagon.

My new function in the Pentagon also meant that I traveled regularly to Kirtland AFB, Albuquerque, New Mexico. Now, this was a good job, and I was doing things I really believed in and hoped that I could positively impact the program. Regarding the A-7D, we had a terrible engine problem because of a very poor engine design. Essentially, the single oil line that carried the cooled oil back to the engine was located in an area that was prone to minor but devastating shifting, causing the oil line to break, starving the engine of oil, and resulting in engine failure. In a single-engine aircraft, engine failure makes for a very bad day; you suddenly become a very inefficient glider! I believe that the Navy was already replacing their A-7 engines with one with a better oil system. The Air Force followed suit, but not before we had several aircraft loses.

The A-10 was a different problem all together; the .30 mm Gatling gun shot all the bullets through the same hole, and with those big, .30 mm rounds; and only limited damage would be done. A "stagger" was built into the gun operation, thus moving the damage around. Other than a need to fly in a combat environment in near full power, there were few problems with this "tank killing" beast. Later, when I checked out in it at Davis-Monthan AFB, Tucson, Arizona, I realized that we had a weapons system that the Army would love, even if it had needed more engine power! I managed the naming of it for the Air Force and was disappointed that my suggestion "The Whisper Jet" wasn't accepted. I suggested the name because on the ground you could not hear it coming as you do most jets! It was named the "Thunder Bolt II" in deference to the earlier WW II Thunder Bolt (P-47).

The A-10 is the perfect aircraft for big old Colonels; lots of space in the cockpit, great air-conditioner, excellent gun sight, carries lots of ammunition, tons of fuel, and armored in the right places, along with a great computer navigation system. However, there were a few unusual problems. Some of the young troops had trouble in weather formation because of the straight wing, unlike what they had learned in the T-38, which had swept-back wings. Qualifying on the gun under initial fighter criteria required shooting at least one hundred bullets, which was difficult to do, since it was a relatively slow-firing gun. I have always been one of the top qualifiers with a fighter gun, but I could never fire one hundred rounds in the A-10. Usually I would have 100 percent of hits with the bullets I would shoot, but I would fire less than fifty rounds. Later the qualification requirements were changed to a percentage of actual hits, with the requirement for one hundred rounds to be fired rescinded. This change also lowered training costs, because .30 mm ammo was costly.

Additionally, because of the lack of power problem, I had proposed to add an engine to the A-10 that would be used in only combat, such as the proven T-38 engine. Many years ago, such a modification was done on the C-119 (Flying Boxcar) to give it more power in high-threat areas. The engine could be fired up when entering combat, thus giving it additional power. Unfortunately no one listened to me and now, years later, they are thinking about re-equipping the aircraft with a stronger and more efficient engine but the loss rate because of the original under-power, I believe, was is too high. Some of the AFOTEC troops at Kirtland were very unhappy with the A-10 (especially my friend Col. "Mr. Earl" Haney, former Thunderbird and truly a feisty little bastard), because it did not meet several of the Air Force required specifications for the aircraft. Mr. Earl is one of those who had encouraged me to write this book, as he has written one.

Regarding the F-15, we sensed that someone was feeding unfinished and negative data to a Congressional Committee, possibly someone working for Committee who was a Navy F-14 champion. Then the data was fed to the dreaded Government Accountability Office (GAO). To confirm this, I was able to get to our flight-test debriefer, explaining the problem. The flight-test debriefer then built phony data in his reports that only he and I knew about. But we did have the false data validated by a certified accountant. Sure enough, at the next meeting with the Congressional Committee, these data surfaced. We, the Air Force, quietly met with the Chairman of the Congressional Committee and showed him the documented false data, thus exposing that someone was illegally feeding data to the Committee, which was then feeding it to the GAO. We had no problems after that of data being provided to GAO prematurely. After having this great job in Operational Test and Evaluation for a few months, I was moved again.

This time I was assigned to Operation Checkmate: a study team built generally by my friend Moody Sutter and the Chief of Staff, General Jones. It was now run by a Colonel who some say may have far exceeded the Peter Principle. Select and very smart young troops who were experts in their field—whether logistic, intelligence, or operational aircraft—manned the study group. Now this was fun—smart, really smart, Captains, Majors and an LtCol or two who were constantly challenging everything. Checkmate was the pet project of Air Force Chief of Staff Gen. David Jones.

Their mission of Checkmate was to fight the war with the "now capabilities" rather than the future capabilities that are usually used in war planning. Checkmate reported directly to the Chief of the Air Force, Gen. David Jones. While Gen. Jones was considered by many to be a SAC puke, I quickly learned that was absolutely wrong, and he thought like a young fighter pilot!

He wanted to rock the boat, and he picked—or actually, Gens. Vandenburg and Ellis picked the right bunch, except for the Colonel in charge.

When I was moved into Checkmate, I was told that although I was only the deputy, I was really in charge, and the other Colonel knew that. The personnel system was searching for an assignment for him. I had been recently promoted to Colonel, and he and I were able to work it out. Occasionally he would say something during the briefing that had to be "tactically corrected," but other than that, he stayed out of the way.

We accomplished so many things with our unique method of presenting our concerns. To do this we formed a Red (Russian) Team and a Blue (good guys) team. The Red Team would actually wear a Commie Red–type uniform. The briefings were extremely dynamic, and tempers frequently increased. My job was almost like that of a "bouncer" or 'arbitrator' who tried to keep the briefing rolling. Sometimes, when the real facts were presented to the military leadership, leaving out the future corrections, tactics, and procedures or planned changes, we would have an explosion from some senior officers from the various services. A few items that were presented addressed real and serious concerns. In some cases the problems were solved almost on the spot.

One example was the lack of immediate on-scene tactical intelligence. With a tactical U-2, this lack could quickly be resolved. As a result, the U-2 program, which had been closed, was opened again. This resulted in a massive improvement in valid, on-scene tactical intelligence and a great boon to those with "boots on the ground" or "jocks in the aircraft!"

An input to the Navy that probably embarrassed them was that we pointed out that there were very limited mine sweeping capabilities. They then generated reserve forces to handle this task.

One item that I became aware of and which was later written about in detail in the book *Red October*, by Tom Clancy, surfaced to me somehow during my research. Our problem was that as we briefed the Secretary of Defense, we realized that he did not know about the Navy's capability relative to the Russian Submarine Skippers. I approached a classmate and a good friend from the Academy who was the key Navy's submarine Pentagon Officer, about our concern. He simply said "the SecDef" wasn't cleared for that information. I probably tried to remind him that the civilian leaders controlled the Military and the SecDef was our entry into the civilian leadership.

My next stop was in response to my friend's boss, who said he would consult with the Chief of Naval Operations (CNO) on the matter. Next, I received a call to report to the CNO's office almost immediately. During my conversation with the CNO, standing at attention, I explained that I was a Naval Academy Graduate and I understood the Navy's concern but we, the military, were set up to be under civilian control. I further explained that we were again briefing the SecDef in a few days, and I was certain the subject would come up. He asked how we learned about it. I really didn't know how I learned about it, and I still don't remember how I learned about it. I said, however, we did know, and it was our duty to talk about it, since we gave a top-secret briefing to the SecDef about our "now" war-fighting capabilities. I was dismissed by the CNO, and he said I would hear from him again. To say that he tried to intimidate me is an understatement, but since I was a combat fighter pilot, I was bullet proof!

The day before we briefed the SecDef, I received a call that the SecDef had been briefed, so the matter died. The SecDef's naval aide, when he arrived for the briefing, assured me that the Navy had briefed the SecDef about the submarine skippers. Of course when the book *Red October* soon came out, everyone now knew about the fact that we had considerable knowledge about the Russian sub skippers.

We also surfaced many logistic problems as well as many cases where airlift was greatly overloaded, as different units were committed to the same airlift capabilities. Our briefings were so successful that future actual military operations were planned by Checkmate, and I was very proud to be part of this program. Unfortunately, I believe that some follow-up leadership of Checkmate pushed their self-generated and individual ideas rather than fully developed and documented ideas, as we always did when Checkmate started, because we never gave personal opinions.

During my tour in the Pentagon, my good friend Moody Sutter and I were involved in the debriefing of Victor Belinko, the MIG 25 pilot who landed in Japan and defected to the US. He was kept in a "safe house" in Washington, DC, and we debriefed in another "safe debriefing area" in DC. He would arrive in the debriefing area early in the morning, and the CIA controlled the debriefing, with us, the Tactical Fighter Pilots getting only an occasional shot at him, as we had to listen in another room. Mostly, we just listened to others debriefing him and made notes that we wanted the debriefers to ask him. He was a typical fighter pilot, aggressive, sometimes nasty, (just like Moody and I) and probably the foulest mouth I have ever heard. I asked one of the CIA troops about his swearing, and he said, "Swearing in the Soviet Union is an art form, and Victor is a Rembrandt!"

One of the observations I made was that Victor had a keen eye of observation as he traveled to and from where he was kept. He observed who drove what, who were bad drivers, and what was wrong at the some of the intersections.

During one debriefing, he kept mentioning a radar switch that he had never touched but that maintenance always had to check after a flight and sometimes before. It was called a "combat switch," and it concerned Moody and me a great deal. No one else was concerned, but we were sure it might be or was a different radar frequency. If the switch gave the pilot a different radar frequency that he could use in combat and thus none of our electronic countermeasures systems would be tuned to it. Then we had a very big problem. We constantly tried to have this switch and its capability confirmed, but since the CIA controlled the debriefing, our concerns were never addressed. I never learned if what we supposed was a problem really existed.

Once we, the TAC forces, took Belinko to a famous Greek restaurant south of DC and located on a river. Many of the TAC Generals and senior officers attended, and probably there were twenty to thirty of us there. For some reason, I sort of managed it, since the restaurant was probably my idea, as I loved this restaurant. When it came time for the check, the TAC Commander said, "Barry, please get the check and take care of it, with a good tip, please." I approached the Manager who was supervising the meal and he said, "There is no charge, Barry," rather loudly and firmly. Of course everyone, including Victor, heard him, and Victor said, "Just like in Russia!" My friend the Manager said in a very firm and even louder voice to Victor, "No, not like Russia, this is America, where I came as a dishwasher and now own the finest Greek restaurant, probably, in America. Only in America can one rise from dishwasher to owner through hard work!" The TAC Commander stood up and said, "Thank you, but we must pay!"

"Not in this restaurant—*now or ever!*" And he walked out with his head held high, and no one would take our money! It still waters my eyes thinking about it, and we never did pay!

One distraction was that in the basement operational organization there was an SAC General, Deputy to Gen. Vandenberg, who really didn't like me. I don't think he knew I started out in SAC intelligence at Barksdale AFB! One time when our two TAC generals were TDY, he called me in to chew me out for something. I was standing in front of his desk, a really big desk, and he said some awful things to me, obviously trying to get me upset. He definitely was succeeding, and I asked to leave as I was close to embarrassing myself, probably by beating the hell out of him. Even his secretary, who heard him, came in and said, "General, we need to get Col. Howard out of here." With that, he said something else about my folks, and I went after him, either across or around his desk! He quickly departed out his back door and locked it, so I couldn't get to him. Later, I believe he was chairman of my Brigade General's board. The only good thing I can say about him is that he had a very charming, beautiful and friendly wife!

After many phone calls, I was able to reestablish my Air War College assignment, so I was able to depart the Pentagon after two years, two days, and six hours. I have to admit that I really enjoyed this assignment, and I was certainly challenged, and I am certain that I was able to contribute to my Air Force. As I was departing on the last day, they were putting new furniture in my office, and I had a red leather chair that I loved to sit in when I read. I asked what was going to happen to the chair, which was in pretty good shape, and was told that it would probably be thrown away. Later, as I was departing from the basement, I had pulled my vehicle to one of the loading ramps to load my things in it, and I saw my chair next to a trash container with other chairs in it. I asked the troop throwing the chairs into the trash container if I could have the red leather chair; he said, "Sure!" I still have my red leather chair, just another case of "*lucky* Barry"! Off to Air War College I went! I did leave my old cornflower blue 311th refrigerator in Checkmate for the late Friday BS sessions!

AIR WAR COLLEGE, FINALLY, 7/1978-6/1979

Attending the Air War College in Montgomery, Alabama, was a great year for the Howard family! We had a chance to visit areas we weren't familiar with, and we really relaxed. Also we were able to build a house with a nice basketball court for Mike on the out skirts of Montgomery. The house was finished in a timely manner; we had some great neighbors, even some from my Air War College class. It was a great year of study, challenge, and partying.

We even had the traditional father-son basketball game, where the wife and daughter were crying, and the battle was bloody, just like in the movie *The Great Santini*, and I think Mike even won the game. Mike did start on the high school basketball team, and for once we didn't get a call from the school about our son being in a fight the first day, as had usually happened. We gorged ourselves with the wonderful oysters available in Montgomery at the various oyster bars!

As we began our Air War College year, we had a golf tournament where I wore a shirt that said, "You ain't shit, if you aren't a fighter pilot!" I don't think it made me any friends among the non-fighter folks, but that quickly died down. On top of the shirt,

I surprisingly won the tournament! As a result, I never played golf again at Air War College; I quit a winner!

On a more serious side, I was very unhappy about the curriculum! It had been designed around examples of civilian management, not military leadership. I believed then, and I still believe now, that the military has better leadership, not management, than any organization anywhere. Men like Perishing, Patton, Halsey, Arnold, Marshall, Eisenhower, LeMay, Puller, and Nimitz, had/have no equals in the civilian world! I fought the curriculum throughout the course, and finally the General in charge of the school challenged me to write a better curriculum designed around military leadership procedures, methods, and how it is to be instilled as one grows in the military. It was a challenge that I couldn't pass up, and I worked very hard on developing the new course. I later learned that I wasn't the only one upset with the course, and much of what I proposed was accepted under someone else's name who was a member of the War Air College Staff. It didn't matter to me, as I was damned happy the course had changed, and the military leadership again was the main thrust of the course.

The year at Montgomery was a very productive year and certainly enjoyable. I learned a great deal about other Air Force challenges from my classmates from other parts of the Air Force. This certainly enhanced my knowledge with regard to being able to function as a senior commander. Initially I assumed I would graduate and become a DO in a fighter or training wing. However, I forgot that my former boss Neil Eddins hadn't finished riding this pony! To my shock, I was assigned to an AWACS squadron at Tinker AFB, Oklahoma.

The house we built made us a pretty decent profit, same as did the house we lived in while I was in the Pentagon. With the profit from Montgomery and the house in Virginia, we were able to build a nice home for our next assignment in Edmond, Oklahoma, about twenty miles north of Tinker AFB.

963ʳᵈ AWACS SQUADRON, 8/1979-5/1981

Departing the Air War College, I wanted to be a fighter wing DO but my former boss, now Brig. Gen. Neil Eddins from Afton, Wyoming, had other ideas. He was to be assigned to the Commander of the Airborne Warning and Control System or WACS Wing, Tinker AFB, Oklahoma, and I was to be Commander of the 963rd AWACS Squadron starting in August 1979. I was told it would be the first fully tactical operational AWACS squadron. What I wasn't told is that **I had to make it tactical.** Needless to say, I was greatly disappointed, but I sure liked working for Neil. Maj. Gen. John L. Piotrowski was the Commander when I arrived, but Neil followed soon after. Gen. Piotrowski eventually and quickly made four stars.

The 963ʳᵈ Squadron was a very large squadron, with many different disciplines including many officers and airmen. The airmen were exceptional and had expertise that only existed in the military. The Officers were the same, but in general were lacking pride and positional confidence and believed or knew they had been treated unfairly (absolutely the truth too!)—and they were very dispirited bunch. I was shocked that such talented folks could be so down on themselves, their system, and the Air Force. The only good thing about the situation in the squadron was that I knew I could fix it with Gen. Eddins's support, which I got. Many had been passed over too. My first attack was regarding OERs, which were well written, but the marks were lower than other disciplines in the Air Force, thus fewer officers were promoted in their career fields. I bumped up my endorsements and had the writers bump up the OERs in the squadron. We, my second superb assistant deputy, Don Riley (Gridley) and I, worked it hard. Don was an absolutely outstanding officer, as good as any I ever have met, and he should have been promoted to brigadier general, which surely would have invigorated the career field. We worked hard on pride in the squadron, and the 963rd Blue Knights patches started appearing everywhere; our light blue scarves stood out and our AWACS tactical work was second to none. I need to add this was my third squadron with light blue scarves.

It became immediately apparent to me that AWACS was designed for strategic or air defense operations, but with some modifications it would be a wonderful tactical force modifier and excellent enhancer in a tactical world.

We had a young, black Administrative Officer, Lt. G. A. Fuller, who worked the deployment package hard and we watered their eyes during exercises. When we actually deployed, we always were ready before the required "ready time." Of course we also received the tougher missions and became very involved in Special Operations. For each promotion cycle, I worked the phone and Gen. Eddins hard, which started paying off, and we started to get promotions for our officers. Our other Deputy Commander who had previously been passed over was promoted to Colonel. That really started a fire in our troops; they now knew things were looking up. We (I believe Chief Johnson) put together a "flyaway kit" which allowed us to improve conditions wherever we were deployed by repairing or building things we needed or wanted for our troops. In any military organization, you have loads of talent, which will surface if you look for it. Pretty soon, when the wing was tasked, many times it was a request for the 963rd Blue Knights!

One of our first deployments was to Korea when President Park was assassinated. North Korea had said that the next time there was political unrest in South Korea; it would attack and retake the country for the North. We deployed on very short notice, and, thanks to our Administrative Officer, we were off and running quickly with all the equipment and supplies we needed!

We arrived at Osan, Korea, and set up our aircraft and operating area. The South Koreans were extremely pleased that we were there, and they did all they could to help us. They truly wined, dined, and even provided me with "backrubs" or other things that I might want. As Commander, I tried to set a good example and did not partake of some of the goodies offered! In fact, it got so bad that I had to get a secret bedroom where I could really sleep without a "lovely" reciting poetry to me in Hangul!

The South Korean Leadership included me in most everything they did during our stay, including visiting the Blue House (like our White House) and working with their tactical folks. The deployment was a superb opportunity to work the AWACS into a truly and actual tactical environment. One day we even considered arming the AWACS but had no Mers or Ters to put the weapons on! As a result of our superior systems experts were able to develop and make recommends for serious and proven needed modifications to the radar system to make the Strategic AWACS also a truly full blown Tactical AWACS.

The North Koreans had many AN-2s, a slow bi-wing transport that they could use to infiltrate into the South because they were quiet and could fly under the tactical radar net and actually drop North Korean paratroopers into South Korea. We were able to successfully change the gating on the radar, which also then allowed us to also follow mass movements of vehicles as well as the AN-2s! Remember, the AWACS was designed as strategic radar to track fast moving attacks on the US. I have many moments in my career that I am proud of but our contribution to the tactical environment by "TACemsizing" the AWAC is one of my proudest accomplishments I have been a part of!

On our deployment to Osan, after we made the needed modifications to the radar system and we were totally integrated with the tactical system we believed we were ready to go home. As the threat for the North subsided, I concluded our further presence was not needed.

Christmas was coming, and I wanted to get our troops home for Christmas, since we were doing very little and frankly not needed anymore. Additionally, we had been deployed for the previous Christmas holidays. Of course I always made sure I was deployed with our troops when they were gone during Christmas, Thanksgiving, or New Years.

However, never let a real warrior send a message, as he might ruin his career! I sent a message saying, "The Army General to whom we had chopped knew little or nothing about AWACS potential" and other choice words to get my Troops home for Christmas. Needless-to- say, I started a fire, and, along with a few other incidents, probably destroyed my chances to make General. However, the General I had badmouthed and I became great friends, and later we frequently laughed about the message.

As we were preparing to leave in early December, the senior Korea leadership had me to a "Gisling party" which was wonderful, great food (I love Korean food), lots of drink, and really beautiful ladies, with one assigned to me, and she was gorgeous! I remember she had on a black and white dress. Having been a good boy for a long time, I think I decided that I needed a "going away" present! For *Gisling Parties* we were normally in a big room, talking, eating, drinking, and surrounded by beautiful ladies. Suddenly every "brick," our personal tactical communications devices, the model for future cell phones, went off, except mine. At that time the bricks were about the size of a small actual brick. Suddenly, the Koreans were speaking urgently in Hangul, and I was begging my friends to tell what was going on. Gen. Kim, the Commander of the Korean Air Forces, finally said, "The damn Army has done a junta and there is great political unrest in South Korea." Since I had been driven to the party by one of the senior Korean officers, we jumped into his car and returned to Osan AB.

As I got closer to Osan AB, I finally was able to contact my personnel and was told that no one was talking to them, and they could contact no one at the Seoul Command Post. I told them to get the aircraft ready, and we would probably launch! When I got to the base, there was still no contact with Seoul. We launched and stayed on station until we got the word from our Korean Air Force friends that the unrest had settled down. We landed, and I expected an ass-chewing, but no one said anything except the South Koreans, who were extremely appreciative of our action. As the new Junta settled in, we were released to return to Tinker AFB on December 22nd. The mission to Korea provided the catalyst to TACemsize the AWACS!

Later, Our AWACS squadron, the 963rd, was selected to support the Iranian rescue, first in training and then for the actual rescue. Naturally, I participated first as simply AWACS commander, and for the second rescue attempt, I would have been the air boss. On the second one, we made it only as far as "outbriefing" at a Florida base, as the Americans were released as President Reagan was inaugurated. Obviously, Iran realized that President Reagan was no one to mess with. Had we gone in the second time, it would have been a very big operation, and I am sure it would have been a disaster for Iran.

The training was conducted mostly in northern Florida and elsewhere. I had a chance to spend time on the ground as we trained at night to prepare for rescue. I traveled around on the night-vision-trained chopper crews and also had a chance to watch ground crews who had no idea what was going on other than, "The sergeant told me to stand here and be ready to refuel a helicopter"—as one of the young refuelers said, "I just stood here in the dark, when suddenly, I hear this 'whop whop,' and damn if a helicopter didn't suddenly land here, without lights" and the old sergeant says, "Go refuel him, soldier, which I do!" Since I had the first pair of night-vision glasses, I let the young refuel put them on, and all he could say was, "Shit, man, mother f—k, I can see in dark!"

The chopper training was impressive but unfortunately, the trained chopper crews were replaced by US Marine Corps Choppers crews on the real mission. I was told that the Marine crews were never told that it would be a real mission before they departed their base for the first rescue! Had they been told, like any other combat organization, they would have prepped their aircraft for combat, had spare parts on board, and the crews would have been highly selected. I don't know where the breakdown was, because the Navy rep, who of course also represented the Marines, was a superb officer. Sometime the Navy plays games, or the Marines Leadership might have played games, but I don't know who was responsible for not telling the Chopper crews that they were going to do the real thing or for using crews that had not trained with the rescue team? I know there was one Marine Colonel who knew it was the real thing as he went along, not as a crew member but an observer, probably illegally.

Later I was told that someone made a decision to make it more inclusive of all military organizations, thus the Marine choppers. Whoever made that decision should have been court-martialed!

The last training mission before we departed for the Middle East was on a Saturday night at Lubbock, Texas, Reese AB. We used, not Marine Choppers, but again Air Force Choppers. Unfortunately, some of our team who were to be on the ground in Iran when the rescue started spent Friday night in a small town southeast of Lubbock. Being especially tough, they got in a confrontation in a bar and were apprehended by local sheriff's deputies and taken to the local jail. I received a call from one of the team's leaders who had not been arrested.

He advised me that some of his "boys" had been arrested in a bar, and he was at the jail trying to get them out, and would I talk to the Sheriff? I asked him to put him on the phone, and I introduced myself, saying "I am speaking for the President of the United States and also, I would have the sheriff of Delaware County, Indiana, call him after I hung up, to verify who I was, as he was my Dad" I also told him "that we need the 'boys' released for a very special mission authorized by the President!"

He said, "I am sorry, but your 'boys' will have to see the judge Monday morning!" Try as I might, I couldn't convince him to release them. The *'boys'* were instrumental to the practice the next night and we needed them! I asked him to put the Sergeant back on the line, and, talking in code, I suggested to him that he get them out any way he could; I believe I said "X-ray" Later, when the Sheriff's guards suddenly fell asleep, the *'boys'* returned to the staging area to prepare for the practice. The Saturday practice went as planned. Unfortunately, we had some deaths during the practice when an OH-58 crashed.

Years later, after I had retired and was attending Texas Tech in an MBA program, I was quail hunting near that town, and it started raining, so we headed for a bar to get lunch. We walked in and saw the local sheriff was also having lunch. I worked up the nerve and finally went to the sheriff's table and asked him how long he had been sheriff; he said for years. I then asked him if he had ever lost some prisoners on a Friday night. He said, "You are the SOB that I talked to; I knew I had heard your voice before." I confirmed that I was the guilty SOB. He then said, "The next night he heard all the radio traffic, and he realized that what I had said was true. Naturally, I said "That I was sorry about what we did." He said, "He was really sorry too and embarrassed about what he did!" We had a good laugh, and I bought his lunch!

As we were preparing for the first Iran rescue of the hostages, we deployed to a former Russia base, we called it Alpha, deep in the desert. It was truly a desert, with lots of sand; however, the living bunkers built and covered in sand maintained a nice, cool temperature for living and sleeping. During our stay at Alpha, our squadron troops, never idle, build a VIP quarters, a small but well-used swimming or soaking pool, and even experienced penetrating an old Russian minefield. Our senior NCOs, I believe under the guidance of Chief Roger Johnson, had built a "flyaway construction kit" that they used to improve facilities wherever we were.

One of the strangest events in preparing for the Iranian rescue concerned an Army surgeon, a Lt.Col. who started shooting his mouth off about he was against war and he wasn't going to operate on anyone. We played a little trick on him, seating him on a folding chair outside the tent where we had the Staff Meetings. The last item on the meeting agenda was discussion of this surgeon. It was loudly stated by the Site Commander that what he was doing was a court-martial offense and the punishment was or could be that he would be shot. Someone who had a .45 automatic pulled it out, slide the slide like he was putting a shell in the chamber, and said, "I'll volunteer to shoot the SOB!"

With that, we heard the folding chair fall to the ground, and we could hear him shouting, as he ran toward his bunker, "I'll operate, I'll operate!" Problem solved!

228

One of our Maintenance officers provided some real excitement after he had a few too many adult beverages and drove his jeep into one of the minefields. Fortunately, he got stuck; he may have fallen asleep in the jeep where he was found. I was called to the site and he, fortunately, when he awoke, remained in the jeep. He then may have been trying to drive the jeep out of the minefield when the tires were shot out by one of our folks, and later proper forces rescued him the next morning. I believe he subsequently made two stars—a lucky guy also!

As I mentioned before, if the US Army Leadership had accepted what President Kennedy wanted long ago, we would have had a Special Ops organization as strong and competent as we have today, which is second to none in the world. I am afraid that the old Army Leadership liked to fight Brigades against Brigades or tanks against tanks, and Special Ops just wants to destroy whatever resistance they find and do it quietly, without making a scene!

As part of the initial Iranian rescue attempt, in spite of all that has been said, I know in my heart that it probably would have succeeded if two things happened:

1. If we had used the chopper we trained with or the Marine Corps had told their helicopters' personnel that they were going on a real combat mission and had prepped the choppers accordingly with spare parts on board. As I said before, I will always feel that at least one Marine Colonel knew what was going on, since he flew along, probably truly unauthorized, to be part of it, and he even wrote a book about it, which none of the rest of us could do because we had signed a Presidential paper saying that we would never talk, write or acknowledge the rescue, which obviously he hadn't signed. Of course, now that requirement is over.

2. At Desert One, a chopper and a C-130 tangled killing some and injuring several others. When the Commander at the crash site, Desert One, advised Washington of the crash, I am told he said we can still go but the mission was aborted at that time. They withdrew and brought out the injured folks for treatment. What probably caused the accident is that a helicopter had a "brown out" of sand and dust restricting his visibility as he lifted off and hit a C-130 on the ground nearby! Just a very unlucky event, but basically the forces were still intact.

At the time of the crash at Desert One, I was at the German air show with an AWACS aircraft as a diversion or to trick the enemy. Previously, President Carter had strangely discontinued the US participating in international air shows. Since it was probably well known by our opposing forces that I was the AWACS Commander involved with the rescue, and since I was at the air show with an AWACS, the bad guys figured that there would not be a rescue attempt at that time. I as a decoy was instructed to "act drunk and bug the Russians" at the cocktail party.

I had experience doing that sort of thing, as I had also done it when I was in the Pentagon. My effort in the Pentagon resulted on one Russian Fighter Pilot being extended in DC because of pictures which were taken of us together, unknown to him, thus embarrassing him with his leadership and making him stay for another year. I avoided him at future parties, having been warned that he was really unhappy with me!

In any case, I suspect our decoy worked, because our forces got in and out without reaction. The Russians would have alerted the Iranians if it appeared that we were launching, and obviously conveyed to the Iranians that our forces would not be going that night, since the AWACS Commander was drunk (not really but acting like it!) at the air show party. In fact, a young Iranian officer at Bandar-e-Abbos did sight us going in, but his higher-ups didn't believe him!

My guys dramatically dragged me out of the party to a waiting car and then to a T-39 that took me back to Desert One, where we had another AWACS cocked and ready to launch. The plan was that we would bring the forces out, but since the Mission had been aborted, we weren't needed, as the forces came out after the accident.

I must mention later during a practice for the second rescue attempt, I finally convinced the General leading the effort to fly on the AWACS during a practice. I had tried very hard to convince him to fly with us during the initial practices for the first rescue, but couldn't convince him and his ground folks that we would really have the big picture. In fact, we probably wouldn't have had it initially. But our AWACS troops learned damn fast, and, after a couple of practice missions, we had the whole picture. After a few practices, we were able to map it out, and it was obvious that the place for the Mission Lead or at least a strong representation from him should be on the AWACS! As the General and I debriefed after the practice was over, I noticed a tear in his eye as he was probably thinking about how he could have controlled things on the first attempt. On the second attempt, I am sure he or someone who had his ear would have been with us, had we gone. Since I was to be the "Air Boss" during the 2nd rescue, I would have had lots of Naval fighter assets for counter air, had there been any!

The Special Ops guys will always be special in my mind because they were very quiet, extremely skilled, and elite warriors who were/are prepared for any challenge. Of course during the actual failed rescue, those "boys" who were arrested that night near Lubbock on the final practice mission, real warriors, were in position ready and prepared to start the rescue. During the after-action debrief, we were fairly confident that we would have rescued all but four of the prisoners. Those four where held elsewhere, unknown to us!

Recently I learned that upon leaving AWACS, a Legion of Merit (LOM) was written and submitted for me. I will put it here, because it best describes what we did in the 963rd AWACS, and I am very proud of what we accomplished, and I had never seen as detailed an LOM and, "to hell with whoever stopped it!" The men of the 963rd deserved to see it, because it clearly documented what they did to develop and enhance the AWACS as a tactical weapons system.

LEGION OF MERIT

Recommend Colonel Barry J. Howard, 511-26-8207FR, for the award of the Legion of Merit. Colonel Howard distinguished himself by exceptionally meritorious conduct in the performance of outstanding services to the United States as Commander, 963rd Airborne Warning and Control Squadron, and Assistant Deputy Commander for Operations, 552nd Airborne Warning and Control Wing, Tinker Air Force Base, Oklahoma, from 6 June 1979 to 19 March 1981. Commanding the largest E-3A operational squadron, Colonel Howard explored new concepts and initiated procedures which gave the Airborne Warning and Control System (AWACS) its first genuine tactical capability. In order to determine what was needed to reach the goal of full tactical versatility, he deployed with AWACS crews to Korea, Egypt, Germany, and Saudi Arabia. The deployment to Korea was directed by the Joint Chiefs of Staff in response to a request by the Korean government following President Park Chung Hee's assassination in October 1979. Colonel Howard commanded this entire

232

tactical operation, code-named Operation Blue Pegasus, from 27 October 1979 to 22 December. The E-3A fully integrated with the Korean Tactical Air Control System and the 6903 Electronic Security Squadron for the first time. Under his guidance, the deployed men and women of the 552nd AWAC Wing flew fifty-four missions and amassed 372 flying hours, providing "deep look" surveillance coverage of Korea and conducting highly classified testing of certain systems. In addition, the E-3A took part in the Korean exercise Cope Jade, which employed naval, ground, and air units, and then in the US/Japanese exercise Cope North, which provided the first E-3A control of Japanese fighters on practice scrambles and intercepts in Japanese airspace. At the conclusion of the deployment, the Korean Air Force Chief of Staff, General Yoon Ja Joong, presented Colonel Howard a plaque that commended him and his personnel for once again demonstrating a "quick reaction and deployment capability" in time of a national crisis. The Chief of Staff, United States Air Force, General Lew Allen, sent a message to the 552nd AWAC Wing Commander which read, "The Air Force effort during the E-3A deployed to Korea was outstanding. Our capability to respond rapidly and to sustain operations provided a highly visible demonstration of support for an important ally during a critical period. Results of this kind can only be achieved with an extremely dedicated and professional team." A few months later, in February 1980, the E-3A was again deployed to serve national interests, this time to Egypt. He greatly improved the living conditions at the bare-essential base in the desert by bringing in lumber and tools, a portable swimming pool, and washing machines. Morale shot upward spectacularly. In December 1980, Colonel Howard led crews on another

JCS-directed emergency deployment to Germany, which was caused by unrest and tension in Poland. He directed AWACS efforts during the difficult first three weeks and met all the demanding and varied USAFE and NATO mission requirements. Later in the month, he deployed with the E-3A crews to Saudi Arabia as commander and established operational procedures which made the airspace in Southwest Asia secure and safe for US and Saudi forces. In addition to his active involvement in numerous overseas deployments, Colonel Howard took charge of the 552nd AWAC Wing's participation in Sentinel Sward, an extremely sensitive inter-service operation directed by the National Command Authorities and supervised by the Joint Chiefs of Staff. He spearheaded the handpicked team, which developed, tested, and refined the procedures to make AWACS an integral part of this unique undertaking in projecting airpower throughout the free world. He made numerous contributions at Tinker AFB. He established the satellite communications requirement for the #-3A. This capability was a vital element of the success of the mission in Saudi Arabia. He created a functional deployment checklist for the 552nd AWAC Wing Commander and his staff. This checklist addressed all personnel and equipment areas affected by a sudden mobilization and lists both mission essential and "nice to have" items. He originated and developed the procedures for having instructor personnel assigned to an operational squadron, thus getting E-3A aircrews fully qualified and operational ready in a significantly more timely manner. The professional competence, exemplary leadership, and devotion to duty displayed by Colonel Howard reflect great credit upon himself and the United States Air Force.

I may not have deserved it, but our troops in the 963rd AWACS sure as hell did! They rebuilt a magnificent strategic war fighting tool into a tactical fighting tool (*truly a force multiplier*) that could function and control the tactical air war and while even provide significant and extremely useful intelligence to our ground forces. Hopefully, the career fields of the AWACS officers are now receiving proper promotions and status as they are real warriors who give our forces the edge!

314th AIR DIVISION, OSAN, KOREA, 3/1981-3/1982

Gen. "Fat Fred" Haeffner made it possible for me to become his 314th Air Division Director of Operations (DO) after my AWACS tour. He had a big project to complete: building the prototype TACC (Tactical Air Control Center) on Osan AB, Korea. I suppose he thought I could help, since in the past I was able to get many projects done that he knew about. The truth be known, he had the right guy to make it happen perfectly: my Deputy, Col. Chuck Link. I simply stayed out of Chuck's way. If I have a strength or skill, it is that I know how to use folks or just stay out of their way as they make things happen. I simply run a bit of interference for them. Chuck didn't need any help! Throughout my career, I have helped, recruited, or stole talented personnel to, I think, make the Air Force a better place or get the job done better. Sometime later, Chuck replaced me as Wing Commander at Osan on his way to two stars—a very talented guy, but that is another story!

My year as the 314th DO was challenging, fun and a some-what relaxing period of my career. The big effort was training and preparing for "Team Spirit" a multi-National exercise which I, along with the 5th Air Force Commander ran, really I did, but General Donnelly kept a close eye on me! One of my big challenges was to select the best Korea barber reviewing all the barbers at the various bases. That was really tough duty, because most of them were the local beautiful ladies and most eventually married a military person. However, it meant that I had to have several haircuts and the associated massages. I drew the line at manicures, not my thing and pedicures were out of the question.

While I was the 314th DO, I had the honor of flying with the Koreans in their F-5s which I had also flown at Willie AFB, AZ. Once again the time I spent at Willie flying on the "edge" or near zero airspeed paid off and the young Korean pilots were amazed at me "whipping" them in the air. After a flight they always asked me, "When I had flown in the Korean War and how many MIGs (Russian fighters flown in North Korea) did I get?" I would quickly explain that I was in school (Naval Academy) during the Korean War. What was bad is that I couldn't adequately explain to them what I did in the air. Like many other pilots they were taught to avoid the "edge" or zero airspeed because their instructors didn't teach it and also were very wary of it. As a result, I usually had the opportunity to either simulate "killing" them either with the gun or Aim-9 missiles. Our young training instructor pilots today know how to explain what I did but being of the old school; I just did it automatically and really couldn't explain it. The Korean government was kind enough to give me Korean pilot wings which I proudly wear.

YOKOTA AB, JAPAN, 3/1982-10/1983

As the 314th DO, having been the Director of Operations for the yearly exercise in Korea, "Team Spirit," I assume I impressed Gen. Chuck Donnelly since he actually commanded the exercise and we sat side by side in the Command Post as the exercise progressed. After the exercise, in March of 1983, I was selected as the 475th Air Base Wing Commander at Yokota AB, Japan, after Yokota had busted their ORI inspection. Gen. Donnelly also had his Headquarters at Yokota AB and he really welcomed me with open arms. I arrived at Yokota AB as the new Air Base Wing Commander and with Dorlyne as the First Lady. Taking command at Yokota, I gave my introduction speech in Japanese—really bad Japanese, but was it a hit with the Japanese! I was told that I was the only American to ever do that.

Because I was the son of an agent of the FBI, which most Japanese greatly respected, I was invited to be a judge at various police-type events like judo and competitive shooting events. At the same time, Dorlyne led a group call the Tanabata Dancers, who eventually won the national Folk-dancing Championship and she was presented their trophy by then Prime Minister Nakasone.

I was given some unusual challenges at Yokota. First, Yokota had been a "homesteading base" where personnel extended and extended; some had been there over twenty years. I had to stop the extensions. Next, I was to fire the Hospital Commander for "alleged" misconduct. And finally, Yokota had failed their Operational Readiness Inspection (ORI), thus another, and probably the most important, task I was given was to pass the next Inspection.

I was at Yokota for only about twenty months, but we did pass our next inspection with flying colors. As I prepared to retrain the wing to pass the ORI, late the second Friday afternoon I was at Yokota, I received a call that someone was going to suicide off one of our high-rise apartment buildings next to the Enlisted Club. I jumped into my staff car and drove to the building. I ran into the lobby, where one of our Air Policemen told me I was at the right place. I tried the elevators, but they all were stopped someplace, so I ran up the stairs. What a dumb decision—twelve floors I had to run up! When I got to the top, I found the Catholic Chaplain trying to breathe and talk to me—we were both panting like horses that had just run a race, having both run up two different flights of twelve sets of stairs! He explained that it was a wife whose husband was in the club with a "girlfriend," and she was going to jump on them when they came out, since his vehicle was parked in front of the apartment building. After I caught my breath, I eased out to where she was standing and began talking to her. I remember telling her that I had just taken command of Yokota two weeks ago, and I needed her help. That sort of stopped her a bit, and it gave me a chance to grab her and hold her until the Chaplain helped me drag her in. Nothing like a fast start!

The next day we had a fire in one of our row apartments. I rushed to the fire and quickly noticed that the Fire Chief was totally panicked and frozen, not leading the fire-fighting team.

Fortunately, a very sharp enlisted black Sergeant had taken charge and prevented the fire from spreading down the entire row of apartments.

The Fire Department under the Base Engineering Department which at Yokota was probably the best Engineering Department in the Air Force with Norm Sapiro and Joe Honma. These two civilians worked for Maj. Brian Lee and, earlier, Lt. Col. Joe Hicks, a grounded pilot, and both were superb engineers. What was unique about those two civilians, Norm and Joe, was that when they arrived at Yokota, within days after World War II had ended, they quickly established an Engineering College that was also fully certified and accredited. They then trained many of the Japanese future civilian leaders as engineers, and several rose to the top of the Japanese civilian leadership. The Prime Minister, Nakasone, who was in office when I arrived at Yokota, had graduated from their school.

I talked to the three of them—Norm, Joe, and Maj. Lee—and said I wanted the Fire Chief removed. They said they would convince him to return to the States voluntarily and to retire, which he did. We were also able to get the Sergeant who took charge a medal and later a promotion.

Shortly after I arrived at Yokota, we also had some VIP visitors arrive who we took out to a unique Japanese restaurant, which had a stream running through it. A lovely Japanese lady would sit by the stream, catch a trout swimming by with her hand, and filet it for Japanese-type snacks for our visitors. They had a wonderful time, and, as we returned to the base, which was probably an hour away, they just raved about the meal and the beauty of the place. As we neared the base, we passed by one of the runway approach areas and lighting system.

I need to digress a bit here: occasionally we had acts of attacks on the base by those Japanese elements that were anti-American. I had met with the local police forces, and they had promised me that they would have our base surrounded within minutes should any of the anti-base groups cause trouble.

As we approached the base, I saw a bomb go off in our approach lights area. I asked the driver to stop the our small bus and told my staff members to generate our security forces and ask them to call the local Japanese police forces. I went to the bomb area and extinguished the small fire caused by the bomb using my big feet! My status with the Japanese Police went up tremendously, standing there at the bomb-site when their security forces arrived! Once again *lucky*!

Yokota had many problems and shortly after that, my wife Dorlyne, who had worked for H&R Block Tax Company several times and was a very good accountant, found that there was considerable embezzlement going on within the Enlisted Wives Club. The Club over the years had amassed considerable amounts of money that they had earned through various social events held on the base, especially the Fourth of July event, which many of the local Japanese attended. Eventually several of the ladies were convicted and might have done some time in prison?

While there, the superb leadership of our Engineering folks designed and built, and we brought it on line, a very "green" system of burning our trash to provide power for the base, and it produced no undesirable fumes or discharges. This was started in 1981 and on line by 1983! I suspect that it was one of the first for our nation, in a foreign country. We knew it worked perfectly because the Japanese government, which can be extremely demanding, was thrilled with it, and none of our neighbors complained! Of course Norm and Joe, sly guys that they were, remained constantly in touch with the various Japanese agencies that regulated or oversaw such projects—and oh, by the way, the projects were led by their former students! Many of the Inspectors sent by the Japanese Government had also been their students, so we not only got accolades but also lots of free technical advice!

Our base was divided up like a pie among seven different Japanese protectorates, like our counties in the US. They received payments from the US for their piece of the pie, so they had an influence on our efforts. The Japanese were very sensitive to fumes or discharges and they were extremely happy with our incinerator because our engineers took them on tours as the facility was being built and when it was finished.

One day I received a call from Gen. Donnelly's office telling me that he wanted to see me, which was unusual, since I was with him a lot, and we frequently had sessions at his house with vodka tonics. When I arrived, he had an aerial picture of our golf course, Tama Hills, best in the Air Force and the entire plot of land surrounding the golf course. During WW II it was a Japanese munitions storage area, and there were many concrete bunkers and a large German-built hotel-type building, and it was just a very beautiful area. When I had toured it when I first arrived at Yokota, I thought it could be made into a wonderful recreational area, but I had to pass an Inspection first. The General said, "Barry, do you think we could build a recreation area at Tama Hills like the military one in Garmisch, Germany?" He added that many troops in the Pacific were on short tours, and they were allowed an extended leave during their tour. If we had a recreational area here, they could bring their families over and enjoy the Orient. Naturally I agreed, and we decided that we would try to build it. He promised some financial assistance, and I said "I'll bet I can get volunteers too to help, and of course Harry Glaze's Red Horse, a group of combat engineers who can do damn near anything and most of it is legal!" which caused the General to say, "Hell, I hadn't thought about Frack and his boys! Do it!"

I got Norm Sapiro, Joe Honma, and Maj. Lee together after the meeting to develop our plan to build a recreation area for the

Pacific. Near Yokota was an Army storage area at Camp Zama with lots of useful goodies in it that could be requisitioned at no cost. Part of the plan we developed was for the engineers to loot the site. We decided to purchase some small, Japanese-built, self-contained cabins, which were really well designed and constructed, for our visiting families. Of course the German-built hotel needed tons of work, and the dining area was large, so we decided that we needed someone talented from MWR (Morale, Welfare and Recreation) to participate in our project. We found just the person who knew how to get things done—actually, too well, as I will later discuss!

We were off and running, buying, borrowing, occasionally stealing, building, and steering volunteers to help clean-up and build in less than two years a first-class recreation area. Our volunteers became totally enmeshed in the project, and the more we did, the more they wanted to do. Their suggestions really added to the facility. We built a first-class restaurant in the hotel, rehabbed the rooms, and installed several Japanese-built cabins. Red Horse rebuilt one of the big former Japanese bomb bunkers into a facility that would sleep and house a fairly large organization for a party. They also installed a hot tub that we found at Camp Zama, Japan. We added a small exchange in a building that we rehabbed, and the tennis courts, which the PACAF (Pacific Air Forces) Commander formally opened, as he was a tennis player. The courts were also named after him—lots of points there!

We elected a pretty young daughter of one of our Air Force personnel as Queen of Tama Hills Recreational Area for the grand opening. We had lots of support from the Japanese, as they could see that it would bring tourists to Japan. We slowly developed transportation for our visitors based on what they wanted to do while there. We did it all in about seventeen months, and since the PACAF Commander participated in opening some of the facility, we didn't have anyone challenging what we were doing, thank goodness! Finally, when Gen. Donnelly officially opened the Tama Hills Recreation Area with our pretty young Queen, we all were very proud.

I, of course, sweated out for many years the fact that we may have stretched some or many regulations to accomplish the project. I was very happy when seven years had passed after we built Tama Hills, since I was told then that the statute of limitation was seven years.

Unfortunately, we had one serious loss during the period of construction and building. The very talented young Sergeant from MWR who had built a truly five-star restaurant and hotel was caught transporting several cases of Black Label Scotch into town—obviously, for the black market. Our Military Court system found him guilty, and we lost him. He was so talented. He came to my office after his conviction and apologized for what he did, and we were both almost in tears, because he was so good at developing the facility, ingenious at obtaining equipment, and creative. Losing him was truly a loss to the Air Force, Yokota, MWR, and especially me, because he was able to make lemonade out of virtually nothing. The Japanese black market is so lucrative that many have crossed the line, unfortunately!

An interesting event occurred at Christmastime! It was traditional that I, as the Wing Commander, present a gift to the leader of each of the seven Japanese protectorates Leaders, normally a bottle of Black Label Scotch. One of the protectorates was very strongly led by an anti-US socialist or possibly communist, and each Christmas he made the presentation a very unhappy and disruptive event. He would have media, mostly anti-US, and others present when the Yokota Commander made his annual presentation. My driver, and elderly but very astute Japanese, and our interpreter, Tsumoto-san, had an idea! He suggested that my very attractive wife, Dorlyne, deliver the gift, since I was "sick."

The Japanese men are very considerate of American women, especially good-looking ones with a fine figure, such as Dorlyne. What a coup!

The socialist leader had many Japanese media there ready for an incident. He was absolutely taken back and the distasteful scene that usually happened became a very positive event. I got a lot of credit, but it should go to Mr. Tsumoto-san and my wife Dorlyne, who handled it so well and had the gentleman eating out of her hand! All the while the assembled media looked on! What a great job she did! And I don't think he ever gave us trouble again!

I did have another call from Col. Brian Shimomura (the top cop) one early morning saying, "I have called the bomb squad; they should be here in six hours; but we have a bomb!" I naturally asked him where and said I would meet him there immediately; it was about 0710 on a workday. I arrived at the scene, which just happened to be the main street into Yokota, with the traffic backed up and out the entrance gate of the base. The procedure when a bomb is found, which we rapidly changed, was to place the bomb as far away from the nearest buildings, which just happened to be the center of the main street. Brian explained that a young troubled airman had set the bomb, they had found "nunchucks" and other unauthorized items in his room, and he was under arrest. He later was quickly discharged, that day, and put on a "big bird" back to the States. As I escorted him to the "big bird," he was given a "nite-nite" shot and slept all the way to San Francisco, where a deputy sheriff awoke him.

Anyhow, we had a bomb in the street, and traffic backed up outside the main gate and tying-up the local Japanese traffic. The bomb squad would not be there for several hours. I looked at the bomb and saw the wires attached to it. Brian had a set of dikes, which I took from him, and I walked to the bomb. As

I got there, I said to myself, "This is the dumbest thing I have ever done, but once there I have to do something, like cut the wires!"

I remembered the "red wire" is normally the hot one, so with great misgivings, I cut the red wire—and nothing happened! I then cut the rest of them, picked up the bomb, and opened the road to traffic—talk about dumb. The bomb looked like sticks of dynamite, but once we took it apart, it was D-cell batteries wrapped in aluminum foil. The young man who caused this trouble departed the base that afternoon discharged from the Air Force. Some folks started calling me "Col. Red Wire"! Dumb, really dumb fighter pilot, but really *lucky*!

We planned a big Dining-Out and we invited my old Boss, Maj. Gen. Willie P. McBride, retired, as our speaker. Gen. McBride was on the way through Korea to Japan but had a personal problem and couldn't make it. Since I used to write many of his speeches, I just put another one together, and I was introduced as a "stand-in" for the missing Gen. McBride.

A very funny event occurred as we sat down for the dinner; I noticed our Top Cop, Col. Brian Shimomura standing in the doorway where one would enter the dining room. It was obvious that he needed to talk to me, so I beckoned him up to the speakers' table. Dorlyne had established on base a house where family members could temporarily live should they be threatened by their spouse. Because it was normally the man beating the wife or children, the "House" was primarily set-up for women and children. The House was scheduled to be opened the next day by Gen. McBride. Brian said, "Sir, we need to open the new House; we have a spousal serious beating with broken arm! I leaned over to Dorlyne and told her we had a lady to enter into the new house, as her husband had hurt her. Brian said, "No, it is a husband who has been beaten by his wife and she had broken his arm!"

I couldn't pass up the chance and relayed the incident to the members of the Wing at the Dining-Out and they all roared, as no one expected a husband to ever be in the "Half-way House"!

One of my major challenges at Yokota was regarding the Hospital Commander which my Wing Senior NCO, the Chief, helped me solve. As I mentioned earlier, it wasn't the Hospital Commander at fault: it was his Administrative Officer who was defrauding the Air Force and starting rumors accusing the Commander of various things to cover the Administrative Officer's series of serious misconducts. An example was one of the Administrative Officer's adult children had an illegitimate child who was regularly treated at the military hospital, without paying. I was able to convince the 5th Air Force Commander, Gen. Donnelly that it was the hospital Administrator at fault, and he was handled properly. The Hospital Commander continued his good work and leadership of the hospital.

Dorlyne and I were honored with an invitation to visit the Imperial Palace to view the Cherry Blossoms with our Interpreter Tsumoto-san. It was extremely beautiful, and the Cherry Blossom trees in Washington, DC, are said to be associated with or from the Imperial Palace.

Dorlyne had many challenges at Yokota. One of them was to lead a group called the Tanabada Dancers, consisting of volunteer American men and women (mostly women) along with actual Japanese who were family members of Yokota military personal. Dorlyne had a lot to learn in short order, but she mastered the task quickly. The first festival at which the Dancers performed was held in July 1982, after we arrived in late March 1982.

The Tanabata Dancers were formed in 1973 to promote goodwill and friendship with the Japanese by learning traditional dances and joining in festivities. The name *Tanabata* means "Evening of the Seventh Star" and the annual Star Festivals are celebrated between July seventh and August seventh throughout

Japan. Our dancers were provided a Japanese teacher or Sensei (Japanese teacher) who travelled to Yokota every Thursday evening to teach the dances.

To carry out our patriotic theme, the summer kimonos, called *Yukata* had a white background with blue cranes and a red *obi* or sash. Cranes are a sign of good luck, and Dorlyne said, "That she needed all the luck that could be mustered," but, true to form, she did learn the dances quickly. As she said, "Thank goodness we wore the flat-soled slippers, but most of our Japanese women wore the traditional slippers with two thin pieces of wood on the soles. Our dancers also wore tabbies, which are Japanese socks that can be worn with or without slippers." As Dorlyne said, "They were hard to get used to as they are split at the big toe and were quite slippery! We had the traditional music recorded and we practiced and practiced with a great deal of concentration and fun."

One of the most beautiful and well-known dances is called *Tanko-Bushi*, which means "the Coal Miner's Dance." Our group got that down to perfection. At festival time, our group danced in all the surrounding prefectures, and always received lots of oohs and ahs!

We were entered into many contests. We were in competition with native Japanese who had been doing these dances for most of their lives. And when the music started, they knew all the steps and movements. As Dorlyne said, "Our Sensi danced in the front row, so we could follow her and try to imitate her." As festivals rapidly advanced, our group got propelled to a competition for our area, which they won which meant that they would compete on National TV!

As I escorted Dorlyne and the dancers to the TV competition at the TV studio, I asked Dorlyne, "Where are your fancy clothes?" I knew or felt sure that her Yokota dancers would win, and Prime Minister Nakasone was to present the award. Dorlyne was in

Levis and a sweater with her costume only to wear dancing. She assured me that, while they were really good, but because they were mostly "gugines" or foreigners, they would not win. When the judges announced the Yokota team as the winner, she panicked a bit and asked me what she could do in her Levis and sweater. I simply said, "Wear your beautiful red, white, and blue costume, the summer white kimono with the blue cranes and red obi." She quickly changed and proudly, on Japanese National TV, received the trophy from the Prime Minister! How proud they all were and I was for them!

As the "make-up" ORI began, our troops were ready, and we were watering their eyes with our performance. Suddenly, I received another call from Gen. Donnelly! As I walked into his office, someone on his staff said, "You'll like this visit," which I really did! I was to Command the 51st TAC Fighter Wing, Osan, Korea but at the same time I would continue to Command Yokota until after the ORI!

My next challenge was truly a dream come true but fortunately I was working so hard with our ORI at Yokota and then with the new challenge of Osan, Korea. As a result, I didn't get to enjoy it as much as I would have wanted. Commanding two wings for a couple of weeks meant little sleep, lots of travel by F-4 or T-39 and two entirely different Command attitudes. However, it was, for me, a dream come true and I am glad I was busy or I would have probably just gone around smiling and laughing. Thanks to the Chiefs of Osan, my fondest dream came true.

51st TAC FIGHTER WING, OSAN AFB, KOREA, 10/1983-7/1984

I really thought I had died and gone to Heaven when I commanded the 311ᵗʰ Tactical Fighter Training Squadron at Luke AFB, but when Gen. Donnelly told me in September of 1983 that I was going to Command the famous 51ˢᵗ Tactical Fighter Wing, Osan AB, Korea, I *knew* I was in Heaven! Osan AB, Korea, was truly the tip of the spear facing North Korea, *which was run by crazy Kim*!

Again, my predecessor at Osan had been relieved, somewhat foolishly I believe, but I was thrilled to get the Command! Even with the hitch that I had to finish the ORI at Yokota AB, Japan before I gave up that Command of Yokota! I think I had both jobs for about two or three weeks. It was a bit challenging, flying back and forth daily, either in an F-4 or a T-39.

Osan, unlike Yokota, was in great good shape morale-wise, because it had a real and visible mission, most assigned there were only there for one or two years, and the North Koreans made enough trouble that our folks were primed for combat, should it come. Since I had been at Osan as the 314th Air Division DO and before that as the AWACS Commander after the assassination of President Pak, I knew most of the senior Korean Military who, of course, at that time, had great influence on the South Korean Government. Especially the Korean Air Force Chief of Staff, Gen. Kim. Later we even hunted pheasants together on Chen Shui Do Island with the PACAF Air Force Commander.

Immediately after arriving from Japan, what we called the *Korean Mafia* (a group of Korean civilians closely associated with the base and extremely beneficial to the base and our mission) took me pheasant hunting west of the base, since they knew how I loved to hunt and it was pheasant season. There were three to four inches of snow on the ground, and I saw some very strange tracks in the snow. Returning from the hunt, I called my Chief Cop and I believe the Office of Special Investigations (OSI) together and briefed them on the tracks I saw. Early in South Korea's development as a nation, most South Koreans wore flip-flops made from cut up old auto tires and in the winter with "tabbies," but by this time, their industry was making modern flip-flops and no one wore the old ones made from auto tires. However, there were tracks in the field that we hunted indicating that someone was wearing the old style flip-flops—strange? My guys went out there, but reported back that they didn't find anything; I told them that I would call in the South Korean KCIA (like our CIA) because I knew there was something wrong out there. Again my guys said, "No, Sir, there is nothing out there!"

I subsequently called my Korean friend who was the head of the KCIA, another Gen. Kim, and, before telling him what I was calling about, I extracted from him if he found anything, I would be part of the interrogation! Of course he agreed. A few days later, he called me back and told me they had found a North Korean in a "spider hole" who had been there about six months recording Udorn's aircraft activities. We had a U-2 detachment,

F-4s, OV-10s, an F-15 detachment from Kadina on alert, and an occasional SR-71. I remind him of his promise that I could in on the interrogation and of course he said I would be there. A few hours later, he again called and said the North Korean had died in an auto accident in route to Seoul!

You bet he did! However, I was very proud of my sighting, and I think it impressed my law-enforcement folks that the old Colonel had a sharp eye (eyes of an eagle)!

My cousin Karen, her husband, Federal Judge John Conway, and his mother traveled to Osan after visiting us in Japan for a short stay in Korea. They really thought I was important to command two locations simultaneously; little did they know that I was merely an available colonel, who was actually a proven good Commander! I was later told by someone who should know, that the senior NCOs of Osan when asked, "Who should be the new Commander of Osan?" said that it should be me! If this is true, it made me damn proud! But I'll never know because I never asked General Donnelly.

Once I was fully operating only at Osan, free from Yokota where we had proudly passed our ORI, and my cousin and her family had returned to the US; I scheduled myself to Davis Monthan (DM) AFB, Arizona, to get an A-10 *quickie* checkout. This was because I had a squadron of A-10s at Suwon AB, Korea, north of Osan. DM provided me a very short checkout, and they had aircraft without the computer navigational system, unlike Suwon's newer aircraft, which had a computer navigational system. Since I had been at Luke AFB, it was pretty easy to know the training areas at DM. However, I did need to know how to use the computer navigation system for Korea. When I got back to Osan, I spent some time with the A-10s that were located at Suwon. The A-10 is the perfect aircraft for old Colonels, big cockpit, good air-conditioner, plenty of gas (seldom have we had a fighter with plenty of gas), and very easy to fly. I did make sure I always had a "seeing eye" Lieutenant who would help me start up the computer system.

On our normal A-10 training missions, we would go to the tactical range with real bombs, connect with a tanker (just getting hookups but no gas was transferred), go to the training range with twenty-five pound practice bombs and the .30 mm gun and then to the DMZ to work with a FAC. My "seeing eye" computer Lieutenant would give me a point to update the computer by flying over it and, then, I was just like the smart kids with an updated computer!

The gun in the A-10 fires very slowly compared to the F-4, and I seldom would fire more than fifty rounds. At that time, you needed to fire one hundred rounds to qualify, *but* of the fifty or so I fired, every one of them hit the target! As I noted earlier, we changed the qualification requirements to an average of number of hits versus rounds fired, making it more realistic and saving money!

The A-10 has proven to be a great support aircraft for the Army. Some in the Air Force, like my good friend "Mr. Earl," Col. Earl Haney (Retired), don't like the A-10 for various reasons, primarily for not meeting design specifications. But as always, the troops who fly a weapons system always make it work and work well in spite of its short comings. As I noted earlier, I managed the A-10 development program when I was in the Pentagon and also when I was at Tactical Air Command Headquarters. To set the record straight, I need to mention the major A-10 deficiency: being terribly underpowered, thus it must normally operate at near 100 percent in combat: loss of an engine on take-off or with a full combat load might cause the loss of the aircraft. However, as always, the fighter pilots will make it work, and they did. In the A-10 we may have had losses that we shouldn't have had because of being underpowered! I must say, I loved to fly it because, in spite of its short comings, I knew, I and others could successfully operate with it in combat and it really felt like a warrior's airplane!

Since we had the relatively new weapons system, the A-10, in the wing at Suwon AB. But we seemed to be forgotten regarding spare parts for the A-10 aircraft. Our "in commission" rate was horrible. Having the best aircraft Maintenance Officer in the Air Force, Kevin Kelly, I asked him what we could do to improve our parts supply. He suggested that we bring the person responsible for supplying our parts, or the PIM, over for a visit and turn her over to the troops and the ladies, his wife Ko and Dorlyne, for some shopping, as Christmas was approaching.

We obtained a ticket for the lady who managed the A-10 parts in California to come to Osan. Kevin and I met her (truly a little old lady in tennis shoes), at the airplane. Later, after we briefed her on our needs, Kevin's wife, Ko, and Dorlyne immediately took her shopping to Etaiwan (Itawan) area, in Seoul or in the local town, Song Tong Shi, outside our base. We also wined and dined her with some of the maintenance troops who weren't shy about complaining about the lack of parts.

After she returned to California, our "in commission" rate went from last in the Air Force to first and remained there for some time! Kevin Kelly was the best there was—too bad the Air Force didn't make him a general, because he was truly a problem solver!

At Osan I was blessed with a superb staff, including a Catholic Chaplain who was probably my final advisor for tough or "sticky" problems. Lt. Col. Julie, now was married to a former Tech Rep and a great guy, was my PR lady. Julie had been passed over for her next promotion by what appeared to be an OER by an officer who obviously was anti-women. We were able to correct that with an excellent 5th Air Force Commander's endorsement, and Julie subsequently got promoted. She, along with the Chaplain became my deepest brain trust, although I had other top notch folks on the staff including the DO, Bob Nesbit, and a very special the Chief of Maintenance, Kevin Kelly.

Osan, being near Seoul, and also, actually, the small town outside the base, which we called "Song Tong Shi," had wonderful shopping; consequently, we had many visitors and many were VIPs. Song Tong Shi was run by what we referred to as the *Korean Mafia* who were true friends of the base and always responded to any request I made of them. Through Dorlyne's efforts, the Mafia started including their wives in social events too! Truly a major advancement in Korean society!

One of our regular visitors was the Navy's first Vietnam Ace (An Ace has five airborne enemy aircraft kills), Randy "Duke" Cunningham, who really treated Dorlyne and Suzi Glaze wonderfully, always arriving with presents for them from his travels. I think he even spent a night or two at our home during his frequent visits. Duke was a real fighter pilot, but I had trouble liking him, and I really don't know why—hell, maybe even jealousy? Duke, after the Navy, was elected to the US House of Representatives from California. Sadly, Duke was convicted of accepting bribes and has just been recently released from jail. What a waste!

We were blessed at Osan to have a Red Horse team assigned and run by my friend and a true warrior, Col. Harry Glaze, a former University of Arkansas football tackle. Harry and his wife Suzi were our next-door neighbors twice at Osan. He and his Red Horse were capable of getting any engineering job done, hopefully legally, but they would get it done, whatever it took! Talk about two peas in a pod—Harry and Barry, who thought alike! We knew that Gen. Donnelly really knew and believed in us, because he named us "Frick and Frack!"

We knew the Russians were experimenting with developing a capability of replacing bomb-damaged runways with premolded blocks of concrete. Harry and his Red Horse established and developed a simple and functioning system to build pre-molded blocks for runway repair and we tested the blocks a bit at Osan. Unfortunately, the Air Force foolishly didn't go along with Harry and his troops who could do anything, and most of it was legal!

The wives of Osan were up in arms about the water system at Osan, as they had run out of water the previous winter. As I arrived as the new Wing Commander, my first visitors were a group of women wearing their grease-stained winter coats who were concerned about making sure we had water the next winter. Thus, when I took Command of the Wing, one of my first questions during my first staff meeting was, "How is the drilling of the new wells coming?"

"Right on schedule," the Base Engineer said. I should have expanded the question more, but each weekly staff meeting I asked the same question and reminded the Engineer that we must have the new wells operating before winter, "Which sometimes comes early to Osan!" If the new wells weren't on-line, we would again be out of water, and Air Force wives can be really tough and mean without water. As freezing weather set in, suddenly the Base Engineer said, "We won't have the new wells on line until next spring!"

"That is unacceptable!" I believe I raised my voice or at least my secretary, Jo Adkins, Gonzo Atkin's wife said it was the loudest she had ever heard from me. The answer I was given was that the wells were working, but because of the early freeze, they hadn't been connected to the water system, and it couldn't be done until spring. I removed the Base Engineer shortly afterward, and he is the only person I ever relieved in my Air Force career. I think he was really happy to be relieved, as he had never been active as field engineer and always had been a desk jockey. That evening, after the staff meeting, I convened a meeting with the Assistant Engineer, also Maj. Lee, and some of his lieutenants in my office. I asked them if they knew what an "Invasion Line"

was, and the Asst. Eng. did know what it was, but he said we had no way to connect the wells to the line.

Knowing that I was going to call on the Red Horse, I had brought a case of beer to the meeting, and quickly called Col. Harry Glaze at about 1630 and told him our problem. He was there before I finished my first beer and came to the meeting with a couple of Red Horse senior sergeants.

By 10:00 p.m. that night Red Horse had solved the problem with the wells on line and operating. They simply, using the quick-drying and extremely strong runway repair patching material, built a housing that connected the "invasion line" to the wells and then to the water system! I have always loved Red Horse, and now more than ever!

Of course with Red Horse, you had to be prepared to come to their aid as they did for you. Harry and his troops had built a "training room"; really a bar for after-hours relaxing for the troops. It had been identified by a previous inspection to be removed, since the inspectors thought that it was illegal—for shame, Harry!

The 51st Wing commander to the rescue! I started having wing training sessions in the "training room" during the day, as at Osan we had very limited training space. Of course, with the cheap Korean help, after the training sessions, it reverted to the Red Horse party room. Gen. Donnelly and I had several adult beverages during his frequent visits to Osan as the months passed. It was not mentioned again in the next ORI!

For future Air Force officers: *Red Horse is a very special asset and a unique outfit that should be encouraged and protected, because they will always get the job done. Usually it will be done legally, but it* will *be done!*

I had asked the 51st Wing DO, Bob Nesbit, known as "Coltong," or in Hangul (Korean), "Bald-Headed Bastard" to develop a simulated combat exercise on the base for the families to view. The exercise would include actual attacks on the runway using our aircraft, but, of course, only simulating dropping bombs. We would also have a demonstration of rescue operations with our Jolly Green (helicopters) detachment. Of course, my staff and I trusted them too much to show good judgment—another lesson learned! They damn near burned up the field with their actions! *But* they put on a show that the families really liked, especially the kids.

I know the Wing Commander (*me!*) was nervous that the results of the exercise would get to higher headquarters. I was especially concerned about the new 314th commander, located at Osan, a Major Gen. "Buck" Rogers, who didn't appear to be a warrior. The only questions he ever asked me were about personal conveniences such as ginger snaps in the commissary or when his new freezer was coming in—never aircraft in commission rates or combat capabilities.

During our important Operational Readiness Inspection (ORI), Kevin Kelly's troops watered the eyes of the inspectors, as did most of the folks in the Wing. I will admit I was a bit unhappy with some of the comments during the ORI "out-briefing" by the Inspectors because real warriors know and believe that they are the best and need to be told so. I will admit, from the Inspectors' view, I was wrong, but our troops were always my concern, and I needed to say what I said—but it may have cost me!

One of the fun things that happened during the ORI was the Inspectors had me killed, and they loaded me into a body bag. The Inspectors said, "I was too strong and too much involved in running the wing!" **JUST WHAT YOU NEED, PEACETIME THINKING INSPECTORS!**

While they hauled me out of the Command Post in the body bag, I received a panic call from Base Ops Senior Sergeant asking me to "Please come to Base Ops." So, even though I was considered dead, I headed for Base Ops. There I found an angry Navy two Star Admiral. He said something to the effect of "I expected better treatment based on my rank here at Osan." I immediately said, "Admiral, I agree; I am a Naval Academy graduate, and I am sorry. However, if I could explain some of our problems, you might understand why? See those flashing lights down south of the field, which is a U-2 with a wing ripped off? Looking the other way, see that bird on final, notice the crash crews and fire trucks lining the runway? It is an SR-71 on an emergency divert with an engine failure. Finally, our ORI Inspectors just killed me probably because I was too strong a Commander, and I was hauled out in a body bag."

The Admiral quickly said, "Colonel, did you get my name?" I said, "No, Sir, I am sorry!" He then said, "Good; forget I ever talked to you, and I will get the hell out of your way, and good luck, Colonel, you have your plate full!"

Our troops did very well during the ORI, but the Inspectors' wording to our troops really disappointed me. When you have an large organization of combat-ready troops who are leaning forward and ready for any challenge from the enemy, you don't say to them, they look pretty good," you say something like, "It is obvious that you are ready for any challenge, and you will defeat it; we are proud of your readiness!" And then the Inspectors could say something like, "However if you did such and such you might get even better results." My attack on the Inspectors probably cost me for a promotion but you don't fool around with Combat Ready Troops!

Our 5th Air Force Commander loved to come to Osan, because our troops were so serious, dedicated, and true warriors. One time when he visited, he had dinner with Dorlyne and me in our apartment (around 1300 square feet). As I was taking him to his quarters, it was snowing, with about two to three inches on the ground. I suggested that we visit a couple of our guards located around the field. These troops were armed and ready for any-thing. We arrived at a young troop guarding the perimeter at his station on the southwestern side of the base. We found him standing in the snow with blowing snow swirling around him. He was a shining professional, dedicated, and, before we left, his obvious warrior-like attention to his duty had Gen. Donnelly in tears of pride. Afterwards, I heard Gen. Donnelly refer to that night in a couple of speeches and again, his eyes always welled up with pride—mine too, as they are now as I write this! I would challenge anyone who might say, "This generation of young folks isn't as good as those in WW II!"

I am a very light sleeper, and, frequently at night after midnight, I would travel around the base in my staff car just "checking things out," and of course the Air Police guards were my special interest. The Chief of the Air Police and his NCO Chief begged me to call in before I traveled on the west side of the base, where our guards were really on their toes and ready for anything, but I said, "I would rather not!" We also had dogs with a few of them. One night I was visiting the guards on the West side of the base, with at least two to three inches of snow on the ground and it was snowing pretty hard and colder than hell! I would travel with my window down so that I could hear the challenge of the guard so I wouldn't get shot!

I heard a "Halt!" and I heard a round chambered in the guard's rifle! I naturally halted put my hands outside my open window and shouted, "Col. Howard here!"

About that time, a *really big white dog* tried to crawl in my window, while a young female guard, also dressed in white, tried to hold back the snarling animal. While I didn't have a personal accident that I would be ashamed of, it did scare the hell out of me!

I thanked her for being so alert and on duty in this terrible weather. She told me that she had just received a call that her dog would be picked up, because it was too cold for dogs to stay out, but, of course, she had to stay. As someone famous said, "Where do we get such dedicated folks?"! My eyes are watering as I write this; DAMN! They are so very good!

After the big white dog event, I gave in and would call the Command Post that I was visiting the guards. Before I started calling the Command Post, I had probably visited our guards twenty to thirty times and I never—repeat, *never* found anything but real warriors ready to defend the base!

Unfortunately, because I had also commanded Yokota AB, I had to give up the wing sooner than I wanted; at least that is what I was told. The good news was that Chuck Link would replace me in July, 1984 so he was well prepared and was also a warrior.

Senator Barry Goldwater was a long time member of the 311th TFTS at Luke AFB, Arizona and frequently attended social events, such as this Dining Out shown here with Dorlyne, me, my cousin Karen, and her late husband, Dick Peterson.

Getting a drink of fuel in my F-4

This is the year we should REPEAT
So let's go out and VOTE FOR FEET!

RE-ELECT
BARRY HOWARD
for SENIOR CLASS VICE-PRESIDENT

Campaign card used at Muncie Central High School to get elected!

Getting a medal from my Luke AFB Wing Commander

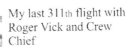

My last 311th flight with Roger Vick and Crew Chief

262

Dorlyne, along
with the Sensei,
leading the
Tanabada Dancers.

My friend, mentor
and warrior, the late
'Willie P.' McBride.

Dorlyne and I, as Guests at the
official Royal Japanese Cherry
Blossom Festival.

Air Force Chief of
Staff, Davy Jones
with members of
Checkmate which
he initiated.

263

The Korean Mafia, my friends from three long visits to Osan AB, Korea, Col. Harry Glaze and Suzi were also close to our Korean friends of the base.

Through Dorlyne's efforts, the Koreans started bringing their wives to social events. A real step forward.

My acting as General MacArthur, Marty McCullough as General Sutherland and Carlito Cunanan, who played Sergio Osmena, the President of the Philippines who's been in absentia.

Temporary Doctor Barry at work at one of the visits with ourMedical Team to a barrio (a small Philippine village).

Sylvia and I off to a dance.

Noel in her car seat enjoying the ride and the view.

Jan Causey and I at a Red River Rats Reunion

My sympathy group, God love 'em!

X-ray of rebuilt right knee with cadaver bone, steel bands and lots of bone cement.

Beautiful Sandra who has made my life wonderful.

Silva's unique and fun filled bar, with the owner standing on a box in the center/back because Big Jeff Hoaglund and I are so tall. Sandra and Christine Hoaglund are the beauties of the bunch.

Fighter Pilots, Bill Ricks and Mac Angel and their wives, Connie and Pam, lead an exciting life.

PHILIPPINES AS 13th AF VC, 7/1984-5/1985

My last assignment that counted!

After I gave up the 51st TFW, Osan, Korea, to Chuck Link, I was assigned immediately as the Vice-Commander of the 13th Air Force in the Philippines. Unfortunately, someone I had always trusted and respected had convinced me that it was to be only a "holding position." Maj. Gen. "Fat" Fred Haeffner, then the PACAF Vice-Commander, said that it was a holding position until I was promoted to Brig. General. It seemed valid, since most everyone told me that I was a shoe-in, since I had successfully had three squadrons and two wings. Additionally, as Wing Commander, the Wings had very satisfactory ORIs. The first wing I commanded was because the previous Wing Commander failed his ORI, but we were able to recover the Wing and had an excellent ORI. Actually both wings I Commended was because the previous Commanders had been relieved when I took over.

Arriving at the 13th at Clark Field, in the Philippines, I suspect that the 13th AF Commander Mike Nelson, didn't particularly like me but that only became apparent after I was there a while. Shortly after I arrived, the Chief of Staff, Charlie Gabriel, visited his West Point roommate, Gen. "Fast Eddie" Ramos, the Philippine military Chief of Staff. After Gen. Gabriel left, all the Philippine senior officers started calling me "General"! It seemed to us that it was really going to happen; I was going to be a brigadier. As a result, we bought an answering machine for our house since, should it happen, many might call us, and we didn't want to miss their calls. I installed the answering machine the day before the list came out, but we never received a call on it, because I wasn't on the list! In spite of our disappointment, I really enjoyed my short tour at Clark Field, Philippines, for many reasons.

Our house maid (of course, we paid her salary) was Gen. MacArthur's former number-two house girl, and was she good! We could call her on Friday night from the Officer's Club, saying we were bringing home four couples, and give her their names. When we got there, she had each individual's' desired drinks fixed (she had a card file on everyone) and *Pu Pus* (finger foods) prepared and placed around the living room for their enjoyment. If we said we were going to have dinner, she would have it ready. She was a wonderful and very talented lady, and she kept a Roladex on everyone we knew, and most of the folks on the base! She sure made our life simple and enjoyable.

Clark Field had the Air Forces' regional Hospital and it was a large and very good hospital. The Commander of the Hospital was a superb officer and a neighbor. The hospital had most modern medical equipment and was well supplied with all medical specialties, as it was truly a hospital set up for combat operations for the region.

For training of our Medical teams, we would deploy them to various very poor *barongs,* (small villages) near Clark Field. Dorlyne and I would go with the teams along with Gretchen Cojuangco, wife of Dang Ding. Dang Ding owned the Philippines Beer company, the Philippine Ice Cream Company and many other important companies. Gretchen was a tall, beautiful blonde, and a wonderful, participating lady. She, Dorlyne, and I did things like pull teeth, remove boils (Pilipino had lots of boils), and other medical procedures.

Those we treated probably had never have had penicillin, so they were given a few pills and frankly, on re-check of the patients, not one I can remember ever had an infection. The people of the locations we visited treated us like heroes; we had warm sweet tea (warm, as no one had refrigeration), nice sandwiches, and fruit that I am sure they couldn't afford, but they were so appreciative. However, I think we and the Medical Teams had enormous satisfaction helping the folks of the barongs!

- One time we were setup and operating providing care and helping the folks. Suddenly, an armed Pilipino confronted me, and, as I looked around, we were surrounded by armed men who looked like rebels. Later, I learned they were Communist rebels. He said something to the effect of "We don't want you here!" Gretchen quickly came to me and said, "Don't do anything, I have called Dang Ding, and help is on the way!" Gretchen knew I was armed, as I always carried a pistol under my shirt for protection.

The fellow who had confronted me, I think, heard her and quickly said a few words in Tagalog to those surrounding our Medical Team, and suddenly they started melting into the woods, as quickly as they had arrived. As they were disappearing, what appeared as an organized, very well-armed team surrounded us; Dang Ding had probably pre-located them there to protect us if needed.

Sometime later, Dorlyne and I were invited to visit Dang Ding on an island retreat, where he was the command authority but a very fair one. It was a wonderful visit, great food, and an exciting tour of the island. That night as we watched a new war movie, Dang Ding gave me, as a present for my service in the Philippines, a 1911 Colt .45 automatic. It was still wrapped in the wax paper with Cosmoline still on the gun. As we were leaving the next day, he asked for the gun back, because he was going to send it to a famous gunsmith to re-work it, since the original 1911s were great firepower but not very accurate. Unhappily, I never got the gun back, since the islands suffered an uprising, and Dang Ding along with Marcos, left the country. President Marcos has since died, but Dang Ding is back running all his companies.

I used to jokingly call the Colt .45 a Philippine personal ID, since it seemed everyone had one, and I sure wish I had the one I owned for a night back then! Once, Dorlyne and I needed to get away for a few days, so we simply jumped a commercial airliner to the southern Muslim island of Mindanao and the city of Davao. A friend I flew the Aero Club aircraft with, Russ Long, had a furniture plant there. We checked into a beach front motel. My friend gave us a tour of the island. He also gave us a tour of his furniture construction company plant. While there, he had a meeting with his employees, and he introduced us to them, which I really didn't want him to do, since I wasn't supposed to be there. He then said to his employees, "This is Col. Howard, the 13th Air Force Vice- Commander and he has asked me why I did not have to pay tribute to the Muslim rebels." His senior or Boss employee said, "We are all Muslims, and that is why Mr. Russ doesn't pay tribute." I jokingly said, "I see no Philippine IDs on anyone; you know, a 1911 Colt .45 automatics." At that, Russ's Senior Employee said something in the native language to all present, and suddenly it seem that everyone pulled out a weapon, and one even pulled out a large machine gun from under his traditional Muslim robe. I was obviously somewhat taken aback, and the Senior Employee said, "Col. Howard, you and your wife can go anywhere in the Philippines; you are considered friends of the Philippines, and we know all about you and what you have done for our country." With that, everyone clapped, which did relieve the tension I was feeling.

The next morning, very early, I received a call from the office of the motel, and a man said in a panicked voice, "Sir, I think you need to come to the office!" I headed for the office, and I saw around the motel an armed force of jeeps, armored personnel carriers with machine guns manned and loaded, and an Army Colonel came to me saluting. He said, "Gen. Ramos said to tell you that you should return to Clark Field under our protection." When I got back to Clark Field, I received a call from the General saying I shouldn't travel around the Philippines without notifying him. I gave him a simple response, "Yes, Sir" but I think I had my fingers crossed!

Throughout this book, I have mentioned events that were challenging, normally resulting in very *lucky* results, professional advancements, and serious military challenges, and I had so much fun and excitement that I really can't remember much unhappiness! I can't deny that there weren't disasters that I had to address, but the most of the time, the challenges were interesting, fun, and a learning experience, and made me feel like I was contributing.

I can only recall only one really horrible occurrence. That was the terrible and devastating fire that destroyed the Hotel Baguio, in Baguio, Philippines, very close to our Camp John Hay military recreation area. Since the fire was late at night, there were many deaths. When it happened, I was at Clark Field, and my General was gone, so I responded for 13th Air Force, generating the Command Post and as much assistance as we had available. The hotel was a wooden structure, so few were able to escape, and there were many burned bodies that needed to be identified and returned to their families. We eventually set up a morgue at Clark Field, but, because of so many bodies and the heat in the Philippines, it was a challenging matter. Military folks are so "can do" in attitude and capability that this unhappy event was handled with skill, human concern, speed, and proper reverence. The morgue was set-up in a warehouse, but we installed several very large, mobile, aircraft air-conditioners into the warehouse, thus protecting the many bodies until they were identified and removed.

Unfortunately, the last body to be identified was a lady from India, so it took quite a while for her family members to arrive. I escorted the individuals who were there to identify the body to the area for viewing of the body. Instantly they identified her by the ring she had on her toe. We had all been very concerned, because she had been terribly burned, and we were afraid that it would be difficult to identify her. The India tradition of wearing a toe ring made it less difficult and frankly, those of us who were handling the identification should have thought about the ring. Especially me, because I spent so much time in India!

I have to admit that I was once again extremely proud of our military and how wonderfully they handled this horrible event and made it easier for the families who came in to identify their love ones. We provided on-base transportation, housing, feeding facilities, and counseling. My chest swells with pride as I remember that most unhappy event!

Regarding Marcos, I need to mention that I talked to a retired Army Lt. General who had fought in the Philippines during WW II, and he told me in all sincerity that he had put "Major" Marcos, after the Philippines were out from under Japanese control, in for the Medal of Honor. Why? Because the American General thought that Marcos was truly the bravest, most successful, and true leader of the Philippine rebels against the Japanese. He said Marcos's men terrorized and did severe damage to the Japanese as they tried to control the Philippines before our US

Forces returned. Unfortunately, he never received it, I assume because of the bad press he and his wife received in the American papers.

The Chief of Staff of the Philippines military while I was there was Gen. Eddie "Fast Eddie" Ramos. One day he approached me about playing Gen. MacArthur for the 40th re-enactment of the Leyte Landing of World War II. It was to be a Joint Exercise titled "Pagbabalik 84" to include US, Philippine, and Australian forces. Of course, I agreed, and then the fun began! First, Gen. MacArthur's personal tailor measured me for a real Gen. MacArthur uniform. Many of the Philippine senior officers were there when I was measured. What I learned at the measuring was that his tailor was very light in his tennis shoes, and the Philippine senior officers had a great laugh when as he measured my inseam!

It was a wonderful opportunity for my wife and me, and the parties seemed to never stop. Of course, by now all of Philippine military started calling me General. I did a serious study of Gen. MacArthur and memorized the speech he gave as he came ashore—which was superb and so deep. Probably the most stirring happenings were when old Philippinos approached me as I walked along the shore in my Gen. MacArthur uniform, lightly touching me on my arm and speaking to me in Tagalong with tears in their eyes. It was heart rending and it was obvious that Gen. MacArthur was loved by the Philippinos!

As we were preparing to land the forces of invasion, we floated around the flotilla of ships from the Philippines, US, and Australia, with me standing at the helm of the landing craft. The ships would call on their loudspeakers, "Attention to port [or starboard]; Gen. MacArthur is passing our ship!" The troops would "man the rails", salute, and cheer—I felt pretty important!

My simulated staff who would wade ashore with me included two of my classmates from the Naval Academy at Annapolis,

Maryland, Marty "Fado" McCullough and Carlos "Carlito" Cunanan, now a Philippine Naval officer who has since passed away from a heart attack. My friend, Marty played Gen. Sutherland and Carlito played Sergio Osmena, the President of the Philippines who been in asthenia. Carlito and his wife were good friends of ours while we were at Clark Field. Marty and I rowed crew together at Annapolis, and we were also very good friends along with his wife, Adrianne.

As my landing craft approached the shore for us to disembark and wade ashore, a Philippine friend who was the official photographer for the event asked if he could jump off the ramp and get in position for a picture of us wading ashore. Of course I said, "Go ahead," which he did. As he sunk out of sight, I said to the Coxswain, "When he gets back aboard, let's pull it forward until you feel bottom!" The picture he took, in color, is similar to the one that appeared throughout the United States as a morale boost after the forces actually landed on October 20, 1944. The picture or poster was in red, white and blue and looks like the ones that were up everywhere in the US during WW II. I have one of the new ones on my wall in my office and it looks just like the ones I remember as a child in Wichita. I remember, they were put on telephone poles and everywhere and with a title saying,

"*I SHALL RETURN!*"

After I waded ashore with my corncob pipe and a pistol in my hip pocket as the General had when he went ashore, I gave the same speech he gave. I still get chills when I think about it: what wonderful words he had designed to arouse those many rebel forces who were still fighting against the Japanese! He beseeched them to increase and continue their attacks on the Japanese, which they did, especially Maj. Marcos!

After I gave my speech, I walked along the shores or rode in a jeep to the reviewing stand set-up for the event. I had watched an old film of the General's actual arrival, and, as I drove around,

I tried to act as he did, with a corncob pipe in my mouth. Later, as I sat down on the stage prepared for the event, President Marcos who was sitting with our Ambassador, walked up to where I was sitting, came to a stiff attention, and saluted me. What the hell should I do?

Fortunately, his aide quickly whispered in my ear, "Remember, General, he was a just a Major then!" I threw him what I think was a "General-type salute," and he did an about-face and marched back to his seat. *Wow!* I was impressed, he remembered!

Afterwards at a gala party, his wife Imelda sang for us, and then she approached me and asked me to sing with her. Little did she know that when I was eleven or twelve at the Walnut Street Baptist Church in Muncie, Indiana, the choir director told me, "never, repeat never, sing! Just move your lips, as you have a horrible voice!" I tried to tell her, but she wouldn't accept what I said, and got very mad at me. What made it worse, a few weeks earlier, she had given Dorlyne and I a personal, very detailed tour of her famous "shoe closet!" I later heard about her anger from many in the Manila diplomatic world, and that, along with some disappointment concerning the promotion, gave us cause to accelerate our return to the good old USA!

Gretchen and Dang Ding Cojuangco gave us a superb going away, an almost formal party. Sometime earlier, I had sent to Dang Ding a letter (on my own, without any approval) almost begging Dang Ding to run against Marcos since he knew, as we in the US knew, that Imelda was truly running the country since Marco was so sick. Dang Ding simply said, "Marcos is like a father to me, and I cannot run against him." However, in 1992 he did run, and Marcos's son beat him for the nomination. Marcos's son was subsequently beaten by Gen. Ramos for the President of the Philippines.

Before we left Clark, the famous Manila Hotel insisted that we spend a weekend in the famed MacArthur Penthouse suite.

It was all free, and it included a wonderful party for local and foreign dignitaries, including the Japanese Attaché! Of course I wore the uniform and smoked the corncob pipe, and we had a wonderful time!

The whole affair was very special and really excited Dorlyne and I. Of course the folks kept telling us that we would be on the next General's list. It did hurt a bit when I wasn't there either, but, in the long run, I had other challenges and challenging opportunities in retirement. I suspect it hurt Dorlyne terribly, because she truly worked her cute bottom off as the five times Air Force Commander's wife. Being a Commander's wife back then, especially in the Pacific, was just plain hard work. Over there, you have no social services and she, along with other volunteers, really worked our social problems hard.

Not getting promoted was a bit of a disappointment, because I thought, and many others told me that they thought, we had earned it. Fortunately, I knew of a few events in my early career probably weighed heavy against me and frankly, guys like me aren't very good in peacetime. However, I still terribly miss the Air Force. Primarily, I especially miss the young dynamic men and women as they are truly superb and they are dedicated to defending this great Nation! In retirement, I live near Kirtland AFB, New Mexico, and I am thrilled every time I am at the base (three times a week because of my knees, which hate me!). As I enter or leave the base, I swell with pride seeing the young troops that we should all be so very proud of, especially those Air Police men and women who guard the base. They are superior!

BERGSTROM AFB, AUSTIN, TEXAS, 5/1985-2/1986

Dorlyne and I decided after I wasn't promoted and with Imelda Marcos mad at me for not singing with her, that it was time to return to the States and join the civilian world. I had been previously offered a job as the manager of the profitable newspaper in the small West Texas town of Graham. Unfortunately, the person a family member, who offered me the job had passed away as we were returning. I arrived at Bergstrom AFB in May 1985. I became a Special Assistant to the Commander of 12th Air Force, a nothing job, but he, the General, also expressed shock that I wasn't promoted. I did clash a bit with his DO, but I only had a short period with 12th AF. We decided it was time to look for other challenges, and I retired from the Air Force in February 1986.

Looking back on my Air Force career, I know I achieved all my goals, really had a ball, and have never regretted a minute of it. As I progressed through the Air Force career my life was always getting more exciting. First a "Trash hauler," then an ATC T-37 IP, Maintenance Test Pilot, followed by a checkout in the F-4, upgraded to F-4 IP, combat tour in the F-4, became a 9th Air Force, headquarters weenie, grabbed by the Tactical Air

Force Commander for his staff, and then my dream job, a fighter squadron commander.

Then it got really interesting: to the Pentagon bouncing around from simulators to Test and Evaluation followed by "Checkmate" and then debriefing the Russian MIG 25 pilot. Finally Air War College and then Commander of the 963rd AWACS Squadron at Tinker AFB and being really involved in worldly affairs. I have to thank my friend and former Thunderbird solo and leader, Neil Eddins of Afton, Wyoming. Some say Neil rode me like a free roam pony, but he always was a good boss. Of course, initially, I wasn't a happy camper at Tinker AFB, but after a few weeks in the 963rd I knew I was going to enjoy this challenge! Later, I was selected to be a Wing Commander twice: the 475th Wing at Yokota, Japan, and later the prized 51st TAC Fighter Wing, Osan, Korea. How about that: a former "Trash Hauler" as Commander of probably, at that time, the most combat-ready fighter wing in the Air Force, Osan AB, Korea? We were truly the tip of the tactical spear in the world. We were located closest to the proven active bad guys of North Korea.

Some of the fighter guys I associated with occasionally give me a bit of hell for being a former *Trash Hauler* but I was always able to demonstrate more than adequate fighter-flying skills and in many cases, better than theirs!

I am absolutely convinced that the training, education, experience, and yes, discipline I received in the 39th Troop Carrier Squadron in France, gave me a real step-up throughout the rest of my career. I have to admit, it probably was the best three-plus years of learning during my Air Force career. However, when I was blowing and going in an F-4, especially in Vietnam, or even leading the 963rd AWACS squadron I continued to learn! I had so much fun and many challenges that as I write this, I just smile and recall very fond memories, which I have remembered and tried to illuminate in this book! Once again, old *Col.Lucky*, *lucked* out again and fate along with my lack of attention to my studying in pilot training, paid off for the long haul! My fighter career was only delayed a bit but my aviation and Air Force skills were magnified in the 39th.

LUBBOCK, TEXAS, RETIREMENT AND GRAD SCHOOL, 3/1986-1987

When I finally retired, 12th Air Force had a very nice retirement ceremony, and Gen. *Willie P.* McBride came to the ceremony in February of 1986. I really appreciated his visit and his concern that I had not been promoted. He gave me a ring he had made, which I still have. He did finally tell me about Mr. Jones of Northrup wanting to hire me at the Nellis AFB Symposium but, true to *Willie P.* style, he said, "He simply forgot to tell me." *Sure, Willie P.*, but I still will always fondly remember working for you and knowing about your talents in combat and for the Air Force!

Austin was a nice location, but I had decided that I wanted to run a hospital in retirement, and I chose Texas Tech to get a Hospital Administrator's MBA! We moved to Lubbock, and a very good friend in Austin, Jesse Henderson, an Air National Guard Colonel, helped us move, bless his heart!

At Texas Tech I began going to graduate school on the GI bill. After one semester, I knew that I didn't want to continue. Having run many training programs and being an experienced flying instructor, I was extremely disappointed on the quality of professors at Tech. In fact, the one good one I had, my Accounting Professor, got laid off by Tech! Although I think I had straight A's the one semester I completed at Tech, I was rescued from college by a series of family deaths, including that of my Mother, *Little Napoleon*!

I did have the wonderful experience of spending the last few weeks with Mom in and out of Ball Hospital in Muncie, Indiana. I did learn that cities that only have a single hospital may not have all of the finer extra amenities as do hospitals where there is competition among the different hospitals.

My Mother, as long as I can remember, hated her hair, and at the time she was in the Ball Hospital, the only hospital in Muncie. As a result, Ball Hospital, since they had a trapped cliental, had few amenities. Ball Hospital had no beauty shop and no valet parking or other perks. Because of the hair she had, Mom went to the beauty shop every other week, and it was time for her visit her hair dresser. I asked the nurse if it would upset anyone if I took her to the beauty shop. That question caused a minor explosion—*it was out of the question for her to go to the beauty shop!* That did it; I visited the Hospital Administer and told him that he had better get security, "Because I was taking my Mother to the beauty shop on Thursday afternoon, period!"

Thursday arrived and, to my surprise, the ward was very cooperative, and no one tried to stop us; I guess my size sometimes pays off. Mother died a few days later, but she died happy with painted finger nails and her hair properly fixed. Mom even said to me just before she passed, "Barry, big bossy brassy Barry, you were a wonderful son and a successful son, and I am so proud of you, and you gave us such wonderful grandchildren! But, you traveled the world and never sent back one picture, ever!" unfortunately, that was the truth, I am a terrible tourist!

Mother had told me that she was ready to go, and she was horribly angry, because one night when she probably had a minor stroke or a minor heart attack, they put a breathing tube in her when she had passed out late at night. She had given them strict written instructions that the hospital should take no extraordinary actions for her. I begged her to just use the breathing tube for a few hours, once it was in, but she was adamant, and, with very angry eyes and hand gestures, since she could not talk because of the tube, she demanded that it be removed. *Little Napoleon* could not speak, but she could talk with her fiery eyes! The breathing tube was removed, and she passed away quietly with me holding her hand. Unfortunately, I spent a lot of time trying to call my brothers, and I probably should have been with her more!

I did close her eyes after she passed. We did *not* bury her in a red dress, as she clearly directed in the first line of the note of *her death instructions* she left on a yellow-lined pad. Her funeral was truly a tribute to her life, by the number of folks who attended—including the man she often called her fourth son but who was also her political enemy, the former Police Chief whom Dad had sent to FBI school. He was now Mayor of Muncie, Jim "Lard" Carey, who Mom dearly loved, and I think when we boys were gone, she considered him her wayward fourth son, a damn Democrat! We did stop in her favorite restaurant and bar, the Flamingo, after departing the cemetery. In fact, the convoy of vehicles just went straight into the Flamingo without any one previously mentioning it. I don't think I had called the Flamingo that we were stopping, but we had previously stopped there after Dad's funeral. I do remember that the owner met me at the door as we arrived and said, "We were expecting you!" The Flamingo staff treated us wonderfully! The owner made a terrific speech about our Mom and it was greatly appreciated. Like for Dad, the billing was a minimum again!

LITTLE CAYMAN, THE SOUTHERN CROSS CLUB, 1987-1988

Because of the several family deaths for which I was the Executor, I dropped out of Texas Tech. My brother Kent asked me to go to Little Cayman and the Southern Cross Club and teach the manager, Mike Emmanuel, along with his wife Donna, to operate the Club using a computer for some management functions. The Southern Cross Club was an exclusive Diving and Fishing Resort owned by several well-healed individuals; we frequently called it the *44 Millionaires Club*.

Shortly after I arrived, the Cayman Island Government demanded that Mike Emmanuel leave for some very minor complaint. I agreed to stay for a while until they could locate an acceptable manager.

Shortly after arriving and being a pilot, I am usually attuned of weather conditions, and I noticed a very rapid drop in the air pressure, which could be an indication that a storm was brewing in the Caribbean. I called the National Weather Agency and suggested that possibly a very strong storm (hurricane) might be developing. I got a "No way!" response, followed by a detailed regurgitation of their scientific data. However, a bit later, they called me back and agreed that a big storm (later called Gilbert) was in fact brewing and heading for Little Cayman.

The Cayman government suggested that we move everyone on the island to the hanger at the airfield, and that they would start sending in aircraft to evacuate the tourists by air. In fact, only one aircraft came in, and the staffs from the various resorts jumped in front of the tourists, even knocking down some of the visitors, and filled the aircraft. Not one visitor or guest was able to get on the airplane! Of course, not another aircraft came to rescue the visitors!

At the Southern Cross Club, we had several daughters of US Senators visiting. Because of this, I called the National Command Center and advised them that many had been left on the Island and I had been a C-130 pilot in the Air Force and I knew that one could land on Little Cayman. It seemed that they reacted immediately, as a C-130 arrived overhead very quickly, but the Cayman government would not allow them to land, so the many tourists and visitors were forced to ride out the storm on the island.

I guess I was either elected or decided to be "in charge" of those left on the island. As I have found in a tense situation in the past, taking charge forcefully—or maybe a better word is *strongly*—is normally happily accepted by those involved. I was concerned about the hanger where the government directed that we stay. Why? Because it was on relatively low ground, possibly the lowest on the island. The highest point on the island was only thirty to forty feet above sea level but it also was a somewhat protected area, with decently size trees, which probably had deep roots for protection, since they had to sink their roots deeply to get water. We quickly established and set-up an alternate or emergency site to move to on the highest ground on the island, should we have flooding at the hanger.

As the rain and the wind became very furious that night, I asked someone I trusted if he would sit outside the hanger in a vehicle watching for flooding. As the night wore on, we had one staff member from another resort get drunk and became a real pain, and we finally had to physically restrain him. Unfortunately, the individual I put outside to watch for flooding, unbeknownst to me, took a case of beer into the vehicle in which he was supposed to be watching for the water rise.

About three in the morning I became uncomfortable and had a very uncomfortable feeling in my stomach! I opened one of the small hanger doors and found the water within inches of coming in the door. I waded out to the vehicle that was supposed to alert us and found a case of empty beer cans and a soundly sleeping "alerter"!

We had a full house or hanger of people who needed to be moved to higher ground, probably to the alternate site we had set-up. Our Southern Cross Dive Master had found one of the big trucks that a contractor had on the island, so we loaded all from the hanger into the back of the truck and headed for the alternate site. As we passed the Southern Cross Club on the way to the alternate site, we found the Club was not flooded and really in an almost normal situation, except for many Palm trees blown down. Some cabins had earlier received severe damage, and the dock had disappeared from the wind, rain, and water surge. Since we had water, food, a functioning kitchen, and bathrooms at the Club, we abandoned the decision to head for the alternate site. At the club we rode out the rest of the storm in a rather pleasant situation!

Prior to the storm, the many boats owned by the Club we either pulled ashore or had taken to a protective cove for anchorage. The Club lost only one boat during the storm, but I later learned that it had actually been stolen, not storm destroyed. Since I was now managing the Club, after the storm passed we quickly began rebuilding the facility. As we waited for materials to rebuild the dock and cabins, I went to the other side of the island where the coconut palm trees grew and dropped their nuts. I gathered many fallen coconuts, which were around the trees. Some of the nuts had already started rooting, and I planted a bunch of them to replace those we lost and even increase the number of trees for future protection of the Club. To plant coconuts, you simply dig a small coconut size hole and put about half of the coconut into the sand and simply keep it watered. Years later, returning to Little Cayman, I found that most had grown, and they looked great! I felt a little like Johnny Appleseed when I saw them!

I had recruited a friend of my son Mike, Carl Chaffin, as a cook for the Club. I had also asked him, when I recruited him, if he knew how to use a hammer. He said one summer he had framed houses—great! After the storm passed, we started on the Dock since we needed it to move in supplies. We built a great dock, but I learned that Carl didn't really know how to use a hammer; it turns out he had used a nail gun to frame the houses. I did give him some instructions on hammers, and he became very good. We were able to complete the dock before governmental staff personnel from Grand Cayman arrived with "*Governmental guidance*" on rebuilding a dock. Jetting in a dock was apparently now a *no-no*, but by the time they got there, it was already jetted in (using a gasoline engine with a hose and air pressure to blast in the pilings), and the dock was beautiful and functioning! One of the other Little Cayman resort owners also had several lumber yards in Florida and started the supplies flowing. He was extremely helpful and cooperative with me, which made it easier to repair the damage.

Carl was not bad as a builder, but he was a superb cook! In his desire to provide great meals, he figured how to catch sharks, which have very tasty meat. The first time he cooked shark, we had almost a revolt from the Cayman staff, who consider themselves "water people" and who said, "We don't eat the shark, and he don't eat us!" From then on, when he prepared shark for the guests, he also prepared spaghetti, most frequently with Spam in it, which the Cayman folks love. I also love Spam!

While on Little Cayman, I became good friends with a Frankie Bodden, great grandson of Black Beard the pirate! He also owned the liquor store over on Cayman Brac, about twelve miles away! He loved to party and his drink was normally Captain Morgan's Spiced Rum. After a few bouts or parties with Frankie, I became and I am still a real fan of Captain Morgan's Spiced Rum! Frankie was someone who always knew what was going on either on the Brac or Little Cayman, and he would always give me great advice. My calling of the hurricane seemed to really impress him, since he was born a man of the seas, and he assumed I was too.

We quickly set to work to rebuild the resort and quickly reopened for business, but first we had to re-build the electrical system, which was somewhat antiquated and without the normal safety features one would expect. We attempted to correct the system as best we could. The water system, which was also rather amateur in construction but somewhat functional, was easy to modify, since it was laid in the sand of the facility.

I certainly enjoyed my almost-year on Little Cayman, especially the rebuilding of the storm-damaged facilities. Building the dock was a learning exercise and something I had never done before. I was amazed the last time I visited Little Cayman how it had exploded with people, resorts, and available functions to include a car-rental agency and grocery store. When I was managing the Southern Cross Club, there were only twenty-three permanent people who were living on the island. Another great learning experience in that I learned to be an almost dive master, re-build a resort, and improve both a water system and an electrical system for the resort.

While on Little Cayman, I received a call from Fort Myers, Florida, and Lee County Mosquito Control District (LCMCD), recruiting me to join Lee County Mosquito Control as their Director of Supply and Resources to recover their supply-system computer program, since it had never really been fully installed and used—another interesting challenge and opportunity!

LEE COUNTY MOSQUITO CONTROL DISTRICT, 1988-1998

Lee County Mosquito Control (LCMCD) is the largest mosquito-control agency in America and probably the world. What they didn't know when they hired me is that when I was at Clark Field, Philippines, as the 13th AF Vice Commander, I had called them about a mosquito problem we had along with the associated malaria. They gave us superb information, and we were able to decrease our mosquito threat considerably. Even in the Philippines with all the rain, it is fairly easy with a few tricks from LCMCD to reasonably manage a mosquito infestation. Any standing water with associated warm temperatures will breed mosquitos in as few as three days—particularly flower-pots that have standing water in them or in tropical areas, air plants, or places in trees where water will stand. Old tires left out lying around are real mosquito-breeding areas. During high temperatures, mosquitos will breed in three to five days, but after our removing the standing water, the mosquito larva and eggs will dry-up.

I was once again *lucky*, as my friend Harry Glaze, former Red Horse Commander, had told Mosquito Control Director, T. Wayne Miller that I was an expert on computer management. Apparently LCMCD had hired a troop to work the computer problems but either he didn't do it or didn't know how to do it. (Probably the latter!) Once we got the system working, we were able to decrease the supply account by several millions of dollars, reduce quantities to reasonable amounts, and actually control the ordering, repair, and issue of items based on usage through the computer management system.

In my long and exciting life, I have had some very funny incidents occur. After I retired from the Air Force and I was working for Lee County Mosquito Control, a hurricane hit the Homestead Air Force Base area. I was sent over there to check it out for mosquitoes and at the same time check salvage for material that we might want to obtain, since I was authorize to representing LCMCD to obtain recycled equipment useful for our operation. Mosquito Control agencies are considered a medical necessity and are given priority to obtain recycled or unused military equipment. While there I was reviewing the damage, which was very extensive, but surprisingly random. For example, the Base Chapel, of an A-Frame design, had completely disappeared, while just across the street the VIP Quarters were hardly touched. Only one room had a leaking roof and otherwise, just cosmetic external damage, and the rooms were fully usable.

While checking out the damage, I visited the location of the house my family had lived in when I was assigned to the 478th TFS first as a Student in the F-4 training program and later as a very unhappy F-4 Instructor Pilot who wanted to go to combat! The house was within crawling distance of the Officer's Club. All that remained of the house was the slab, a few pipes, and some bushes. However, the famous banana tree that our son, Mike, managed to get in trouble over was growing as if nothing happened. Many years ago, when I was a young Captain stationed at Homestead in the F-4 program, Mike and a young friend decided to cut down the banana tree. The tree, of course, regrew but we did let him experience going to the Air Police office and being questioned about cutting down the tree. I believe Mike learned a lesson and didn't give his Mother further problems; in fact, he was wonderful and filled in as the man of the family while I was gone off to the war.

Back to the visit to Homestead AFB: I subsequently received a call from one of the managers of the salvage facility, who I knew, at Homestead. He asked if I would come to the salvage facility to help a Colonel from the Pentagon. I quickly drove to the Salvage office and was introduced to the Colonel who was from the Pentagon and was checking the damage to Homestead as a Civil Engineer. He had a large set of base blueprints with him. I asked how I could be of help, and he pointed out a building near the salvage area that had very little damage, and he said, "That building isn't on the base blueprints, as all buildings on Homestead must be on this plan!"

I knew the building very well, because twice I mission-briefed in it for the Iranian rescue, the last time being just before President Reagan took office. I said to the Colonel, "It is a black building," and he quickly said, "No, it isn't, it is brown [painted brown]!" I asked him if he knew what a black building was, and he said "Sure, I know the difference between black and brown." Not wanting to embarrass him in front of the others, I asked him to walk outside. Outside I suggested he call his office and ask them what "black" buildings were, which he did. "Black Buildings" are buildings built with special funds that are not put on base blueprints and are used for classified missions or programs. In this case, I had out-briefed in this building as we were preparing to depart for the Iranian rescue attempts. Of course the Iranians released the prisoners before we could go the second time. They knew the strength of President Reagan, and I wish every future President would remember that President Reagan made it clear that he wouldn't fool around with them and wanted the Americans home, *now*! Strength is the only thing many world leaders understand; words do not work but strength does!

Anyhow, it was obvious to me that even the Good Lord didn't know about "black buildings" either. Because everything around the *black building* had been destroyed but the *black building* had hardly any damage to the paint, shingles, or anything else. Also, now the Pentagon Colonel now knew about black buildings!

I really enjoyed my time with LCMCD, as the folks for the most part were very professional, dedicated, and fun to be with. A group of us became fishing buddies and made many fishing trips, where we sometimes even caught some fish but also consumed lots of cigars and adult beverages.

While in Ft. Myers Sylvia (an English Lady) and I met an English couple who became our great friends and part of our partying team, Jane and Peter Ray along with their beautiful daughter, Louise. They had been fighting the immigration battle but while doing that they always worked, started businesses, and paid their taxes. Fortunately, through some friends I had and their lawyer we were able to solve their problems after I officially vouched for them. Sylvia being English really enjoyed them and frequently translated for me when we were partying and they went "Bloke!"

Back to LCMCD, once we got the computer system working, I became the organizational "scrounger" for available recycled military material, very useful for LCMCD. We needed some new helicopters (UH-1s) and I learned that six of them were available in Alaska, all with very little flying time on them. Knowing that National Guard outfits with transports (C-17) needed training missions, I spent some time on the phone and found one that would pick up the six choppers in Alaska and fly them down to us in Florida. The Guard outfit got tons of practical training, including loading six UH-1s, which was a challenge but very excellent training. We sent a troop up to Alaska to manage the pick-up and to fly down with them. They landed at Patrick AFB, Florida, from where our chopper pilots then flew the choppers down to Homestead. This action probably paid my salary for several years, as did much of the other "stuff" I picked up (say, *scrounged*) from the various military recycle locations.

DIVORCE FROM DORLYNE and MEETING SYLVIA LITTLE, 1990-2005

One day while working at LCMCD, a Deputy Sheriff arrived at my office and presented me with divorce papers! What a shock it was to me! I didn't have inkling that we were having trouble, and I certainly wasn't misbehaving, as I may have done earlier in my life. I have to admit that the surprise truly shocked me and angered me a great deal.

There had been absolutely no conversation between Dorlyne and me about divorce. After receiving the papers, I was allowed to talk only with her lawyer, a really mean lady. Yes, I was forced to talk to a mean lawyer rather than to my wife, Dorlyne. The anger I had was only increased by the conversations with the Lady Lawyer. I think I said to hell with it, I will become a bachelor. Later I learned that Dorlyne was upset that I was asked by my friend Don Meyer's widow, Carol Myers, to represent my deceased friend Don when his son, Donald, was married. Dorlyne thought she had not been invited to the wedding, but she had. In her mind she had not been invited, and I assume this was

295

the driving factor, among others concerns, that resulted in my receiving the divorce papers.

The divorce battle became the playground of the lawyers; mine really didn't like Dorlyne, and I really didn't like her lawyer. I could not have had a divorce at a worse time. Beloved Patsy Schroeder, (just joking!) the Colorado Congresswoman, passed some laws that resulted in Dorlyne receiving not only considerable liquid funds from me but also about 46 percent of my retirement, and I agreed to give her another 2 percent with a short term insurance policy on me which runs out this year. At least I now have someone regularly praying for me! While the amount Dorlyne gets from my retirement does hurt me financially, she does deserve it because she worked very hard assisting me in my Air Force career and especially the five times I was a Commander.

I did do one not so-nice trick concerning my 1964½ Mustang Convertible built on the 23rd of April 1964—one of the very first Mustangs ever built with the famed 289 motor in it. It was the same color as the convertible that Lee Iacocca drove out on April 17, 1964, when he introduced the Mustang to the world. Dorlyne and I had been at the beach in Fort Myers, and a gentleman tried to hand me a check for my Mustang for fifteen thousand dollars, like it stood. Naturally I thanked him but said no deal. Dorlyne wanted, as one of the divorce settlements, ½ of the value of the Mustang or $7,500. To avoid that, I quickly signed the Mustang over to my daughter, naturally in anger.

As I write this, I can now say finally in our old age we have resolved our anger and get along pretty well. In fact, Dorlyne visited me three times when I was in the VA hospital, in a wheelchair or in bed at home, representing Barrie Lynn, who was living in London, England. Our divorce took years to finalize, and it cost a bunch. I am sure that I would have enjoyed retirement with Dorlyne, but it wasn't to be.

As a result of the divorce effort, I began some dating, but nothing exciting until one day, around Christmas, while shopping I stopped in a bar in the Edison Mall in Fort Myers to have a drink. There I met an English Lady named Sylvia Little who was very exciting and beautiful. Sylvia and I had a slowly developing romance, and we grew together as time passed. We talked about the West, and I learned that she and her late husband had lived in Albuquerque, New Mexico, my favorite place in the world. We had two allegedly Mexican food restaurants in Ft. Myers that frankly the food ran from hot to cold. Additionally, I had found a very small place in Fort Myers that made the best tamales I had ever eaten, and I am a tamale expert, Rosa's!

When I first met Sylvia, I offered to take her to dinner at one of the Mexican Restaurants, but she declined. However, she did give me her phone number for the future. I did not realize that I had slugged down two tall Vodka tonics when I met her, because I was damn thirsty and most probably because I really hate shopping. She thought I had a drinking problem! Anyhow, after calling her several times, I finally was able to take her out to dinner and we became a team. It was a good team, and we had lots of fun together. Later she decided that I needed to move in with her in her apartment.

We became the supplier of fruit and vegetables to many of the little old ladies who lived in the other apartments in her building. Sylvia had a house east of town with many fruit trees. Additionally, when I went to Miami and Homestead AFB pretty regularly to look for recycled military materials for LCMCD, I would stop by the vegetable market in a town east of Fort Myers, Immokalee. There they sold vegetables just picked by the bushel at a very cheap price. Thus we had fruit from the trees and vegetables from the market, and the ladies of Sylvia's apartment building loved it!

One of Sylvia's old boyfriends had left his tractor at Sylvia's house out on the river and I used it to fix up the place, remove some old palm trees and just generally clean up the place. Also I modernized the inside of the house as it hadn't been lived in for some time. Eventually my Naval Academy "wife" and his family lived in it for a while as did Al Thunyan, my Saudi student.

One funny incident concerning the "little old Ladies" occurred. I had put a steel re-enforced screen door on Sylvia's apartment, and it fit perfectly, taking me no more than thirty minutes to install. All the little old Ladies suddenly wanted one too. After installing Sylvia's, I guess I installed several others, and *not one of them took less than three hours to install* because the door frames were not square. But the ladies really liked them!

One Christmas, I flew to Texas to be with my grandchildren for Christmas. While there, I visited an auto auction and picked up a small Nissan pickup and drove it back to Fort Myers. I arrived late at night and parked in our assigned parking place, and one of the tires went flat. Early the next morning I found a very nasty note on the windshield saying that pickups were illegal and "to remove it immediately." Now, others in the apartments had pickups, but they parked them in the back where they were unseen. The note was signed "The Homeowners Committee" and insisted that I "move this vehicle immediately." That did it; we decided to buy a house and move out, which we did very quickly. The little old ladies revolted against the Homeowners Committee and voted them all out at the next election. Those committee members had caused the fruit-and-vegetables man to leave!

Once we got settled, we did invite the little old ladies to our house on the water with a swimming pool. I bought the house but put it in both our names. Sylvia loved it. The house had two formal dining areas and one informal one, three bedrooms, a garage office for me, a large living room, and a screened-in pool with a great party area. The pool area also had a bathroom with a shower. The only flaws were that a well for watering our two-lot yard had a very high content of iron in it, and the house had only a single garage. We did have an avocado tree, which produced hundreds of very large avocadoes, and three fruit trees (lemon, grapefruit, and orange). Florida is fun, except for the summers which is terribly hot and humid, especially if you have a big yard to take care of, which we had!

After about ten years with LCMCD, since I had accomplished my goal of making the computer system one that "Christmas help could use," I was let go with a fairly nice package—it was a bit of a shock to me, but it probably shouldn't have been. I had designed the computer program so that I wasn't needed and those who worked with me could handle it, but I thought that my re-cycling efforts were still needed.

After the end of my career at LCMCD, I became a truly retired guy, the third time. After I ran out of "honey-dos," I started volunteering with the State, primarily to help retrain recently laid-off mid-level managers who had frankly failed to update themselves with the various new technologies, especially computers. It was a very satisfying challenge to help someone who was shocked by being laid off and who probably had a house, car, maybe a boat payment, and very little money in the bank. I used to keep count of those I or we helped regain employment, and it was significant: well over two hundred!

How did we do it? Primarily we taught them how to use a computer, which many of them had not personally trained themselves to use. Then we built their résumé on it. It is amazing how, when working on a personal résumé with a newly learned tool such as a computer, an individual will dynamically and rapidly grow in their ability to use and their knowledge of a computer.

Notice I said, "Our successes," which was because of the fact that the individuals being retrained all worked as a team, and when someone figured out a procedure on the computer that enhanced a résumé, they then told the others. It was truly heart-rending to watch this occur. First, we had to attack the "I am defeated mentality" and, once that was accomplished (and it was always very visible), I could nearly always predict when the individual would get a job.

An incident that occurred during that period that I will always fondly remember when Sylvia and I went to MacDill AFB, Tampa, FL for an Air Force Association meeting. The retired former Air Force Chief of Staff, General Ron Fogelman was to be the speaker. We ran into General Fogelman as we entered the dining room and he said something to the effect, "Aww, Barry, my hero, it is good to see you" as he shook my hand and of course I introduced Sylvia to him and his wife, *Miss Jane*! An astonished Sylvia said, "What was that about?" I said, "I had no idea?"

When the General started his speech he mentioned that, "It is good to see my hero, Barry Howard in the crowd, he is the one who proved that we always will need a gun in a fighter!" Wow, sure made old *Lucky* feel good and damned important!

CALL FROM NEW MEXICO, 7/1997-8/1999

A couple of nice articles were written about our successes with the State getting middle-managers back in the employed world, which were read in New Mexico by someone in a key position, probably Pete Rahn, the Highway Department Director. I received a call one Thursday asking if I was interested in working for the New Mexico Highway Department as a consultant. Of course I accepted the offer, since I always believed that New Mexico was the greatest place to live in the US and still do, in spite of the crummy politics. I was quickly on my way to New Mexico! I departed Florida in my little Nissan pickup with over two hundred thousand miles on it, with my computer and clothes. Sylvia, soon to be my wife, put the house up for sale, and off I went. I arrived in New Mexico and was at my new job on Monday. It quickly became obvious that I had something to offer the Highway Department besides the program I was asked to build. Engineers are scientifically oriented and not too politically or organizationally oriented. Consequently, I contributed in many ways to the Department.

Fortunately, my cousin Karen (Howard) Turner lived in Albuquerque, and she took me under her wing. My cousin Karen was my closest relative, and, since I moved to New Mexico, she has been a wonderful friend and explainer of New Mexico customs and traditions. She had a very special husband (and now my close friend) known to me as my "Doctor or Hawkeye" (Iowa Hawkeyes) Dr. Bob Turner. Hawkeye and I go to the UNM college basketball games together and we truly speak the same language.

Karen had suffered some previous marital challenges that had somewhat tainted her political thoughts and beliefs, but her family orientation is second to none. Karen and I had always clashed, even when my brother Kent and I at a young age lived with her family as our Mom and Dad searched for a place to live after one of Dad's FBI moves to Muncie, Indiana. This was shortly after the war and housing was always in short supply. Karen and Kent constantly challenged Karen's late sister, Lynn and I. Lynn and I were really the "good children," of all of us living with my Aunt Idris and Unk Eddie (Dad's brother) as young children. Lynn, Karen's sister, tragically was murdered as a college student in Colorado. Lynn and I were of course always right, but Karen and Kent continually made life miserable for us by being "tattle-tales" and "Goody Two-shoes."

Karen at one time was a strong member of the Republican Party and married the State Chairman of the party. Unfortunately, that marriage suffered from being on very rocky grounds that were not Karen's fault, but to me, it resulted in her change from a solid-thinking "real American" to an ACLU-supporting liberal/progressive. While I tried to avoid political discussion with or around Karen, I frequently failed in this effort, I guess because I was and am so concerned at this perilous time in our nation.

In spite of her thinking faults, she has been a family strength and an extremely strong worker for and continual volunteer and contributor to disadvantaged folks. She is a woman of action, unlike many progressives or liberals who only speak or demand actions but do not actually provide effort and real support to those who need it.

MARRIAGE TO SYLVIA, 9/26/1997-12/7/2005

Later, returning to Florida for a few days, Sylvia and I were married, with Sylvia's daughter Melanie's son, Logan Jones, who was one-and-a-half-year-old, as the only witness. That night, we did invited some of our friends to a dinner at our favorite Greek restaurant on the beach, not telling anyone that we were married, and during dinner I happened to call Sylvia "Mrs. Howard" Someone at the far end of the table, my friend and buddy Brian Cotterill, heard me and called everyone's attention to it. Also attending our *marriage dinner*, were Jane and Peter Ray our good English friends but their daughter Louise couldn't make it. Later we helped them gain legal status in the US.

Sylvia gave me a great second family with a great daughter Melanie and Grandchillen; grandson Logan and granddaughter Devon. Both Logan and Devon are exciting children who are also great athletics. Logan was probably the best child athlete I had ever seen!

After we were married, we moved to New Mexico, built the home I now live in, and were having a wonderful life when colon cancer struck Sylvia. The sad part is that five years before her death on Dec. 7, 2005, one of our employees on the US 550 highway construction project I was helping to build died of colon cancer. Because of his problem, I insisted that everyone get a colon test. Unfortunately, Sylvia, who was terribly afraid of doctors and hospitals, she refused to have a colon-check. I even cried and got on my knees begging her, but to no avail. Had she had the test, she might be here today. She passed away on Dec. 7, 2005, in Florida with her children and grandchildren.

Sometime after Sylvia learned that she had cancer, she was sitting in the backyard reading when this little, cute dog jumped in her lap! She had her cell phone and called me at work at UMN University saying, "I think the neighbors' new dog has escaped." Since she didn't have their phone number to check with them, I quickly called our wonderful neighbors, Rita and Jim Peaslees, and they said their dog was at home. The dog was a Miniature Pinscher (Min-Pin) and by the time I called her back, the dog had run off.

It seemed that the Min-Pin had been running loose in the neighborhood for some time, and, as you drove around, nearly every house in our neighborhood had food and water out for her by the street. As far as we knew, she ran loose in the neighborhood for three months prior to our catching her, sleeping on various neighbors' back porches. Our neighborhood had lots of coyotes that were enjoying meals of the many rabbits and quail that were growing in the area. That the little dog survived the coyotes was amazing. In any case, Sylvia put out the word that she wanted the little Min-Pin.

Our friends, Jim and Sue Lloyd, borrowed an animal trap, baited it with Kentucky Fried Chicken skin, and caught the little doggie that had been sleeping on their outdoor couch. Sylvia was thrilled and she named her Noel, since she came into our lives at Christmastime, December 7, 2002. Instantly, Noel won our hearts, and, along with our adult male cat, Churchill, who had been with us for eight years, they became our children. Noel was such a great pet and buddy of mine. But unfortunately, after Sylvia passed I met another Lady, "Jan" Causey who was also widowed and we became friends. Noel would go with her to Colorado during the summers. While there Noel, chased a ground squirrel up a tree, made it up about ten feet, and fell backward on her back, hurting herself permanently.

One night a year or so after we caught her, Noel escaped from the house; she truly had a traveling heart, and I was trying to catch her with a bacon trail on the ground and a swing on the door so if she should come in, I would snap it shut. I heard her scream—a bloodcurdling scream! A neighbor and I both ran out to her as she came limping up to me with blood running down her back, as apparently a coyote had tried to get her around the neck. As soon as she saw me, it appeared that she headed back after the coyote, since she now had support. The next day she received eighteen stitches and several drainage tubes, and the Vet said she probably wouldn't survive the attack. BUT no hill for a climber like Noel—she lived for many years after that horrible night!

Recently, my constant companion, Noel began failing and had to be put to sleep during September 2012, and I miss her terribly.

ENGINEER WITH FLATIRON CONSTRUCTION, 9/1999-12/2002

Flatiron hired me away from consulting with the Highway Department to work on Highway 550 from north of Albuquerque to Aztec—114 miles. I need to digress a bit here to explain why I was working for Flatiron Construction Company. Dipak Parekh, along with his assistant, Tom Rath, had recruited me away from the Highway Department, which was easy, since I felt that few challenges remained for me as a consultant. In my two years with the Highway Department, I had really felt useful and accomplished much. I had partnered with Max Valerio, who was one of the sharpest top-level managers in the Highway Department. I would hope that Max would someday run the Highway Department; he is truly an extremely mature, honest, and competent engineer and is a class act!

One of my major accomplishments consulting for the Highway Department that I think demonstrates how important it is for an outsider to review operations, particularly of government agencies, was regarding the computer program that was used for scheduling and managing of highway work. I was asked to review the Highway Department's Computer Management System used to "Manage their work schedule." The program appeared strange and was not functioning like a computer-managed program should operate. I finally was able to learn the name of the company that had built it. I called the company that developed the program, and they said the program had been "dead" for several years. This meant that it should not be used, had not been updated for some time, and should be replaced. We then had a competition for a replacement program, and it became apparent to me that there was some *hanky-panky* going on with one of the competitors, which ultimately was selected by the committee.

As a result, I had to "fall on my sword" and challenge the committee to the individual ultimately responsible for making the replacement-competition decision. I gave him a signed letter telling him that the committees' recommendation was extremely faulty. Fortunately, this classy and strong management leader disregarded obviously strong inputs from the less-than-honest engineers and determined that another competitor's submittal was the best and most useful program and it should be selected. He then selected the correct competitor, not the one who tried to *hanky-panky* the committee's selection process.

Later when I went with Flatiron, I had several titles such as the Training Officer, the point of contact with the Native Americans units along the road, and later operational point of contact with the Highway Department since I obviously had maintained some respect and friendship with members of the department.

I was the one engineer on the project who was having a truly learning situation of learning about highway construction. I was once again truly drinking from a *fire hydrant* and learning from sunrise to sunset! Because of my past leadership experience, I spent a lot of time with Dipak Parekh, the actual program manager, addressing complicated management problems, and I was really enjoying myself. I learned tons from Dipak and his assistant, Tom Rath, and I was able to contribute, because I examined problems from another viewpoint. My viewpoint was still from an engineer's perspective but not just a highway-construction viewpoint. Also, when we had Technical equipment problems, I solved a few of them, which really stood me in good stead with the company's technical expert, John Ross. I was able to read the technical material, which many find hard to do! John Ross was acknowledged as the technical or scientific road-building expert. I think I was able to impress him which really pleased me!

One of my duties was solving problems with the Native Americans or other folks along the road we were building or where we were getting materials. We had a very large gravel pit in La Jara, New Mexico, north and east of our Cuba office. We had a couple of neighbors in La Jara who were just plain— pains in the butt. One fellow who came to our meeting with the La Jara folks as we tried to solve their complaints was a very serious fellow named Jack Leaf. Jack had been a cross-country truck driver and a certified carpenter. Jack had been seriously burned, which was caused by a bombing of the house he and several others rented.

I believe that Jack's body received 80 percent of third-degree burns (with half of them to the bone) and 15 percent of his body had second-degree burns. He arrived at the University of North Carolina, Chapel Hill Burn Clinic in a coma and later they further induced his coma which resulted in about six months of coma as they worked on his body. He also had received artificial knees, but you would never know it, as I have never noticed him let his condition bother him a bit. His recovery can be attributed to our advances in burn treatment and his just plain extremely strong will-power. I also believe the burn center realized his extra strong desire to survive and made him their model! He even served as a volunteer Fire Fighter and drove the large water-truck to the fires.

He studied the material we gave them and soon he became our friend in La Jara. With his help we were able to solve all the complaints and we eventually had one of the contractors put several thousand dollars into neighborhood facilities. Jack has become a longtime friend, and it turns out that he has one brother who made Lt.General in the Air Force and two others associated with the military service. He certainly is a model who demonstrates to me that life goes on with aches and pains. He once said to me, *"Ninety percent of recovery is having a positive mental attitude, and you must just attack!"* Having watched Jack over the years has been a great help to me with my flipping knees!

In my work with the Native Americans living near the area of our work, I found the older Navajos to be very unhappy with the younger Navajos. The reason, even though I set up a training school for those unfamiliar with road construction, none of the young Navajos showed any interest in being trained for the relatively high paying jobs. The old Navajos said to me, "They had built the road we were working on and they wanted the young Navajos to help built the new one!"

I don't believe one young Navajo had the training nor worked on the road for Flatiron but several other young men living along or near the road took the training and developed life-long careers. It was obvious to me, that maybe the young Navajos would rather receive welfare than earn a living and it made the older Navajos very angry!

9/11/01 CHANGED EVERYTHING

9/11/01 will remain in the minds of most Americans as the first actual violation of America's homeland. As I watched it on TV that day, my mind switched back and forth between being angry and sorely sad that I will be too old to be part of this Nation's response. *Being old really sucks!*

Later that day I had a planned meeting as I was assigned as the Flatiron Rep. with New Mexico Transportation Department. Our meeting with them was to be at their offices on University of New Mexico campus, in David Albright office. I assumed that because of the attack in New York, only Transportation Secretary Pete Rahn, David Albright, Steve Roehrig (Sandia National Laboratories), and I showed up. The attack was discussed at length, and, since it was an attack using transportation vehicles as the weapons, strong consideration was given to starting a group to address preparations for future attacks. Secretary Rahn directed Albright to organize a group to address the matter. Because of my military experience, Secretary Rahn asked if I could be involved. I told him I would ask my boss with Flatiron, Dipak Parekh, if I could participate. Dipak immediately agreed that

I should be a member of the team. That night I talked to Chief Federal Judge John Conway, of the Federal Court in New Mexico. He agreed with Secretary Rahn's direction and added that we should involve Los Alamos and Sandia National Labs along with the New Mexico National Guard. I believe he also contacted Secretary Rahn, who he had mentored when the Secretary was a student in high school.

Once officially on the team, David asked that I help him recruit potential members because of my past military experiences. Our team grew at a rapid rate, and members like Col. Greg Zanetti, New Mexico National Guard (later promoted to Brigadier General); Col. Jay Wilson, USAF, M-Day assignee, and many other extremely knowledgeable and experienced individuals who, to me, demonstrated that they were real warriors and volunteered their time to the team.

To ensure we had proper security for our meetings, Ron Grist, a former law enforcement officer, was recruited. Ron was a super Cop and really added to our operations and efforts. He was the strong silent type but when he spoke, you should listen closely, because he kept you secure and out of legal trouble!

Judge John Conway also a warrior, a Naval Academy graduate, and had been an Air Force Fighter Pilot, who flew F-86s and later was dragged, probably kicking and screaming, into B-47 Strategic Bombers! I suspect that is was why he left the Air Force and became an attorney. He, along with Secretary Rahn, became the sponsors of our group.

Judge Conway was also involved as a "Select" Judge who attended special judicial meetings in Washington, DC. I proudly acknowledge that the warrior Judge, John Conway, is my friend and a true patriot!

Our group first addressed what we considered were immediate New Mexico matters but always keeping kept in mind that New Mexico was just part of the whole United States. It became absolutely mandatory that there be direct involvement with the Federal Government. Naturally, because it was transportation-oriented, our first effort was to involve the U.S. Department of Transportation, Washington, DC, which was slow to realize that they had a major part to play in this challenge to our National Security.

Our contact with the FBI, which had legal and direct authorization to be involved, appeared ready to be involved, although it was somewhat disappointing to me as to their lack of initiative and serious concern. I later became aware that my Dad's beloved FBI had become a "Pretty and Politically Correct (PC)" agency. The warrior ethos was still there, but it was immediately obvious that not everyone in the FBI was a warrior!

I later learned what had happened to the FBI through a little personal research. Unfortunately, Congress and the Church Committee had destroyed the former FBI and forced them to become a Politically Correct (PC) organization. This change of the FBI was clearly obvious to me when I visited the FBI Headquarters in the Hoover Building, right after September 11, 2001. I spent several days in the FBI's Hoover building, and, each time I left the building, I stopped under a tree near the exit. I said a little prayer to my Dad who worshipped his FBI and Mr. Hoover, "Saying I was really sorry about the damage that had been done to the FBI."

The New Mexico 9/11/01 team addressed many Homeland Security items, but one area became central, and that was a computer system that could tie the Nation together. Fortunately, the National Laboratories were champions at computer design and functions, and we worked on a nationwide computer netting system. Our team developed a computer system that we tested in five states: Florida, Texas, New Mexico, Missouri, and Maryland, along with units in the FBI's Hoover Building and the Washington, DC, Headquarters of the U.S. Department of Transportation.

We ran a bread-board (first stage of development) operational test just prior to July 4, 2001, as we were concerned that there might be another terrorists' event on July 4, 2001. The test to some degree demonstrated the system, but, unfortunately, a Highway Department computer tech unilaterally made what he thought was a minor program change which really glitched the system. A few months later we ran another test, which was very successful. For both tests, I was in the Hoover building, and the second test clearly demonstrated the utility of the system and most importantly, the security of the system.

During the first test, it surfaced that the FBI used only contractors for their IT operation. This was a bit shocking to me, because there are two things wrong with contractors in the IT world. First, for the FBI, security really matters, and it is difficult to fully and quickly vet contractors. The second, which I have learned through a great deal of computer IT experience, is that contractors always want the next advance in technology and usually work in that direction. Frequently the next technology just doesn't work as advertised until long after it is released and the everyday geeks get to use it regularly, finding or correcting the faults!

As an aside, one of our computer techs who really helped build the system, Lyle Cates, fortunately was so good and unique in the IT world that he was able to make the next generation of security devices work as advertised right from the start. The company that built the devices actually acknowledged that he, Lyle, knew more about the device than the company did. As a result, the company stayed in touch with him as he continually discovered additional capabilities of the device.

The contractor's control of the FBI's IT or computers was clearly demonstrated to us as we tried to sign on the FBI system for the second test. The fact that no FBI person could sign us on the FBI computer system but only a hired contractor could was very concerning to me as a warrior! During a real emergency, there is no assurance that contractors will show up; rather, they might be more concerned about their families.

After the two tests, we thought we had demonstrated to the FBI that our system would give them a capability that would allow their Command Post to stay in contact with the states and the Department of Transportation (DOT). Of equal importance, it was a secure system, and it worked in both directions. The states could make inputs to the FBI or the Transportation Department and the states could receive inputs from the FBI or Transportation Department, securely. This was truly a first in the US: a secure system that worked both ways quickly and dynamically. In the past such systems worked primarily only one way, downward from Washington, DC, to the states.

After the second test, I attended a senior FBI staff meeting and offered the system to the FBI. Shockingly, the senior FBI lawyer said that the FBI could not accept a secure computer system. The system had been built by Sandia and Los Alamos *National Laboratories* along with the New Mexico Highway Department. The system had been developed in Albuquerque for the FBI and the US Transportation Department as a result of the terrorist attack on September 11, 2001. Obviously the FBI lawyer did not realize that the Nation Laboratories exist to develop for other National organizations like the FBI?

Why did he reject it? He said because the computer system cost more than fifty dollars, and the FBI could not accept a gift of this value as per one of the laws governing federal organizations. I asked him if he knew what the National Laboratories were, but received no answer. I was truly in shock!

Today, I am still shocked, especially since recently the FBI's third attempt to install a somewhat similar system to what the geniuses of the National Labs and a few others in the New Mexico Highway Department had offered them for nothing has again failed, as their previous attempts to build a system had failed. And, oh, by the way, the FBI has spent millions on those failed systems! I do blame some of this refusal to the fact that the FBI IT system at the time was in the hands of contractors and they failed to alert the FBI leadership and legal department about the utility of the system offered to them at no cost other than equipment.

Again, we offered them a proven system, which was secure, and at no cost, because the National Labs were involved and New Mexico cares! We had demonstrated the system to them by tying in the five test states and another Federal agency, securely! I know that J. Edgar Hoover would have had a heart attack over refusing the free computer program, since he had a history of always returning some of his budget. He probably turned over in his grave knowing that the FBI has spent millions trying to get what we offered them for free and today, they still lack a fully functional system like we had offered!

Besides building this advanced state-of-the-art system for the FBI, our 9/11/01 group accomplished and developed many security procedures that were copied by other state organizations that had groups similar to ours. During an emergency it is mandatory that the roads be kept open, and, as we explored this area, it was learned that no procedures were established for National Emergencies in the state. The National Guard, the State Police, and associated law-enforcement agencies are key players, and cross-agency procedures needed to be developed. One of the key hang-ups was the need to protect a so-called crime scene. Protecting an event that could be considered a crime scene is important, but if it impedes keeping the roads open in a National Emergency, someone needs to address this matter, possibly even a lowly "On scene" law enforcement officer or young National Guardsman.

As a result of our group's efforts, the New Mexico State Highway and Transportation Department developed a training program that alerted all employees to being the eyes and ears for National Security. Highway Department employees clearly demonstrated this in Florida, where a lowly, unskilled highway department worker observed questionable people who were photographing their roads and bridges.

Exercises were conducted with the State Police, local Law Enforcement agencies, and the National Guard, which has considerable trained personnel, material, and equipment that would be critical during a National Emergency. Through the involvement of outstanding patriots like Tim Olivas, we enjoyed strong involvement of the New Mexico National Guard. Tim was a former Guardsman who was the best deputy I ever experienced. He could find a fault in a plan or program that everyone else missed, including me!

We also recommended that the state make agreements or contracts with those private companies that had the available necessary heavy construction equipment for opening damaged or destroyed nationally strategic roads. At this time, the owner of the biggest equipment company in New Mexico was a West Point graduate and would have been happy to support the state during a National emergency. Unfortunately, I don't believe this ever happened.

History has been re-written about J. Edgar Hoover, but this I know: he made the FBI into the supreme law-enforcement agency in the world, and they were the best, and the world knew it. When folks in Korea, Japan, and the Philippines learned that my Dad was an FBI agent, it opened many doors for me.

The successful efforts of our 9/11/2001 Team began ending when New Mexico elected Governor Bill Richardson. First, I noticed several of his very competent staff members on the state staff retired, resigned, or just disappeared. However, because I was working so hard on what I thought were very important matters, I failed to realize that the program had been seriously undercut. Suddenly the leadership of our team, Brig. Gen. Sobel and Dr. David Albright, were under attack. I was told that someone I already considered a disgrace to his Academy background, a person in a key position, was responsible. In my opinion, he was a very disgusting individual, who, I was told by a very reliable source, generated the attacks on Sobel and Albright. Gen. Sobel and Dr. Albright led a team that produced procedures and material for New Mexico that were copied or used as models for procedures developed by many other states. However, suddenly the team became non-functional, as Sobel and Albright were replaced and now the team was managed by a political hack. In fact, the state then brought charges against one of the most honest, patriotic, moral, and upright person I have ever known, Dr. David Albright. David, besides being the leader of the Highways Research Division, he was also an Ordained Minister. Fortunately, I was asked to testify for him, and the truth came out, and Albright won the case. The function of Homeland security in New Mexico, though, suffered a setback that continued until the Administration was changed.

One fact became apparent to me as we addressed this national emergency was; many in key positions as national leaders were unaware of the utility, creativity and uniqueness of our national laboratories. The following two developments are just examples of the many products from these super labs which truly demonstrate their unique and special ability to develop and provide new capabilities for our Nation. The first was the 50 caliber sniper rifle and the second was a computer program to be used during a medical emergency to address the spread of a serious disease, possibly having been use as a weapon by an enemy. The Labs have the facilities and the brain power to develop and build unique capabilities that maybe needed or just plain dreamed of by the thinkers of our Nation!

SYLVIA'S CANCER, 7/2003-12/7/2005

(I have included parts of my diary which I had established during her sickness with details of this tragic story so that others experiencing cancer could learn!)

While working of the US 550 Highway from Bernalillo to Aztec, one of our key workers developed colon cancer. He had a family history of Colon Cancer and, in fact, he told me that he knew he had it and expected to die of it. As he suspected, he died of it less than six months after that conversation and we lost a great worker and a friend!

As a result, I insisted, though Dipak, that all employees get a checkup and a full scope, if necessary. Fortunately, no one else had problems, but it did start the folks thinking about it. I wanted Sylvia to get checked, but she refused! I begged, pleaded, and even cried on my knees trying to get her to be checkup in late 1998 or 1999, since there was a history of colon cancer in her family. Unfortunately, she continued to refuse to be checked.

Late in July or early August 2003, she realized that she was having problems and visited a very competent PA, Lynn Healer, of Lovelace's Rio Rancho office, who arranged a scope for her in two days, on August 25, 2003. After the procedure, it was apparent that she had a problem, and a doctor at Lovelace, Dr. Jean Wright, scheduled surgery for her and removed a cancerous growth. At the time Doctor Wright indicated that Sylvia might consider having chemo, but the odds were only 1-3 percent that she needed it. Further, her CEA, which is used to indicate colon cancer, was a wonderful 4.8 on September 23, 2003, and fewer than 5.0, was considered-cancer free!

We visited the UNM oncology and Dr. Binder, the Department Head, who asked why we were there? We indicated that we would prefer to start Chemo just in case, so they started the procedure soon afterwards.

Unfortunately, Sylvia's CEA jumped to 107 eight months later on March 4th, 2004. We immediately scheduled, through Dr. Binder, a visit to MD Anderson. At MD Anderson, Sylvia was fortunate enough to be assigned to Dr. Steven Curley, formerly of Albuquerque and a superb Doctor and the head of the Department. He adjusted her chemo and scheduled her for an operation to remove the spots on her liver either by surgical cutting or by burning them off. Sylvia had the operation at MD Anderson and, much to our dismay, after Dr. Curley opened Sylvia up, he realized that the cancer had metastasized to her abdomen. She was closed after he burned a few of them off her liver, and her only hope was further chemo including a new combination of drugs which Dr. Curley recommended that she start.

Unfortunately, in the middle of the night on October 23, 2004, Sylvia indicated that she might be having a heart attack! After giving her aspirins, I got her to Loveless in fourteen minutes racing an ambulance traveling from US 550 and beating them there by five minutes. They were able to put a stent in her, and she recovered very quickly. We flew her to Florida after the heart attack, and I drove my truck down with the dog, Noel, and Churchill, the cat!

Sylvia had previously had some chemo in Florida and had also previously visited a heart specialist, Dr. Hoffman, in Florida. On November 5, 2004, Dr. Hoffman gave her a clean bill of health for the heart! Our next visit was back to MD Anderson on January 31–February 2, 2005. Dr. Curley indicated that the tumors were stable and no increased size was noted. We returned to Albuquerque and another visit to a heart specialist, Dr. Kim, who again confirmed that no damage was done by the heart attack.

As a result, Sylvia started her third series of chemo at New Mexico Cancer Center (NMCC), which was closer to our home. We were impressed with the New Mexico Cancer Center, and the professionals there appeared to be very competent, and they had a great dietitian!

She completed the series and did quite well. We then went to Florida for ten days so that she could spend time with her children and grandchildren. Returning from Florida, she started chemo at the NMCC again, but this time the new chemo caused her considerable troubles. She suffered from diarrhea, mouth sores, and neuropathy. At the same time at NMCC, her Oncology Doctor, Dr. Merin, thought that she found some cloudiness in a chest X-ray possibly indicating Fibrosis. Fortunately, a visit was scheduled with Dr. Archie Sanchez, a Fibrosis specialist, and he indicated that her lungs were OK and she had no sign of cancer in her lungs! At last, some good news!

Again we visited MD Anderson June 4–8, 2005, and Dr. Curley indicated that there was no increase in the liver tumors, no sign of lung problems, and only a slight increase in the abdomen tumors. He directed a new and possibly better chemo, which had never been used in New Mexico before. It was Ceturimab or Erbitux (called the Martha Stewart drug) and Irinotecan.

Sylvia suffered problems with the chemo and several times had to have emergency hydration. All the while, I am searching for possible help by contacting every known cancer facility in the US. I do need to add that the NMCC nurses and dietitian were very good and professional. Later, it was determined that some of her problems were caused by a stomach toxin called *Clostridium Difficile*, and she was given a two-week prescription of Metronidazole, which helped a great deal. We even went to a UNM football game for five hours, and she enjoyed it. Happiness was when she was feeling good!

Because Sylvia's children and grandchildren lived in Florida, I started contacting the cancer research hospital, Moffitt, Tampa, Florida, that we had been told was a very good cancer research hospital. With Dr. Curley's approval, we traveled to Florida to try their facility.

At Moffitt, she was assigned a Dr. Catherine Chodkiewicz, and Moffitt gave her a CT scan (9/16/05) and I delivered a CD with all of her previous scans from MD Anderson. After Dr. Chodkiewicz reviewed her scans, she told Sylvia and me that she was doing well, and "There is no rush for further chemo." She did add that there was an additional tumor on the liver to make three (we thought it might have been the one that Dr. Curley burned off). Dr. Chodkiewicz seemed very professional and competent. She did notice that Sylvia's stomach was distended and thought that she might be constipated and recommended that she take laxatives to solve it. While Dr. Chodkiewicz was good, the staff at Moffitt was not impressive.

After taking the laxatives, Sylvia felt terrible, and her daughter, Mel, insisted that she go to the Emergency Room in the hospital where she worked, on October 8, 2005. She had an X-ray, CT scan, and a Doctor's examination. Based on her blood-work, it was decided that she had a urinary infection, and she was given five tablets of Levaquin 500 mg. She continued to feel bad and started turning yellow.

We finally heard from Moffitt around 1800 on October 17, telling us that Sylvia had missed an appointment at 1600, of which neither she nor I had been notified. She was given an appointment the next day with Dr. Chodkiewicz along with a sonogram, blood test, and a visit with a Dr. Suspect who believed she had a bile duct blockage.

On October 25, after being unable to get any response from Moffitt between Oct. 18 and Oct. 24, we went to Moffitt without an appointment, and they realized that she was seriously ill and admitted her to the hospital. Once she was admitted, they considered a stent in the bile duct to open it, and on October 26, 2005, Dr. Barthel tried putting the stent in with no luck! Next they decided to put a drain in the bile duct and Dr. Choi (SP) did the drain procedure. His efforts, briefing, and the team were the most outstanding we had observed at Moffitt, and their team was as good as anyone we ever saw during this terrible time. Once the drain was installed, when Sylvia was released from the Moffitt hospital, no follow-ups were indicated. Having dealt with several other hospitals, this had to be the worse we had ever seen, especially regarding administrative procedures. I would add that in the Air Force, I had senior management responsibility for three different hospitals, so when I say going to Moffitt was a serious mistake; it is based on my extensive past experiences. I provided the hospital administration a detailed letter addressing our concerns but never received a response from them. After dealing with MD Anderson and Moffitt, I would never recommend Moffitt!

After many phone calls to Moffitt, we were able to get an appointment with Dr. Chodkiewicz at 1400 on October 26, with Sylvia getting blood work at 1100. She met with Dr. Chodkiewicz and another doctor discussing her future and they stated that she would be around for next Christmas.

I need to digress: once Sylvia refused to enter a test treatment program, it seemed that Dr. Chodkiewicz lost interest in treating Sylvia. It was obvious that Sylvia was going downhill rapidly, and her pain was increasing tremendously. She was entered into the hospice program for home care. The hospice nurses and doctors, especially Dr. Guthrie, were wonderful and helped relieve her pain. They began shots of Procrit and provided bandages for changing her dressings. Sylvia, being the tough lady she was, continued using the bathroom, and helped change her own bandages.

On December 5, 2005, Dr. Choi changed her drain, again demonstrating the wonderful competency of their unit. That same day Sylvia's son, Chris Thompson, strongly urged us to admit Sylvia to a hospice facility where she could get constant professional help.

Once the decision was made, which she agreed with, I made a terrible mistake by having her taken in an ambulance rather than in my truck. I rode with her, and the ambulance absolutely terrified her, and I will always be sorry that I didn't take her in my truck!

The Sarasota Hospice facility was magnificent, and the care was the best she had ever received.

They immediately put her on high levels of morphine, and her pain subsided almost instantly. Mel, Chris, and I spent the night with her. I blew my stack at a nurse who turned her over during the night. The nurse said, "She didn't want her to get bedsores." Unfortunately, Sylvia moaned and cried when she was turned. Early the next morning, December 7, 2005 (the same day, years earlier, we had obtained her dog Noel!), I jumped in my truck to run back to the Mel's house to feed the animals around 0630. Sylvia was sleeping soundly without moans of pain, looking at peace and beautiful. Around 0730–0745, I was talking to my brother Kent on my cell phone while driving to Mel's house in Punta Gorda, and I heard someone trying to call me. I then received a call that Sylvia had passed around 0730; I was told that she had a smile on her face and Mel and Chris were holding her hands when she passed.

I immediately returned to the hospice facility, and she was still in her bed looking beautiful and with a smile on her face. I knew she was in a better place and finally free of pain!

I have to say Moffitt was a great disappointment because of their terrible operation, especially administratively, which lacked professionalism and lacked the loving care that we had seen every other place, particularly at M.D. Anderson where we had taken Sylvia several times earlier. M.D. Anderson is absolutely the first team concerning cancer!

We had Sylvia cremated, as she had requested. We held a wonderful service in Punta Gorda with the Catholic Priest who had earlier given her full entry into the Catholic Church, which gave her wonderful relief and religious satisfaction. After the service in Punta Gorda, we moved to Sylvia's favorite Irish bar in North Fort Myers, where many of her friends helped celebrate her life. It was a wonderful event that we all were very satisfied with. Additionally, Chris had put together a wonderful collage of her life. Chris still has her ashes.

During the whole process, I don't believe I was ever told that Sylvia was a stage IV cancer patient, but maybe I just didn't want her to be and avoided acknowledging it. Sylvia spent only one night in hospice, but it was absolutely perfect and made her passing as good as it could be! I have told this entire story in hopes that others will benefit from it. My greatest concern is that there doesn't seem to be a central point of knowledge for cancer in this nation, but M.D. Anderson is *absolutely* the best starting point.

JANICE MARIE "JAN" CAUSEY, 2/1/2006-7/24/2007

Dick Desing, an old fighter pilot friend, insisted on having me meet someone he had known for a long time, Janice Marie "Jan" Causey. I hesitated to meet her so soon after Sylvia's death. Initially, I resisted meeting her, but he tricked me into meeting her much sooner that I should have. Dick and I occasionally had lunch together, and he brought her to one of the lunches. Jan and I talked a bit, but nothing happened—no bells and whistles sounded. Sometime later, two or three weeks, I asked her out to dinner, and we had a great Italian meal, and the bells and whistles started sounding. It started when I picked her up; Rush Limbaugh was on her radio, and, when we returned home, she put Patsy Cline on the record player. I think every man has a "dream woman" in his mind. Mine was a tall, slender, athletic, beautiful, very conservative, and strongly independent woman with red hair. Jan doesn't have red hair, but she has everything else that was in my dreams. She does have beautiful naturally curly dark hair, which is always perfect. Little Napoleon would have loved it! She is graying a bit, and it looks like it has been done in the beauty shop. She truly filled the role of my dream woman.

We were together for over a year, and I wanted to make it more permanent. At the time, she agreed, but we realized that we had a problem about where we would live, since I liked my western house, which was truly out in the country on an acre of land, and she truly loved her more formal cosmopolitan or Victorian house in town on a quarter of an acre but on a very nice golf course.

Then one day, Jan, without a word of discussion, said, "We are finished." Shocked, I asked why, and she said something about she would make me miserable, and she wanted to be alone. I tried for months to convince her otherwise but no luck. I must admit I was heartbroken! We still haven't completely talked about how what was so wonderful, suddenly died? During our time together, she also fell in love with Noel, and, after our split-up, she still got Noel when I hit the gym/pool or would go someplace. I deliver Noel to her "Mommy" rather than leaving her home alone. At Jan's house she was spoiled rotten, and, of course, Noel truly loved Jan!

Once Jan came into Noel's life, Noel would travel to Colorado with Jan, where she normally spent the summer with her friend of over forty years, Fay Dillis. During the second summer while visiting Colorado with Jan, Noel chased the ground squirrel up a tree and fell backward, permanently and seriously hurting her back legs. Noel responded well to Depo-Medrol (steroid) shots for some time, and each month she got one. I also found a car seat that allowed her to see out of the car even better than she could before she was hurt, and she was extremely happy riding in her seat! During her final days, we did all we could to make her life good, and I think we succeeded, with Jan spoiling her horribly.

During this time, Noel had become my constant buddy or sidekick, going with me wherever I traveled. Unfortunately, in middle of 2011, the shots became less effective, and she became somewhat infirmed. The vet, Sam Shook, and I knew the end was nearing, but Jan resisted that thought. Unfortunately, I was in San Diego 7–11 September, 2011 with my new Lady friend, Sandra, at a Naval Academy class of 1958 reunion. Jan was taking care of Noel when, unfortunately, it became time for Noel to be put to sleep. Early Saturday morning, the 10th of September, I received a call from Jan, who was in tears, stating, "It was time for Noel." Jan impressed me with her strength during this trying period.

My neighbor and Navy fighter-pilot friend, Jim Lloyd (Jim was shot down in an A-7 and rescued the furthest north of any Naval pilot), after I called him, he quickly drove to the Veterinarian office. Dr. Shook was also my good friend and Noel's vet; he also helped Jan. What friends!

My children Barrie and Mike weighed in and called Jan to support her while Dorlyne called me. My very good friend, Mike Hughes, quickly dug a grave in my backyard for Noel, and, after Noel was buried, he built a wonderful burial site for her. I visit her almost every morning, and I sure miss her, as does Churchill the cat. I think Jan has only seen Noel's grave once. Churchill seems to be concentrating on helping me accept Noel's demise. Noel is missed by all of us; she, like all family dogs, was special. Churchill has been in the family for over eighteen years and truly seemed to realize that I needed support, Additionally, Churchill now runs the house, especially when it is time to get up!

PHOEBE WANTZ, 2/2008-7/2008

Sometime later, my oldest friend in Muncie, Jan Etchison, called me and asked me to help out a friend and a high school classmate of my brother Alan, Phoebe Wantz. Could she come to New Mexico to get her artistic juices flowing again? Of course, I agreed, so Phoebe arrived a few days later. She had planned to rent a car and travel the state. I happened to be without any commitments at the time, so I became a tour guide, and I learned about New Mexico art while Phoebe toured the various artsy areas of the state.

My cousin Karen Turner, who used to have an art studio, started her off on her tour of New Mexico and gave her some great advice about the New Mexico art world. I have to admit, I enjoyed the tours, although I am a terrible tourist! Along the way, several of the artists gave Phoebe, whom I now called "Little Bit," some great advice, and she returned to Muncie fired up. She did over a hundred paintings when she got home.

We have kept in contact, and I visited her once in Florida, where she goes for the winter, since she hates the cold winters in Indiana, as anyone could hate Indiana in the winter!

MY KNEES, 9/10/2003-PRESENT

It was obvious long ago that I was going to have knee problems, and I decided that I wanted to have an operation while my Cousin Karen's husband, Dr. Bob "Hawkeye" Turner, was still involved with the operations. He was, before he retired, Head of Ortho-pedic Surgery at the famous Lovelace Hospital, which handled the initial astronauts' training program. He was retired, but he still, to keep his hand in it by assisting Dr. Tom McEnnerny during sur-gery. I was able to have McEnnerny do my first knee operation on September 10, 2003, primarily because Bob Turner would assist.

The first surgery went very well, and I recovered quickly. Dr. Tom mentioned that I could do anything I had previously done with my knee, which probably was a mistake, because I am a bit of an exercise nut. I was exercising in the Kirtland AFB gym and the pool, where you can do much more with your body in the water than in a gym! Additionally, I had been given Zocor by my personal Doctor, a Lovelace General Practitioner (GP), because my cholesterol was a bit high.

Unfortunately, I had a classic statin (Zocor) reaction where the muscle structure weakens, and, unknown to me or my doctors, the kneecap, which was metal, slipped out of place. Now I had metal-on-metal, and the leg filled with metal filings. This was confirmed by a "soft tissue" X-ray on a Thursday late afternoon. Unfortunately, it appeared to the doctors that my leg was infected, not knowing that the kneecap was rubbing on the titanium plugs put in the lower and upper bones of the knee. The X-ray was taken on Thursday, July 8, 2004, and I was operated on Friday evening, July 9, 2004. The only nice thing about the surgery was the nurses were very good-looking on a late Friday night!

My right knee has never recovered properly after my second operation. Sometime later, it became apparent that I needed another operation. When I couldn't get a response out of Dr. Tom, I contacted Dr. White, at Presbyterian Hospital, who had a reputation similar to Hawkeye Turner, my cousin-in-law. In fact, when I told him that Dr. Turner was my cousin, Dr. White said, "He is the only one I would let do a replacement for me!" He was retiring and assigned my knee to his new replacement, Dr. Mike Archibeck.

Dr. Archibeck removed the prosthesis on June 9, 2005, and had me in bed for six weeks having antibiotic IVs (Vancomicin) morning and night to make sure I didn't have any infection. After many, many tests, it was confirmed that no infection existed. On August 8, 2008, he then replaced the prosthesis, and I was off and walking again. However, the swelling never subsided, and a large bump appeared on the right side of the knee, which was frequently drained of fluid and tested for infection, but there never was an indication that an infection existed.

Being disappointed with Dr. Archibeck, I did not realize that I was his first patient at Presbyterian. I was very disappointed that he had not developed what I thought were good doctor's *bedside manners*. But several of my friends who have been operated on by him lately, rave about him, and he even told a friend he operated on to tell me that he had learned about *bedside manners*!

As I continued to have problems with the knee, I visited Dr. Dan Berry at Mayo Rochester, Minnesota, to obtain his opinion. He said he could fix it, but he refused to tell me what he intended to do and how many operations it would require.

Once again, I felt as if I wouldn't be part of the solution, so I visited the VA Orthopedic department and saw Dr. Joel Cleary, the Chief of the Orthopedic Department, who had initially been partially trained by my cousin Dr. Hawkeye Turner. Hawkeye was very impressed with Dr. Cleary, and so was I: a big man from Helena, Montana, my kind of guy, and his confidence made me confident! He said, "You aren't going to Mayo; I am going to fix you!"

Initially he also treated my left knee with "rooster comb injections," because it was now very painful, and, from the X-rays, it was as bad as or worse than the right one, which had previously been operated on! Normally, Dr. Cleary gave me the knee injections, which were virtually painless, but when a nurse did it, they were brutal. I only let a nurse do it once, and I suggested to Dr. Joel that he instruct the nurses as to how to give the injections, fast! Probably because I was favoring the right knee, the stress on the left knee was increased and subsequently the pain increased dramatically. I was up to 10 mg hydrocodone (Vicodin) about three to four times a day. However, I now constantly wear a brace on it, which prevents radical movement and my pain has subsided. I now control my pain with "over-the-counter" Aleve and very occasional a 5 mg hydrocodone pill.

Dr. Cleary, in February, scheduled me for right knee surgery June 16, 2009. However, by the end of March, the pain was so bad that I dropped by the VA orthopedic clinic on Friday, March 27, 2009, and was going to ask for a much sooner operation. At that visit, Dr. Cleary said the Ortho Board had met and decided that I needed surgery sooner and, was I, "Ready for surgery the next Tuesday [March 31, 2009]?" Of course I was, and the surgery was performed early on March 31, with part of the existing prosthesis being removed, and a medical plug with antibiotics again being installed. This put me into a wheel-chair until the next operation, with my leg rigid and straight out!

Also I was put on very strong antibiotics, Cephalexin, four per day. Going into the operation, the operating staff wasn't very encouraged, but after the operation they were ecstatic and very positive. I was told that had I not had the operation, I might have lost the leg, because the bone was deteriorating, cracking, and collapsing. So on March 31, 2009, I climbed into a wheelchair, since I had no functional knee, and little did I know that I wouldn't climb out of the wheelchair until late in July 2009!

Having built several houses, I always made sure that they were handicap-capable—but not the one we built in Placitas in 1998. What a horrible mistake, because being in a wheelchair is bad enough but being in a house that isn't handicap-capable is a real pain! I had to buy a small refrig, since I could not get into the big one in the kitchen, and I have destroyed most doorways getting my wheelchair through.

During this period of "Barry in the wheelchair," I was blessed with family and friends who helped this widower in a house that was definitely unfriendly to a wheelchair. The night before my first operation, there were seventeen friends and neighbors at the house for Italian food, primarily prepared by Kat Hite, my friend Art's girlfriend. Art of course has been my friend, driver, and helper throughout this period.

My ex-wife, Dorlyne, was here from Texas three times "kicking ass and taking names (mine)": April 11–17, May 3–13, and June 21–July 1. My son Mike was here the night before my operation, on April 20, and stayed through the 23rd. Barrie was here May 11–21.

I assumed that the next operation, scheduled for April 21, 2009, would be when the part of the prosthesis previously removed would be replaced, and I would be off and walking. However, Dr. Joel warned me that he might have to do more "clean-up" in the knee and take more cultures. I even wrote him a letter saying I was willing to chance future problems, but *please* put in the prosthesis! I lost the battle, and again I was still in a wheelchair after an April 21, 2009, operation to again "clean out the knee!"

I did leave the hospital on Saturday, April 25, 2009, on no antibiotics but self-injecting Enoxaparin, a blood thinner, I believe. I have been trained by the VA medical folks to give myself injections and the use of a "pick" for putting medicine into my body. I was told that during the next operation, on May 21, 2009, the prosthesis would be put in the knee.

Later, Dr. Joel said maybe it would be May 26 before the next operation. I again pleaded with him that he had previously scheduled me for May 21, 2009. I told him that my daughter, Barrie, would be here from England for the operation, but she would have to go back after the 21st. He then mentioned that possibly he would do it on May 19, 2009.

The stitches were removed on May 8, and the entire staff suggested that I needed the next operation on the 19th or 21st of May, not the 26th.

I had really worked on leg exercises as Hawkeye (Dr. Bob Turner) had suggested before the operations started, so my legs were in good shape. However, after the operations, I slept fairly well, but I could not get enough exercise. On May 9, 2009, I was able to climb into the backseat of my Toyota pickup truck and, again, I was mobile! I had started traveling more. I could get in the backseat of my truck, and Dorlyne was able to load my wheelchair in the back bed of the pickup, so we could do more.

Unfortunately, the operation scheduled for May 21 was moved to May 26. Barrie had returned to England, but she had been with me from May 11–20. The May 26 operation went well, with the prosthesis inserted along with a cadaver bone, a metal band and lots of bone cement. I had very little pain (I seldom have much pain), but there was still some swelling and the blood-pooling problems.

On June 2, 2009, I was released to Advanced Heath Care of Albuquerque for rehab, since I was a widower with no one to help me at home. Advanced Heath Care was truly a dream rehab facility. The rooms were private, food exceptional, and the staff superb. Having been to a few rehab centers, this was head and shoulders above any others I had visited!

I do need to digress a bit about Advanced Health Care: it is a fantastic facility, both concerning facility and the staff. It is a facility that can have a patient up to one hundred days, and their whole effort is to rehabilitate the patient. They are very tough but extremely sensitive and kind to the patient. I, of course, was in their physical therapy program, which kept me in the gym area a great deal. Since I wanted badly to be rehabbed, I would start working out around 0630, which probably I wasn't allowed to do, but they knew I was doing the right procedures, and the PT staff usually arrived around 0700.

I worked with four ladies whom I called Torture One (Sarah), Torture Two (Ruth), Torture Three (Susan), and Torture Four (Claire), but what dedication and professionalism those ladies demonstrated! Since I spent so much time in the workout area, I had the opportunity to watch all the efforts of the Physical Therapy and Operational Therapy professionals. I watched them take patient in a fetal-position and get that person up and walking and truly rejoining society. It was absolutely a wonderful thing to observe! I watched them go to the rooms and get those who wanted to be fetal and coax them to the training room. I watched them take individuals who had literally given up and eventually in the Operational Training (OT) kitchen, preparing meals—what a thrill!

I had another appointment with Dr. Joel on June 9th at the VA. Dr. Cleary opened the bottom of the incision and drained lots of junk out of the wound, much to my sad disappointment, because I assumed I would then be released to go home!

Dr. Clearly warned that he might have to go back into the knee and clean it out again! At my next appointment with Dr. Joel, June 19th, he admitted me to the VA and scheduled me for surgery on June 20th. Needless to say, I was shocked, since again I had thought I would be going home, as Dorlyne was arriving on Sunday, June 21st. He indicated that he would open only about four to six inches of the knee, but in fact he opened more than twelve inches of it, and again cleaned it out. On Monday, June 22nd, he released me home to the care of my ex-wife, God bless her!

Dorlyne Bailey Howard was the star of this show, along with others such as Sandra Schakel a neighbor I had met and I had an interest in. Dorlyne made my life livable, visiting me three times. During those periods she reorganized this widower's house: threw out lots of stuff, mostly outdated foods, and just plain took charge. She didn't baby me, did some nursing, and most importantly gave me companionship, great food, and a better-organized house. Of course, after she left, I couldn't find a damn thing!

I continued in the wheelchair as directed and by now, I could handle it pretty well. I continued to destroy several of the door jams and parts of the wall about two feet high. I had lots of painting and repair to do once I returned to an operational status. I loved walking Noel in my wheel-chair. There is a hill to the east of my house, so we would climb the hill in the wheel-chair and then race down it, almost a fighter pilot again! Now the knee has a cadaver bone, a couple of steel bands, lots of bone cement, and I could now walk!

Sometime during this period Mike Hughes started working for me since it was obvious that I was unable to do many things around the house. Mike, his three dogs and cat, lived with me for a while since the place he was supposed to live was denied to him. Dave Hite, a neighbor who had recently married Judith Acosta, my beautiful neighbor. They had met on the Internet. It seems to be a great match, and he lived in Montana when they started communicating! Dave has cut the yard several times, and it appears he really likes doing it since he has no yard here to cut.

During this period I tried to change some of the sprinkler heads to improve the watering pattern. I changed four from the wheelchair, and three of them worked and improved the pattern—one didn't. Mike Hughes to the rescue!

On July 13, 2009, at 1030, Dr. Joel Cleary cleared me again to start physical therapy (PT) and rejoin the world of walking, working, and contributing to my environment! He cleared me for walking at 20–percent of my weight with crutches or a cane and I could resume PT sessions (gentle and non-stress for now) three times a week for fifteen sessions. The ladies at Advanced Health Care (Tortures One through Four) again started the PT and really worked me out as follows, starting on July 15, 2009:

1. Warm-up exercises designed by Tania from Operational Training department.
2. Using an exercise machine for twenty minutes with adjustable resistance, which exercises the knees and arms.
3. Weight machine at forty pounds level to strengthen the arms.
4. Numerous leg exercises on a table, forty to sixty at a time in reps of ten.
5. Using parallel bars for leg exercises that work on the hip area.
6. Knee-bending exercises, stepping type.

7. The last event was using an exercise machine that runs the knee the full gambit from 0 to 90 degrees for thirty minutes.
8. Finally, Susan started giving me a massage on my right leg that really gave me some relief; God love Susan!

I normally would start at 0730 and finish at 1000 or 1030 sweating a bit. It sure felt good, but I would take an Aleve gel after exercising. On Monday, July 27, 2009, I started working out at the base pool again with my old water-aerobics class, which I had been part of since at least 1999. During this PT period I was still restricted to only 50 percent of my weight on my right knee, which required me to use crutches, wheelchair, or a cane. During this period, my life was somewhat disrupted and frankly lonely, because the relationship with Jan Causey had stopped. I was experiencing an unpleasant existence! When a neighbor I had met earlier, Sandra Schakel, entered my world, soon Sandra and I developed a slightly more than social relationship, since my ability to mess around was non-existent, but I did get a lot of sympathy!

Susan or Ruth continued my Physical Training (PT), and their massages are the best part of PT! Once again, I was relying simply on an over-the-counter Aleve to deaden the soreness that followed the workouts! Unfortunately, the ability to regenerate my endurance was challenged, and I extremely slowly recovered, as my COPD from the aircraft fires seemed to control my distance-walking ability.

I also received PT from the VA Physical Fitness folks, especially Rob Garner, who is every bit as good but tougher than the Torture Ladies from Advanced Health Care of Albuquerque. Rob is known throughout the PT world, and most rave about him. He is a good bit tougher, and he had me doing harder events, because I hurt a bit more after his sessions. I still frequently stop by to see him, as he is a special guy!

I realized that recovery was a long, slow process, and there will be pain or soreness, and I must just work through it! I was very fortunate or *lucky* again because I could walk and had a functioning right leg and a very strong desire to return to normal life as best I can. Jack Leaf was a model for me, and he has proven to me by example that a positive mental attitude is the key! Of course, I did get lots of sympathy.

Unfortunately, around December 20, 2011, my right thigh started seriously acting up and I was again using my old walker and was suffering more extreme pain than I ever had, any time before! I was certain that the muscle or ligament of the right thigh, where the cadaver bone had been placed, had severed. With all my operations, I seldom used serious pain medicine, but this pain was more intense than I ever had experienced! Fortunately, after I had a nuclear full body scan and a visit with Dr. Shelly from the VA (who assisted on my four knee operations at the VA), it was determined that it was bruised muscle or ligament, and around Valentine's Day the pain began to subside. Another visit to the VA PT man, Rob Garner, and I began a very light weight work, again on my legs, on February 27, 2012! I had never stopped my water aerobics, where I concentrated on my upper body, which I needed to be able to get up from sitting. However, in my old age, I was getting smarter: a cane painted like an American flag colored of red, white, and blue with stars has become my constant friend! Barrie, my daughter, brought it in Texas. I have since found them on the Internet and give them to special friends.

I need to expand a bit on the patriotic cane which Barrie bought me when I forgot my cane, flying to Texas. I called Barrie and asked her to pick one up for me at Walmart. She initially selected a PINK one which, when my ex-Dorlyne saw it, said, "Barrie you know your Dad will kill you if you give him the PINK one!" She quickly replaced it with the one I love, the Red, White and Blue cane and many folks I pass comment on it!

Recently, at the suggestion of an older Doctor friend, I have had some of the veins in the right leg removed. I have learned that vein removal has been going on for over 60 years and it is a very well established procedure. So far, only minor pain or discomfort and the swelling of my right leg is down considerably and the proper color is returning to the lower leg. To me, it has been extremely beneficial series of operations and I wish I had had it done or it had been recommended to me long ago!

Anyone who has had a serious operation knows how concerned the nurses are about the patient getting sick when he eats the first meal in Recovery. I am a rare duck in this regard. I am starved after surgery and want spicy hot food, lots of it. Usually someone will bring me some hot and spicy Popeye's chicken, which I love. It is fun watching the nurses peek in to make sure I don't get sick, which I never have! They normally put a pan near me in case I get sick, but it has never been used! I tell everyone I am Hispanic in gringo disguise since I love spicy hot food! Sandra says I have destroyed my taste buds since I put hot sauce on nearly everything.

SANDRA SMITH SCHAKEL, 3/2009-PRESENT

Sometime in March of 2009, I met a neighbor who had lived just down the street from me for many years, Sandra (Smith) Schakel. Beautiful Sandra was a neighbor that I had seen only once in the twelve years I lived in Placitas. She was only seven houses away, and I had to pass her house whenever I departed or returned home. She is an exotic beauty with a history that hopefully someday she will write her story of her exciting life. Since meeting her, our lives have been exciting, fun filled and truly unbelievable!

Sandra's life has been storybook, and at age eighteen, immediately after she graduated from high school in Studio City, California, she married Steve Reeves, Mr. World, Universe, USA, and probably the first of the generation of clean bodybuilders whom Arnold Schwarzenegger and others modeled themselves after.

Sandra is probably the original Valley Girl, and with Mr. Universe after their marriage, they immediately departed California for NYC, where Steve was in a Broadway show. They had two exciting years together, traveling with the show and later opening a gym in Miami.

After she and Steve split, and because of her proven leadership abilities and intellect, assisted by her natural beauty, she rose above the well-known glass ceiling that many women have suffered. She quickly advanced to become a Vice-President of a Savings and Loan (S&L). Over time she was a VP for several different Savings and Loans. At one time, she managed seventeen branches of Savings and Loans. After Steve, she had a very dynamic social life. Eventually she married Chuck Schakel, a veteran of WWII who, as a Marine, had hit many of the islands in the Pacific that the Marines hit. She and her late husband, Chuck, had moved from California over twenty-three years ago to Placitas. They were married for eighteen years before he passed from a staph infection. At the same time, she was taking care of her Mother who had Alzheimer's and was bedridden for ten years until she died. Chuck died four months before her mother died. Sandra later worked for JC Penny in their call center at night. Sandra is a dynamo and never seems to have idle periods; she can wear me out.

Once we got together, did we shine! We met one day when I saw her trying to lift a large item into her red Jeep. I stopped and asked if I could help her. Of course, she, being the independent lady that she is, said, "No, thanks." Later that day, at Walgreen's, I was there wanting to copy some pictures on their machine, and Sandra was using and using and using it! Finally, after I walked by several times, she realized that I was waiting to use the machine and asked if I wanted to use it. Naturally I said I did, but once I tried to use it, I realized that I was "The dummy in Walgreen's!" She helped me, and then our friendship began. Actually, a few days later she was putting her trash can out for pick-up, and I was driving by. I asked her to go to dinner—soooo we met at the trash can!

She loved my lifestyle, partying with military folks, my fighter pilot reunions, and my social life. Being with her was unbelievable;

when she walked into a room, everyone stared, and before too long she would know everyone, and they really loved her. Good-bye hugs and good-bye kisses were her specialty, and they were just her way. Having her hanging on my arm, I felt like a king, and my status certainly rose.

On top of her beauty, she also treated me like a king since I am not as agile as I used to be. She fixes dinner most every night, fixing me drinks when I arrived, and really making my life wonderful. I do try to get the groceries we need, however. At this time, I was not the most agile or without pain from my knees, and being waited on was wonderful! She was great handling my wheelchair when I was in it, and, though she said she frequently considered it, she never pushed me over a cliff.

Unfortunately, we were the same in many ways, and over-time people who are the same develop irritants, which can cause flashes of anger. We had scheduled several events in the future, but one day I guess I made her unhappy, and when I got home from a meeting with the boys, she had filled my garage with most of the presents I had given her, along with some of my things that were at her house. A short e-mail from Sandra told me that the end of a uniquely wonderful relationship had arrived. It was a great two years.

From our discussions, I assumed that she had many very inter-esting men in her life, and many of them were very distinguished. Most of them were from different worlds than mine. Before the blow-up, I had already told her we were going to our favorite res-taurant, Blades, for her Birthday. I called her and said that I still had a key to her house, and I was going to take her to Blades even if she was still in her pajamas! When I arrived she was dressed magnificently, as she normally is and off we went. We resolved our problems and now see each other more regularly.

Since I am a fighter pilot, I must go to the Air Force bar, if available, on Friday nights. Now Sandra accompanies me to what used to be the Officers Club at Kirtland AFB on Friday nights. Our longtime friends are also normally there on Friday night—Les (Fighter Pilot), Joe (Nuclear scientist), Rob (Air Force Retiree and High School teacher), Chuck (Sandia Technician), and his wife Jane—and while there we are *managed* by normally either Miriam or Gale of the club staff.

Afterwards, on the way home we often also stop at Silva's bar, run by our friend and the son of the man who began the bar long ago, Felix Silva. Felix's father received the very first New Mexico liquor license for his bar after Prohibition that was issued.

Silva's bar is, to say mildly, unique. It was opened on the day after Prohibition ended and has been run by the same family ever since. I always try to take visitors there, because it is truly a family bar where everyone knows everyone else, and it is loaded with history. Especially if we can encourage Felix to start talking history! Sandra and my pictures are on the wall too, along with many others. It is presently on sale for $1.5 million. If you are ever in or near Bernalillo, New Mexico, for a quick review of history, visit Silva's bar!

Also in Placitas we are blessed with a great restaurant, Blades Bistro, run by two sons of an Air Force pilot who served in WW II and the Korean War. The food is marvelous and it is our place like Silva's Bar!

CHECK-6 CABIN AND OUR TEAM, 2007-PRESENT

Recovering from the death of Sylvia my friends Art Flynn, John-Olav Johnsen and Steve Langford (Old Two-Alarm) found a cabin in southern Colorado, which provided the distraction I needed. The cabin was in a valley just a mile or so from the northern edge of New Mexico, in a beautiful and remote valley about five miles south of Mogote, Colorado. The first time I visited there, I saw a herd of deer, probably thirty to fifty in numbers. The cabin is also located about five miles from the nearest house.

The cabin, corral, a metal-framed barn covered with plastic sheeting, and horse stalls on 43 acres were listed at $153,000. Art, our sly money negotiator, got it for us at $60,000. My son Mike helped us build a team of six that included three of his rugby teammates from Texas Tech to buy the piece of "Heaven on earth." Since Art and I are fighter pilots, Art suggested we name it Check-6 (Ck-6), which is what fighter pilots frequently say to tell a wingman to look behind them for enemy sneaking up on them. It is now used by those in or from the fighter world as a greeting or anytime one signs off!

The cabin, corral, and horse stable were solidly built but needed considerable updating: adding external security, and some electrical improvements. Apparently the previous owners had a large generator able to run a refrigerator, standard lighting, and other electrical items. We had only a small generator. We needed some modifications to the lighting system to a low-voltage system and replaced the refrig they left us with a propane one. Unfortunately, we have never been able to get it working properly.

Art (Max), John-Olav Johnsen (JO), and I (Bear) began construction on increasing the external security for the cabin. We built heavy-duty shutters for each window and the front door. Additionally, we worked on the plumbing in the kitchen and bathroom, added a large elevated tank for the bathroom, and rebuilt the bathroom, adding a sliding door for privacy. Plumbing in remote areas requires management of waste through an associated septic system which was there.

Art and I tried to see the cabin a couple of times but were blocked by snow and couldn't get to the cabin. Finally, we were able to drive on the County Road 9 to the cabin. We missed the turn off but found ourselves east of the cabin in Art's "war wagon" that he thought was a tank or an overland vehicle. Instead of returning to the road that we missed, he started directly toward the cabin across a fairly densely grown field of typical remote growth. We bounced along over some very rough terrain. Suddenly, I strongly felt that we were making a mistake! *Lucky* again, I screamed "Stop this flipping vehicle right now!" Art responded to the Colonel's commanding voice and instantly stopped. We got out, and, if we had traveled five feet farther, we would have fallen into a very deep cut that we probably couldn't have gotten out of, and possibly we would have been seriously hurt. We then returned to the county road and the correct turn off for our cabin.

Art is my neighbor, a former Navy F-14 fighter pilot, and I considered him as a son. Recently he was married to a lady he met, Margaret who seems to be making him very happy. I served as their best man when they got married.

Art and a longtime friend, Andor Abonyi, who initially was a member of the cabin team, had a terrible auto wreck returning from Ck-6 one evening. They were both very beat up but they recovered from an accident that could have killed both of them. Art and I usually spent lots of time together on various projects. Additionally, I was able to help Andor's son, Michael, get admitted to the Naval Academy, where he should do very well. Of course Andor has a marvelous Lady, Karen, who is the class of the family.

Back to Ck-6: once in the cabin, we were shocked at the condition inside the cabin—hundreds of aluminum soda cans, a meal or two left on the dining table, and trash everywhere. What was shocking was there were no beer cans or whiskey bottles, which in the future we quickly and seriously corrected that faulty condition. We also found lots of useful supplies such as over fifty roofing sheets (worth about $1,600 at the time), PVC fittings, PVC pipes, electrical fittings and electrical conduits/pipes, some good wood, and other useful items. Unfortunately, lots of junk too, and later we made several visits to the authorized trash areas. Later we had a team "workday" with most members attending. Our two Texan Ck-6 members, Dr. Eric Darrow a famous Pediatric Anesthesiology and Neal Braswell our resident architect built a tower for the main water tank when they were there at another time.

As time moved on, we repainted the whole external cabin, repaired leaks, JO attacked our mice problem, and later we hired help to modify the wooden stove piping to satisfy our insurance company. We added a new flush toilet and a shower with hot water! We have a pump and trailered tank to get water from the Conejos River for our kitchen and bathroom tanks.

We are blessed with wonderful neighbors like Danny O'Grady and Jim Duran of the nearby famous Elk ranch who make our cabin situation so much better. They also keep an eye on the place, offer suggestions to us, help us modify the facility, and share a beer with us. The real bottom line is that our Ck-6 is Heaven on earth!

POLITICS: McCAIN'S PRESIDENTIAL CAMPAIGNS, 1999-2008

Since I had been in the military for years, I was always outside the political arena, but once retired I started participating a bit, primarily financially. Then my Naval Academy friend, John McCain, was making a go for President in 2000. I, along with Benny Montoya (also a Naval Academy Classmate and a retired Admiral), became the co-chairmen of *New Mexico's McCain for President* with Lt. Gen. Leo Marquez as Honorary Head of the team here in New Mexico. Leo is a New Mexico hero, former Air Force fighter pilot, and a very longtime friend. Leo was probably the key to retaining Kirtland AFB, even though many others claim credit for it! Unfortunately, my longtime friend, General Leo passed away recently from a re-occurrence of cancer. Kirtland AFB astutely named their base park, the *Leo Marquez Park!*

We operated that year on $522. Most of which I donated, and we did damn well here in New Mexico. I am confident that the Senator would have won in 2000 except for the professionals consultants in his campaign who failed to listen to all his classmates supporting him. His classmates normally had the true pulse of where they lived and frankly, those involved locally throughout the Nation, were just not listened to, nor were their inputs accepted. We had someone in every possible location. The key or quarterback to our Academy supporters for Johnny was Eileen Giglio, wife of our classmate, Mike. She had tons of info but no one would listen! After dealing with them through three campaigns, I have developed a great distaste for professional GOP consultants!

For example, I was in Florida when Lawton M. Chiles beat Jeb Bush. Bush had a 5 percent lead the day before the Election Day. However, the Chiles organization had callers, the night before the election contact the older Republicans, telling them that Jeb would cut Social Security for them. Absolute BS, because Social Security is a federal system, and the state has no control over it. But it worked; Chiles beat Jeb by a tiny margin, and most agree that the phone calls resulted in older Republicans either not voting for Jeb Bush or voting for Chiles.

In any case, I knew that the Bush family learned from this defeat, and I tried to warn the professionals in Johnny's campaign, who, of course, disregarded my inputs as they did any inputs from other classmates throughout the Nation. The Bush organization copied the Florida Democratic operation in the Carolinas. This broke the McCain campaign's back, and George Bush went on to win.

Unfortunately, as the McCain campaign was cranking up for 2008, I was in China visiting my Daughter, Barrie Lynn, as the Olympics were starting. She was the only foreigner to carry the Olympic torch in China. My ex-wife, my granddaughter Bryn, and I went to where she was to carry the torch. There were busloads of children (with political advisors, I assume) bused to where she was to run. We arrived early, and the young schoolchildren of course wanted to test their English with us. I was able to organize the kids to shout in unison, as Barrie arrived with the torch, "Barrie Lynn Howard." It was not appreciated by those monitoring the students, as they were supposed to sing a song. Good guys 1, Commies 0.

Back to the McCain campaign: The John McCain I knew for many years was the toughest, most hardheaded person I had ever known. Unfortunately, it was obvious that his Presidential campaign was weak, wrong, and, as time wore on, utterly hopeless. I expressed some of my concerns to John when he was in Albuquerque, but obviously, as I am an amateur, it fell on deaf ears. His defeat has proven to be a disaster! I kept a log of the entire campaign, which I have provided to the GOP state party so that hopefully the mistakes made in 2008 will not be repeated in the critical 2012 election. Unfortunately the mistakes of 2008 have been repeated for the 2012 campaign with the GOP consultants calling the shots to the detriment of the candidates!

Finally, the biggest failure of the 2008 campaign in New Mexico was not taking advantage of the Straight Talk Express bus that traveled the entire state of New Mexico. The bus crew couldn't have been more professional, politically astute, or dedicated. Lee Dickens is a typical Marine: aggressive, attuned to existing conditions, and prepared to be in charge. Bob Martinez is an absolutely special person; he is smoother than Lee, politically extremely knowledgeable with regard to New Mexico and nationally. Of course he was born here and knows and understands New Mexico culture. If I had my way, he would be state Party Chairman; he knows someone in almost every town, speaks Spanish, and is Hispanic. Finally, the bus owner and driver, Tom Greer, like Bob, knows many folks around the state or how to find someone in any city, county, or gathering of houses, who could be useful.

Senator Domenici, Congressman Pearce, Sheriff White, and members of their staffs and others of the Party running for office realized the utility of the bus and frequently traveled on the bus. Unfortunately, the State Director for McCain never did! Had she simply ridden on the bus once, for a few hours, I am certain that she would have understood the utility of it, as everyone else did. Of course my friend Senator John McCann was badly beaten by what I call a "Chicago an amateur who has no belief in our American Constitution."

FAMILY TIME: BARRIE AND MIKE, BLH 9/20/1960 & MSH 12/2/61

Dorlyne and I have been blessed with two wonderful children who constantly make us very proud. This is not to say that occasionally one of them, usually Mike does not try to drive us crazy, but I know of no other parents who are more pleased with their children than we are! Barrie is the oldest and was born to Dorlyne in Muncie, Indiana, while I was at Stead AB, Nevada, going through survival school, as I mentioned earlier. Mike on the other hand was born in Evreux, France on the day of the famed Army/Navy football game.

The tale of my Dad, Mom, and Grandma Mac getting Dorlyne to the hospital so Barrie could be born always makes me smile. Grandmother Mac was rushing everyone, and, of course, Dad couldn't find his hat, that FBI fedora! Barrie was born just as I was completing survival school after the "night trek" early in the morning. As you may remember, a friend, Jim Blackwell, woke me to tell me she was born, but the next morning he didn't remember doing it although everyone around me confirmed he did! I did receive a note the next morning telling me that my daughter really had been born. Once I saw her, to say she immediately won my heart is a gross understatement; she was beautiful, happy, and she seemed to like me!

Barrie was a great and very happy baby (and remains very happy, even today) with a deep and truly from-the-heart laugh. I dreamed that she would be the first female fighter pilot, but she was just born a bit too early, even for Title IX women's college sports scholarships. I am sure she would have received one in college basketball, as she was a great point guard! She was, as a young girl, fearless, and always wanting to do what I did or learn how to do what I was doing! She was great on my motorcycle when she was young, but as she got older, the motorcycle wasn't as much fun as it used to be—she was becoming a lady!

She finished high school in Virginia while I was in the Pentagon, and then she went to Texas Tech University, Lubbock, TX to start college. One of the thrills of her daddy's life was visiting her there. We went to Coldwater Bar and Restaurant, and I was able to watch her do a Texas line dance. She seemed very happy there, but, after two years, she changed to Indiana State in Terre Haute. Larry Bird, the outstanding basketball player, had already departed their men's team! Compared to Texas Tech, Indiana State appeared to be the pits.

Little did we know that she did it to be closer to my mother, *Little Napoleon*, in Muncie, about whom she was worried? Upon Barrie's graduation from Indiana State, we invited her to Osan AB, Korea, for an Asian experience, as I was the Director of Operations for the 314th Air Division working for my old boss, Maj. Gen. "Fat Fred" Haeffner. He was again a joy to work for! Just to be around *Fat Fred*, the Pepsi-drinking fighter pilot, and his wonderful wife, Sis, made life a challenge and fun.

Barrie came to Korea to visit, and, while there, she applied for a job at Yokota AFB, Japan, as Youth Director. Naturally she was chosen. Two weeks after she received the job, the Wing failed its Operational Readiness Inspection (ORI), and I was chosen to replace the Air Base Wing Commander. Dorlyne and I talked it over, and we decided that it just wouldn't work, her being the Youth Director and me being the Wing Commander. We sat her down on the couch and told her that she couldn't have the job; some say I *fired* her!

I did call Gen. Chuck Donnelly, who was the 5th Air Force Commander at Yokota, and he said he would help her find a job, which he did. The many accomplished older Japanese who really run Japan, thought what we did about Barrie was wonderful, and they said they would help her too. She was hired by the American Club in Tokyo, Japan as the kindergarten assistant, and various large Japanese companies started hiring her to travel to various locations of their Headquarters to teach the young executives English and American customs. She would be put up in the finest hotel, have meals with the executives, and just spend time with them, speaking only English. She would also ride the bullet train to the various cities. Surprisingly, she quickly picked up some Japanese, Kanji and Katakana. She later taught in a private Japanese high school as the only foreigner. She stayed in Japan five years after we left.

After we returned to the US, Barrie's apartment was robbed, even though there is a Japanese Policeman on every other corner. The Chief of Police of Tokyo wrote me a letter apologizing and said that he would resign because of her robbery. I quickly called him and told him we appreciated his letter, but I would be offended if he resigned. The potential for my being "offended," as the son of an FBI agent, was very serious to the Japanese. Had I not called him, I am sure that he would have resigned, as the Japanese are very conscious about their duties and responsibilities.

When Barrie returned to the States, I had retired, and we were living in Lubbock, Texas. I was going to Texas Tech to get an MBA in Hospital Management. While Barrie was visiting us, Texas Tech advertised for a manager for the federally funded Japanese American program. She applied for the position and she was chosen, probably because she spoke, read, and wrote Japanese! Unfortunately, the federal money for the program never came through. However, she was really enjoying herself, living at home, running around with her friends, and living off her savings or what she could wrangle out of us! Unfortunately, she had rented a storage unit for her many wonderful remembrances from her travel and work in the Pacific, and it had been broken into, and all the valuable items were stolen. No one offered to resign over that, as they did in Japan!

Once again we sat her down on the couch, put our arms around her, and said, "You have thirty days to get out of here!" "Oh, Daddy, you can't be serious!" Within a few days she left for Dallas for a job as an $8.50/hr. Japanese interpreter for a company that provided insurance claims processing for credit card companies, living with her cousin Belinda. However, because of her management and leadership skills, one year later she was in charge of the company's operational bunch. Her big challenge at the time was to buy new computers to set up a credit card call center for the organization. I begged her to buy IBM-type computer, since the Macs, at that time, had very few programs available. She listened to her Daddy and bought the right computers. Sometime after that, VISA, which had a working relationship with her company, hired her away, and then the fun began!

VISA was a major sponsor of the Olympics and Barrie had the opportunity to manage a Customer Service Center during the Atlanta Olympic Games. VISA leadership directed Barrie to develop a briefing for the Olympic Committee, which included mostly very senior Japanese businessmen. She gave the briefing to several older Japanese gentlemen since the next Olympic event was to be in Japan. From my experiences, decision-makers in Japan are normally very senior. After she gave the briefing in English, the Chairman of VISA said, "Of course Miss Howard could give the brief in Japanese too!" Barrie then replied very humbly (as a Japanese woman would) in Japanese, "Oh, my Japanese is weak, my pronunciation is poor, and I have a limited vocabulary."

The men being briefed were impressed with her humbleness and shy approach, realizing that she truly understood the true character of Japan! When Japanese are impressed, they appear to be trying to suck out their front teeth, which they did after Barrie spoke to them in Japanese. They agreed that VISA should continue as a major sponsor if Barrie would be part of the team that handled it; thus, she was first involved with the Winter Olympics at Nagano, Japan. (I have to digress a bit here, my daughter and I differ on the above two paragraphs but I did talk to someone who was escorting the Japanese team and I have written what he told me. Barrie is still a very low key person and her Daddy has a bit more fire about her efforts! My impressions still stand!)

VISA has been involved in all Olympic events ever since, and for the Beijing, China, Olympics, she was made a Vice-President, responsible for all International Sports that VISA sponsored.

After Beijing, she moved her office to London for the 2012 Summer Olympics; after they were over, she said they were the best run that she had been associated with. Now, as VP, she also has other events in Germany, South Africa, Canada, New Zealand and of course Brazil for the FIFA World Cup (2014) and next the Summer Olympics. She visits or talks by telephone to VISA folks she is responsible for at all sponsored events regularly. She is a busy lady! Recently, VISA has changed her title to Senior Business Leader rather than her previous title of Vice President as they did for the rest of the VISA. Sounds commie to me; I guess Obama is maybe really getting to our businesses.

Our son and daughter, Mike and Barrie, were staying with us when we had the 475 Air Base Wing in Yokota AB, Japan. We had big and uniquely fun living quarters, which were initially built for Gen. MacArthur right after WW II, although he only lived in it for a short period. However, Air Force Gen. Emmet "Rosie" O'Donnell did for some time. It was made with several Quonset huts and very well done to make it feel like a home. Shortly after I moved into to it, I had it declared as a historical building called "Rosie's Place" so that it couldn't be torn down and replaced.

Our son, Mike, was twenty years old and had two years of junior college at Northeastern Oklahoma A&M in Miami, Oklahoma. Mike's story really starts after we moved to Langley, Virginia. There, I helped a friend, a fellow officer and Academy graduate, Mike Stevens, start, organize, and run an elementary-school-level football team. Mike Stevens had been a high school all-American fullback in Illinois. But because of injuries, he had rowed crew at the Naval Academy with me or me with him, as he stroked the first boat, which I was always in as the *bow rower* at the first of the season!

As we gathered the neighborhood kids who wanted to play football, it was apparent that many were somewhat underprivileged, and their families couldn't afford to buy them uniforms so I visited the Langley MWR (Morale, Welfare and Recreation) Boss and explained our dilemma. It just so happened that the base had obtained new uniforms for their base team, and they gave us their old ones! Mike and I then purchased team jerseys for our players, because we couldn't find a sponsor to help us. My son was known as Big Mike, and Mike Steven's son was known as Little Mike, even though his dad was also called Big Mike. The first year I was the assistant coach to Mike Stevens, Big Mike.

Our first year was fairly successful, with Big Mike's son, Little Mike, who was about five foot two, as quarterback and my son as an end. They both loved to hit, as did most of our hardscrabble kids, and our defense was really good. We concentrated on the basics and teamwork. Our players were quickly learning teamwork and discipline, something that seemed to be missing in their everyday lives. The next year, Big Mike Stevens returned to Southeast Asia (Vietnam), and I took over as coach, but, smart man that I am, I recruited Moe Severt, whose son was on the team. Moe had played college and service football as an offensive player, thus he ran the offense. Moe really knew his football. We made a major change to our offense by moving my son, Big Mike, who was five foot eight or ten at that time, to quarterback. We had learned the first year that our offensive line always stood up, and our quarterback, Little Mike Stevens, couldn't see over them. But Big Mike Howard, being tall, could see over them. Little Mike moved to end, and he was a great offensive end and damn fast. With Moe's offense leading the way and with our solid defense, we won the city championship.

One incident I will always remember was when Big Mike Howard got the wind knocked out of him and his Mother, Dorlyne, ran out of the stands onto the field to her "baby," actually beating me to him! Everyone in the stands could clearly hear Big Mike Howard crying and struggling for breath, loudly moaning, "Mom, please go away, you are embarrassing me!"

Mike also played baseball at Langley, and he led his league in batting, so he made the All-Star team. Unfortunately, in the All-Star game, he made a couple of errors, and, as a result, I can't remember him ever picking up a baseball again.

Mike, our French born son, was a true service brat or vagabond. He attended a different high school for each year of high school. To attest to his basketball skills, at each new school he attended, before the season was over, he was always on the starting team. We moved to Edmond, Oklahoma, for his senior year. Mike and I visited most of the high schools in Oklahoma City and determined that we wanted to live in Edmond. Why?

Because the Edmond High School coach, Mike Delagarza, said he needed Mike. Mike had a great year there, and his team played in the Oklahoma State high school Championship finals against the team that had the Daniels brothers, both approaching seven feet tall. Mike's team was beaten, but barely, and he held one of the Daniels brothers, who normally averaged over twenty points per game, to either six or eight points, and Mike out-rebounded them both. After the game, I was in the locker room with Mike, and the Daniels brothers came in to talk to Mike. He introduced me to them. The brother that Mike had guarded said, "That can't be your Daddy; the way you jump and play basketball, you must have a black Daddy!"

After high school, Mike attended a junior college on a basketball scholarship at Northern Oklahoma A&M, Miami, Oklahoma, and he achieved junior college All-American. I never understood why he did not go on with his college basketball. Recently, he told me he quit basketball because it was now a business, with folks giving him money and other things, which he just didn't like—and many of the players who received more money weren't very nice.

At Yokota, Mike was living the good life, and Dad and Mom were busy with the Wing Commander's job. Mike had a VW to drive and a very attractive and athletic girlfriend, Linda Sapiro, who I hoped he would hang on to; she was the daughter of a senior base and very famous engineer, Norm Sapiro. She was a dynamite racquetball player and may have beaten Mike on occasion. He was really living the good life!

One night, about 0100, I received a "hot line" call from the top cop, Brian Shiroyama, probably the best cop in the Air Force. Having dealt with three "Top Cops" as someone who commanded them, Brian was absolutely the best for many reasons but, most importantly, because of his leadership and common sense. His troops loved him, were disciplined, and never—repeat, *never*—got into trouble. The Air Force made a terrible mistake when they didn't make him a general and the Air Force top cop!

Back to son Mike! When Brian called me, he said something to the effect of, "Colonel, unfortunately, we have your son, Mike, here at our office. He hasn't done anything wrong, but my guys found him in a fight with a Yakuza mobster in town, and they took him in, so that other mob members wouldn't beat him up—although when my Security Police arrived, he was winning the fight, big time!"

I said, "I'll be right down to get him!" Brian again said, "There are no charges against him, and we just brought him back to the base to protect him, and, in fact, maybe really protecting the fellow who started the fight with him! Your Mike is really a tough kid!"

I drove to the Air Police station, went in, and thanked the officers for handling the problem, and I took Mike home. In our home he had his own bedroom that was a small Quonset hut with a hot tub. Every bedroom (four of them) in our house had a hot tub! While Mike wasn't belligerent, he was a bit unhappy, because the guy had jumped him while he was sitting with his girlfriend. I told him to go to bed, and we'd work on it tomorrow.

About three hours later, my "hot line" rang again, and it was Brian again! Brian said, "Sir, I am sorry to bother you, but we have your son, Mike, here again!" I said to Brian, "I already picked him up!" He said "No, we have him again, and he hasn't done anything wrong; he just had a fight with a truck driver who forced him off the road. Several Japanese witnesses told my people that the truck driver was forcing everyone off the road, including your son. Mike caught him at a stoplight and pulled him out of the truck so that Police could arrest him. The driver made a serious mistake and hit Mike, and Mike responded accordingly. Local police arrived, charged the truck driver, and called

my folks to come get Mike, who was in no trouble, just mad!"
"Your daughter helped calm him down!" Barrie Lynn was driving
by, going to the beach, and stopped to help.

Apparently Mike's girlfriend had given him a gold necklace
for his birthday, and it had been ripped off in the first fight. After I
sent him to bed the first time, he decided that he was going back
to find the necklace when the truck driver ran him off the road.
Once again the Wing Commander visited the Air Police station
early in the morning. Somewhat forcefully, Mike was sent to bed,
and Dorlyne and I discussed the matter in detail. We decided
that maybe it was time for Mike to return to Texas.

Shortly thereafter, he caught the "Big Bird" back to the States
and returned to Lubbock, TX. He then chose Texas Tech University to finish his interrupted college. Mike fit right in with the
tough West Texas folks and was very talented, popular, and knew
how to organize and run things.

At a very young age, he had started working at a restaurant
on Eagle Lake in Texas as a bus boy. Before the summer was
over, he was running the restaurant! Returning to Lubbock from
Japan, he was hired to supervise and build a bar and restaurant
called, *Toucan*, near Texas Tech University. He not only led the
construction of the facility but also hired the initial staff and managed Toucan which was very successful. Along with running the
Toucan, he attended Texas Tech University and also joined the
rugby team and became a real star—not only in drinking but also
in rugby. I think they even eventually modified the game because
of his jumping ability. Although only six foot six, he could out
jump anyone they played, so I was told that they changed the
rules to allow players to boost up a teammate. Mike's successes
at Texas Tech pleased me, and, of course, as a result, I had fewer
late night hot-line calls!

I need to digress a bit here and mention a procedure that
our son Mike developed for his first day at any of his many

schools that he attended. Usually when Mike attended a new school, by late of the afternoon of his first day of school, we would get a call from the Principal or someone from that office. Mike learned early in his nomadic life that a fight in a new school would establish him socially. He said I told him that, but I suspect it was his Grandpa Howard, since he was tough and I was a skinny talker, not a fighter. I think that every time Mike started at a new school he would have a fight on the first day, and he probably started, before college, ten different schools. I even remember calling Dorlyne one afternoon—I think when we had moved to Edmond, Oklahoma—asking if she had received "The call, yet?" She said no, but after I hung up, a few minutes later, she called back and said the Principal's office had just called, and she was going in to talk to them! The fight at Edmond seemed to work, and Mike really enjoyed his senior year at Edmond High, and he was crowned as the King of his graduation class.

Mike later in his life really hurt his Mother. Dorlyne had special affection for Mike as most mothers do for their male children. Unfortunately, he rejected her somewhat after I retired. However, after rebelling against his mother, he realized the damage he had done and she again became his, *Mommy*. Mike was always able to turn on the charm and undo mistake he had made by being especially sweet to his Mommy or even his Grandmother!

He became a wonderful father, and he and his lovely wife, Marla, had two delightful and amazing daughters, Evan, and the youngest daughter, Bryn, who is so brave and is very close to Sinky (Dorlyne). Evan graduated from Oklahoma University (it was almost a stake through the heart for me, a beautiful Texas lady at OU!). Bryn, our tall, beautiful, and talented young lady, entered Texas University at Austin in a special engineering program that she competed for and won along with two financial scholarships!

Dorlyne and I were very *lucky*—actually, truly blessed, as we had two wonderful children who were goal-oriented and not the least bit shy or had trouble adjusting to new surroundings from our frequent moves! Actually after a few moves, they seemed to look forward to the next move.

MY EDUCATION AND LESSONS LEARNED,
3/25/1936-PRESENT

My life-long education has been a result of my exciting and challenging life, starting with my early jobs, Muncie Central High School, the Indiana National Guard, the US Naval Academy, followed by Photo-Intelligence School, then Jet Pilot Training, instructing in the C-130, T-37, and upgrading/instructing in the F-4. Early in my military career, I completed several correspondence courses, which included the Squadron Officers School (six months), and Command and Staff (one year) and one or two others. I did actually attend the Air War College at Maxwell AFB, Alabama for one year. Probably my most educational experience was gained during command positions at any of the three squadrons or at the two wings I commanded. Commanding the Wings overseas provided insight into many areas that stateside Commanders do not have to address. In the States you have local police, social facilities/services, and various medical services. But overseas, these are lacking, and your unit provides them, either through Volunteer participation, or, on rare occasion, there might be a professional assigned. Dorlyne and I did lots of marriage counseling and addressed family problems associated with being overseas. I think today this area has been strengthened for overseas Commanders.

My varied military experience and education became very useful on the afternoon of 9/11/01. The Chief Federal Judge in Albuquerque, along with the Director of New Mexico Transportation (DOT) initiated a group to address New Mexico's security. I was one of the initial four involved and remained with the team for several years. We visited the Twin Towers site and the FBI Headquarters within days of 9/11/01. I was following in my family's history of government service as my Father did it all; a policeman, one of the first FBI agents in the newly restructured FBI by Hoover, and later the Sheriff of Delaware County, Indiana.

I had many very demanding challenges throughout my life, especially concerning my various occupations. Prior to attending the Navy Academy, as I previously indicated, I had a newspaper route, worked in a drug store, a grocery store, worked the wheat harvest in Colorado for two years, and was a *gandy dancer* on the railroad. In the AF, I was an Intelligence Officer, and, after pilot training, I was a C-130 pilot traveling a great deal of the world and later became a C-130 Instructor Pilot. In ATC, I was an instructor pilot in the T-37, later a Maintenance Test Pilot in the F-5, T-38, and T-37. In the F-4, I had combat in the F-4D, where I was a Flight Leader, Strike Force Commander, Instructor Pilot, Maintenance Test Pilot, and a FAST FAC.

I was blessed with the opportunity to command five outfits ranging in size from fifty folks to the largest of more than fifteen thousand folks. I am proud that I have 229 combat missions under my belt, of which forty were as a FAST FAC and well over one hundred were over North Vietnam in the F-4!

After leaving the AF, I managed an exclusive Fishing and Diving Resort in the Cayman Islands, the Southern Cross Club, owned by several millionaires. After that I was then hired to re-organize the Lee County, Florida, Mosquito Control District's supply and resources system. After retiring from LCMCD, I volunteered with the State of Florida working with recently laid-off middle management folks. We were helping upgrade their capabilities and computer skills so that they could fine work.

Following that I was first a Consultant to the Director of DOT for New Mexico. I then joined Flatiron Construction Company as an engineer, helping build the US 550 a 114-mile road in New Mexico from north of Bernalillo, NM to Aztec, NM. Following that, I served as a Homeland Defense consultant for the state of New Mexico.

In association with my military career and the command positions that I held, I have had numerous radio, media, and TV interviews and/or appearances in this country and in Korea, Japan, and the Philippines. During these events, what worked for me during those exposures was speaking honestly, only giving the basic details and, as a result, the media seldom challenged me.

In my spare time, hunting, golf, repairing things along with lots of reading and now writing are my hobbies. When I am not involved in my hobbies, I participate in several various organizations such as the Quiet Birdmen, Dandelions, USNA Alumni Association, and the fighter pilots' Red River Rats Association.

I have had several life-altering experiences: the first being selected for the US Naval Academy; the next was having Maj. George Patton, the son of *the* Gen. Patton, as my TAC Officer at the Naval Academy who convinced me of the rewards of military life and command. One of the uniquely challenging commands I experienced was being involved with the failed Iranian rescue. I am convinced that any actions or decisions made once the military action had started needs to be managed primarily by the military, as President Reagan and both Presidents Bush did.

The last terrible experience I endured was the death of my wife, Sylvia, December 7, 2005, from colon cancer, which probably could have been prevented if I had been more forceful. The thrills of my life have been Barrie, Mike, the women of my life, my unbelievable career in the Air Force and my challenges after the Air Force. I have been blessed in all the jobs I have had. I suspect I said, "Wow, and they even paid me!" the most when I was in the Air Force. But most of my life has really been good and paid me well in personal satisfaction. I hope my efforts have repaid those that I have worked for adequately, especially the Air Force.

I have been truly the *luckiest* guy I know; there is no hill I wanted to climb that I didn't have the opportunity to climb! If I have any sadness in my life it has been the loss of my parents. Coupled with the loss of my parents has been the loss of Sylvia and later Noel. Of course, retiring from the wonderful folks of the Air Force who are capable of anything was less than fun!

Some might wonder why I didn't mention not being selected to Brigadier General as sadness in my life. It actually gave me a chance to explore and do other exciting things. My life has been really wonderful, exciting, and with many challenges; I have no complaints!

My lessons learned. Because of the challenging and exciting life I have had the pleasure to live and because of my instructor mentality, I think I should try to pass on the lessons I have learned. Many by actions I have taken or a result of watching others or learning from others, and some from really dumb mistakes, I or someone else made!

1. **Major lesson I learned in flight: Let God have the aircraft if you really screwed-up and have lost control of it, He will probably save you, if not, bailout!**
2. **Major lesson from my parents and the USNA: To be honest with integrity.**

3. Major lesson from my life experiences: Thoughtfulness, planning, determination, along with hard work, and sincere personal involvement will normally result in success.
4. Major lesson learned from my commands and George Patton Jr.: Leadership requires knowing, caring, managing, directing, and, most importantly, to lead from the front and strongly protect and support those who are under you.
5. Major lesson about the men and women of the Air Force and military: The young men and women of today's military are dedicated, will face any challenge thrown at them, and are brave beyond belief and are as good as, or better than, any previous generation.
6. Major lesson and a biggie for those in leadership positions: Logical, well-written communications when dealing with various governmental agencies are the only way to challenge or redirect regulations, directions, or procedures that need to be changed. Especially do not use telephone calls or e-mails—just plain old official letters, which then become official documents, and can be deadly to bureaucrats!
7. Leadership, while it can be very challenging, is extremely satisfying and fun and should be desired!
8. I have found that a positive and good attitude with a smile can and will always make life better.
9. My book would not be complete without a clear statement of my faith in God. For me, faith is less what you say and more what you do with the gift of life. I have acted to the best of my ability to defend freedom, including precious religious freedom, for each and all. Throughout the book, I use the word

"lucky". What I mean is "blessed". God has blessed me in so many ways, and continues to bless me every day. (I really think I am one of His favorites because He made me so *lucky* or blessed!) God has never given me any challenge that He knows I couldn't handle. May it be so for the balance of my days?

Sincerely,

Barry J. Howard,

In this book I have shared my life experiences as I remember them. In a few instances, they have clashed in small details with some with whom I have conferred. In most cases, I have vivid memories, some notes and recollections which I trust. Frankly, my remembrances are more fun or interesting.

Da Bear—trash hauler, flying instructor/teacher, fighter pilot, and leader.

THE END

Should there be profit from this book, it will be donated to an organization, supported by the Air Warriors Courage Foundation (AWCF) whose volunteers work with Wounded Warriors (WW) right at the San Antonio Military Medical Center. They are members of the Parr River Rats Force and are all volunteers receiving no pay but do receive supporting funds from the AWCF. The work they do is exemplary and greatly appreciated by the Wounded Warriors and their families. This River Rats Force of volunteers has been doing this for 8 years along with also donating considerable personal funds for their projects. Every penny donated to them goes directly into helping the Wounded Warriors, unlike some WW projects that have a very well paid staff (a CEO making over $300,000/year) with an almost 30% overhead.

The Author, Barry Jack Howard
Colonel USAF (Ret.) FP

Barry Jack Howard was born in Wichita, Kansas, to Martha and Harry Howard on March 25, 1936. His father was a Night Captain on the Wichita Police Department and later was considering going to the Texas Rangers, but J. Edgar Hoover recruited him to the newly restructured FBI. As a result, young Barry traveled with his family to Baltimore, Maryland; Boston, Massachusetts; Duluth, Minnesota; Wichita, Kansas; Kansas City, Kansas; Houston, Texas; and finally to Muncie, Indiana. He arrived in Muncie in the sixth grade, where he stayed until he departed Muncie for the US Naval Academy, Annapolis, Maryland. He attended Wilson Junior high school and graduated from Muncie Central H.S, (420 grads) where he had an exciting and dynamic high school career playing (sparingly) baseball and football and was the class Vice President all three years. He joined the Indiana National Guard in 1953, rising to corporal. He competed for an Academy appointment and won a slot to US Naval Academy for the class of 1958.

He joined the Brigade of Midshipmen in June of 1954 and eventually graduated in June of 1958. He chose the US Air Force, as at that time up to 25 percent of the Academy graduates were allowed to join the Air Force. After attending the Photo Intelligence (PI) Officers course, he was assigned to Barksdale AFB, 2nd Recce Tech. He was able to quickly depart for pilot training at Marianna AB, Florida, first in the T-34 (prop) and then the T-37 jet.

From there he went to Laredo AFB, Texas, for advance flying training in the T-33. Dropping from first in the class to eighth after failing his instrument check ride, he chose C-130s in Evreux AB, France since *luckily*, all fighter slots were taken. It was probably the best thing that could have happened to him, as he developed advanced flying skills and knowledge, and, because of the experienced he gained in that assignment, he became an Instructor Pilot (IP) in C-130s.

He then joined Air Training Command at Williams AFB, Arizona, as a T-37 IP, later he chose to become a Maintenance Flight Test Pilot (MFTP) after he was selected as ATC instructor of the year. After many volunteer requests for fighters, he was sent to Homestead AFB, Florida, first as a student and then, much to his dissatisfaction he was held as an F-4 IP. From there he went to Udorn AB, Thailand, in the 13th TFS. While there, he was a Flight Leader, MFTP, and Mission Commander. He later established a FAST FAC organization where his PI experience paid off. While there, he received a Silver Star, Bronze Star, three DFCs, and 17 Air Medals. He was wounded twice but did not receive the associated Purple Hearts.

From Thailand he was first in the 9th Air Force fighter shop and then to the TAC Headquarters' fighter shop. From there he went to Luke AFB, Arizona, as the Commander of the SAT squadron and later the 311 TFTS. Then he went to the Pentagon, where he bounced around, and finally managing Project Checkmate. After

2 years 2 days and 6 hours he then went to the Air War College, Montgomery AB, Alabama, followed by being the Commander of the 963rd AWACS Squadron. He then was the 314th AD, Osan Korea, Director of Operations followed by then being the Commander of the 475th Air Base Wing, Yokota, Japan. Finally, for the crown jewel of his fighter pilot life he was selected as the Wing Commander of the famed 51st TAC Fighter Wing. He then was the VC, 13th Air Force at Clark AB, Philippines Islands. He then retired in Austin, Texas.

As a civilian he first managed a unique Fishing and Diving resort in the Cayman Islands on Little Cayman, the Southern Cross Club. From there he was the director of Supply and Services for Lee County Mosquito Control District, Ft. Myers, FL for ten years. He then became a consultant to the Director of New Mexico State Highway and Transportation Department, followed by working for Flatiron Construction, building a 114-mile road in New Mexico. Following that he was deeply involved in development of procedures and efforts regarding New Mexico's Home Land Security following the attack of September 11, 2001.

He has lived in Placitas, New Mexico, in the home he built in 1998 and he still can walk and goes to the gym and then swims three times a week at Kirtland AFB, NM. He is the very proud father of Barrie and Mike Howard and all of their accomplishments.

Made in the USA
Charleston, SC
27 March 2013